The Women's Movement Inside and Outside the State

The Women's Movement Inside and Outside the State argues that the mobilization and success of the U.S. women's movement cannot be fully understood without recognizing the presence of feminist activist networks inside the federal government. Utilizing in-depth interviews and historical sources, Lee Ann Banaszak's research documents the significant contributions that these insider activists made to the creation of feminist organizations and the vital roles that they played in the development and implementation of policies in many areas, including education, foreign policy, and women's health. Banaszak also finds that working inside government did not always co-opt or deradicalize these activists. Banaszak's research causes us to rethink our current understanding of many social movement concepts and processes, including political opportunities, movement institutionalization, and confrontational tactics, and it alters our conception of the interests and character of the American state.

Lee Ann Banaszak is currently associate professor of political science and women's studies at the Pennsylvania State University. She is the author of *Why Movements Succeed or Fail: Opportunity, Culture and the Struggle for Woman Suffrage* (1996) and the editor of *Women's Movements Facing the Reconfigured State* (Cambridge, 2003, with Karen Beckwith and Dieter Rucht) and *The U.S. Women's Movement in Global Perspective* (2005). Her articles have appeared in such journals as the *American Political Science Review, Public Opinion Quarterly, Political Research Quarterly, Politics & Gender,* and *Electoral Studies.*

The Women's Movement Inside and Outside the State

LEE ANN BANASZAK
The Pennsylvania State University

CAMBRIDGE
UNIVERSITY PRESS

CAMBRIDGE UNIVERSITY PRESS
Cambridge, New York, Melbourne, Madrid, Cape Town, Singapore,
São Paulo, Delhi, Dubai, Tokyo

Cambridge University Press
32 Avenue of the Americas, New York, NY 10013-2473, USA

www.cambridge.org
Information on this title: www.cambridge.org/9780521132862

First published 2010

Printed in the United States of America

A catalog record for this publication is available from the British Library.

Library of Congress Cataloging in Publication data

Banaszak, Lee Ann, 1960–
The women's movement inside and outside the state / Lee Ann Banaszak.
   p.   cm.
Includes bibliographical references and index.
ISBN 978-0-521-11510-0 (hardback) – ISBN 978-0-521-13286-2 (pbk.)
1. Feminism – United States – History.   2. Women in the civil service – United
States – History.   3. Women in politics – United States – History.   4. Women
social reformers – United States – History.   5. Feminist political geography – United
States.   6. Feminist theory – United States.   I. Title.
HQ1426.B27   2010
305.420973–dc22   2009015986

ISBN 978-0-521-11510-0 Hardback
ISBN 978-0-521-13286-2 Paperback

To Joyce and Len,
the feminists who raised me

And to Clara and Isaac,
the future generation

Contents

List of Tables and Figures

TABLES

FIGURES

Acknowledgments

I am the offspring of the modern women's movement. My mother was among the first women to run for mayor of a major municipality in my home state of Missouri. In middle school I remember the boys joining for the first time our required home economics class. As I considered where to go to college, I received a recruiting letter from West Point urging me to consider being in the second cohort of women there. While I encountered only a few women professors in my undergraduate and graduate studies, they were present enough that I never questioned my own career path. As I entered the ranks of academia, the university child care facilities that allowed me to combine my research with a family life were the product of the battles of an earlier generation of feminists and female academics.

The women's movement I knew from my formative years was one of grassroots activism – women's music festivals, local organiza-tions fighting for the Equal Rights Amendment, and the neighborhood women's health cooperative – and famous feminists like Gloria Steinem and Betty Friedan. It was a feminist movement that stood outside of the State, sometimes pressuring it to incorporate feminist policies and often opposing its institutional biases and conservative actions. Yet, on the other hand, I also was cognizant of a growing list of famous women politicians – Bella Abzug, Shirley Chisholm, and (coming from University City, Missouri) Harriett Woods – all of whom I identified less with the women's movement than with the national political scene that fascinated me. Completely off my radar were feminist activists working inside government, although I now see that they very much influenced my experiences as well.

While the story of second wave feminism has been told by many scholars more skilled than I, the story of this particular set of feminist activists – those that worked within the federal government – has largely remained untold although participants in the movement such as Betty Friedan and Jo Freeman have long noted their existence and the important effects they had on the movement. Where I have been overzealous in stating their achievements (and I do not wish to underplay the important contributions of those outside the state), it is perhaps because their story has been under the radar of most scholars of second wave feminism.

I would not have developed this book without the support of those feminist activists I studied. As should be clear by the description of the development of this project, I owe a great debt to all of the feminists who took the time from their very busy lives to give me a glimpse into their experiences and thoughts, and read my drafts with a careful eye to detail. Despite leading busy lives usually combining activism and the long work days of professional careers, the feminists I interviewed opened their homes to me, handed me valuable primary sources, and were ever accommodating when I would follow up on a specific question even years after the initial interview. I hope that I have done justice to all that they have told me.

There are many feminist activists who served in the federal government but died before I could talk to them: they include Catherine East, Morag Simchak, Caruthers Berger, Marguerite Rawalt, Sylvia Ellison, B. Ann Kleindienst, Elsa Chaney, Barbara Good, Anne Armstrong, and Caroline Cox. Some left extensive archives or oral histories that I could examine; others I know only because they lived in the memory of the activists I interviewed or were briefly mentioned in the historical record. Each of these women came alive, to varying degrees, in the course of my research, and each played important roles in the women's movement from inside the state.

Even with the extensive support provided by these feminist activists, this manuscript could not have been written without the additional help of a number of individuals and institutions. Several social scientists provided valuable assistance during the course of my research. Jo Freeman gave me an initial list of insider feminists to interview and helped to introduce me to many of the first women I interviewed. Laura Woliver and Betty Glad shared archives from the National Institute of Health's Self Help for Women's Rights organization while Alice S. Rossi aided me in the search to find the data from her 1982 book. Numerous scholars took the time to comment on earlier drafts including Mark Anner, Frank Baumgartner, Karen Beckwith, Francis Chen, Cynthia Harrison, Valerie Jenness, Sally Kenny, Mary Katzenstein, Miki Caul Kittilson, Patrick Le Galès, Joni Lovenduski, Susanne Mettler, John McCarthy, David S. Meyer, Sue Tolleson Rinehart, Dieter Rucht, Marian Sawer, John Skrentny, Winston Tripp, S. Laurel Weldon, Celia Valiente, Angelika von Wahl, and Edward Walker. I am particularly grateful to the three anonymous reviewers for Cambridge University Press who provided me with wonderfully thoughtful comments on an earlier draft of the manuscript.

I am also exceedingly grateful to the graduate and undergraduate students who provided research assistance in the course of my work, including Jeremy Deck, Hilary Ferrel, Corrine Harkcom, Petya Kirilova, Tiffany Yankowski, Aleks Petrykowska, and Marie Pierson. Jiso Yoon deserves special mention, because she provided invaluable aid at the end of the process, helping develop the comparative perspective of the final chapter and undertaking the numerous tasks that are needed to create a polished manuscript.

I have also benefited from comments and suggestions that I received at a number of conferences. Early on, a conference in Social Movements and Public Policy supported by The Center for the Study of Democracy at the University of California Irvine provided initial opportunities to examine the theoretical implications of movement–state intersections. A conference on the American State at Oxford University organized by Des King and Larry Jacobs allowed me to hone the argument about how movement–state intersections have affected the American State. Input from a number of scholars at the first European Conference on Gender and Politics in Belfast convened by Karen Celis and Johanna Kantola helped me better to understand how my research speaks to current feminist scholarship on state feminism. Finally, I have benefited from the input of scholars at successive American Political Science Association meetings where I have presented parts of this research. I would like to particularly thank Joyce Outshoorn, Karen Celis, Johanna Kantola, Alice Woodward, Laurel Weldon, Eileen

McDonagh, Fiona McKay, Louise Chappell, and Jill Vickers for
insightful questions or comments on the work. If any errors or problems remain with the manuscript, it is certainly my own fault and not
because I lacked excellent feedback.

Good librarians and archives are vital to any research endeavor,
and I have benefited throughout from both the holdings of a number
of fine institutions as well as the librarians that make them accessible.
The Schlesinger Library at Harvard University's Radcliffe Institute for
Advanced Study provided a wealth of archives of the modern women's
movement and the librarians there – particularly Sarah Hutcheon, Ellen
Shea, Diana Carey, Katherine Kraft and Anne Engelhart – were incred-
ibly helpful. At The Pennsylvania State University, Lee Stout helped me
locate materials in the "A Few Good Women" collection even as it was
being developed; and Helen Sheehy and Stephen Woods in the Social
Science library of Paterno Library provided considerable aid, particularly in locating the census and historical materials in Chapter 2.
Finally, Heidi Rubenstein at the Lauinger Library of Georgetown University was especially helpful in providing information and locating
materials from the Georgetown Foreign Affairs Oral History Project.
I have benefited greatly from all of their expertise.

As Virginia Woolf understood, writers (even academics) need a
space in which to work. In the course of this project, I have benefited
from the provision of physical space offered me by a number of institutions and individuals. Pennsylvania State University has been my
academic home from the beginning of this project and deserves much
thanks for its support. But I also began and ended this project during
research leaves at the Wissenschaftszentrum für Sozialforschung, Ber-
lin. I am particularly grateful to Friedrich Neidhardt who provided me
an academic home in 2000 as I was developing the idea of movement–
state intersections that eventually became this book, and to Dieter
Rucht and Dieter Gosewinkel who hosted me in the Forschungsgruppe
Zivilgesellschaft, Citizenship und politische Mobilisierung as I made
the final edits. Equally importantly, Anny Wong, Sara Banaszak, and
Koa opened their home to me and plied me with good food and conversation during my many research visits to Washington, DC. In all these
cases, the intellectual atmosphere was as important as the physical
space that was provided.

Other institutions provided the financial means that allowed me to complete this research. Research leaves in 2000 and 2008–09 were funded by The Pennsylvania State University and by the Alexander von Humboldt Foundation's Bundeskanzler Fellowship. I also benefited from the financial support provided by a grant from the Research Office of the College of Liberal Arts at Pennsylvania State, which supported travel for interviews and a research assistant. A Research Support Grant from the Schlesinger Library at Harvard University's Radcliffe Institute for Advanced Study financed a three-week trip to the library that allowed me to delve deeply into the archives there. In addition, a Carrie Chapman Catt Honorable Mention Prize for Research on Women and Politics helped to pay for additional research assistance at a critical juncture.

I also want to thank those who have helped move the manuscript into published form. Lew Bateman has been wonderfully supportive as an editor throughout the writing process. Mark Fox, Emily Spangler, and Shelby Peak have done a great job of marshalling the manuscript through the production process. Jennifer Carey provided invaluable help with the production of the book. Oxford University Press kindly granted permission for me to republish parts of my chapter "Moving Feminist Activists Inside the American State" from *The Unsustainable American State* edited by Desmond King and Lawrence Jacobs (2009).

Above all, though, this manuscript owes its existence to my family. The Herculean abilities of my spouse Eric Plutzer, who balanced unconditional support for the project with thoughtful criticism while assuming the lion's share of the household tasks and child care during many periods were critical to the manuscript's completion. Isaac Banaszak Plutzer and Clara Banaszak Plutzer also contributed to the manuscript's completion in part with comments (such as the need for more pictures or a catchier title like *Little Dog Lost in Forest*) but more significantly in giving up a large number of days with me while I interviewed, wrote drafts, and polished the manuscript. Thank you for putting up with it all.

Blurring the Conceptual Boundaries between the Women's Movement and the State

In 1966 and 1967, a newly revitalized women's movement organized the first protests that would expand to become a second wave of mobilization. Hundreds of scholarly works have documented, described, and analyzed this movement. The common narrative of these treatments is a familiar one: Despite having a few allies among government officials, feminist activists operated outside of and often in opposition to a government apparatus that contributed to maintaining women's unequal status. Most contemporary accounts of feminist protest events described the movement in these terms as well. A photograph caption in the December 15, 1967 *Washington Post* is consistent with this narrative, both for what it describes but especially for what it omits:

Mary Eastwood pickets the offices of the Equal Employment Opportunity Commission during a demonstration yesterday sponsored by the National Organization for Women. NOW was protesting what it considers the EEOC's discriminatory ruling permitting employees to place job ads under separate Help Wanted – Male, and Help Wanted – Female, columns. Similar demonstrations took place in New York, Atlanta, Chicago, and San Francisco. (*Washington Post*, December 15, 1967: B3)

There is nothing extraordinary about this caption nor about the accompanying photo showing a woman carrying a sign that says "Equal Employment Opportunity for Women NOW." The picture differs little from others taken at hundreds of feminist protests that occurred across the country during the 1960s and 1970s. However,

there is more to the story than the caption reveals: Mary Eastwood herself was a government employee as were a large percentage of those
who planned and organized the event. Both protesters and organizers
worked in such places as the Department of Justice, the Department
of the Navy, the Central Intelligence Agency, and the Department of
Labor. Some of these government employees helped organize events
but preferred not to demonstrate, fearing negative consequences from
their supervisor (Interview, March 25, 2002).

Most overviews of the women's movement have focused on movement activists *outside* of the government that they are trying to influence (see, for example, Carabillo et al. 1997; Ferree and Hess 2000;
Ryan 1992; Tobias 1997). Indeed, the view that social movements are
clearly and completely "outside the state[1]" prevails throughout both
theoretical and empirical discussions of social movements generally.
Yet many, if not most, of the activists picketing on December 15, 1967
were upper-level employees of the federal government. They constituted
an important network of women's movement activists who permeated
the state and engaged in oppositional actions; they often worked in
ways that remained largely unnoticed both by the movement and by
the bureaucracy that employed them. Contrary to the view that social
movements exist outside the halls of power, this part of the women's
movement existed within the state from the movement's inception.

In this book I examine feminist activists who were upper-level government employees in the period from the Kennedy to the Clinton
administrations. I show that the boundaries between the state and the
movement, often conceptualized as distinguishing two separate collective actors, are fuzzy. More generally, I argue that social movements
often overlap with the state through their activists located within the
state. In the case of the U.S. women's movement, that overlap had
important consequences: It directly influenced the creation of movement organizations, it affected the political opportunities that were
available to the movement, and it furthered some policy outcomes
while constraining others. Understanding the legacy of the women's

---

[1] In this chapter, I use the term "the state" in the same way as other scholars in
comparative politics to indicate the institution with a monopoly on the legitimate use
of force (Moore 1999: 100; Poggi 1990). Generally, when the term is used it does not
reference one of the fifty state governments of the United States unless that is clearly
signaled.

movement – indeed, any movement – requires the development of a theoretical framework for examining the intersection of the movement and the state, and an empirical assessment of movement politics at this intersection.

I begin this chapter by discussing why scholars and activists need to understand how movements and states overlap. I argue that social movement scholars must pay more careful attention to the intersection between social movements and the state – to what constitutes an insider and an outsider. Otherwise, we are likely to miscategorize parts of the movement as allies, overstate the degree of institutionalization and cooptation in social movements, and exaggerate the relative importance of external factors (such as political opportunities) in comparison to internal movement factors. This miscategorization has the effect of underestimating the agency and influence of many feminist activists. Moreover, it is precisely where movements overlap with the state that one can see most clearly how social movements can mold the state to their own political advantage – *creating* political opportunities that can help them in the future.

While gender scholars have long debated the role of insiders in the women's movement and examined the policy effects of women's policy agencies, I also argue that more attention is needed to individual feminist activists as a form of movement–state intersection and not just to the bureaucratic structures of the state. The presence of women's movement activists influences the way state bureaucratic structures function. Moreover, insider feminist activists are located throughout the state, often outside of agencies devoted to "women's issues," and even in these locations, insider feminist activists had and can have significant influences on policy. Although studying insider feminists is difficult because their actions often occur "under the radar" (see for example Kenney 2008: 717–18), the significance of these networks of individual activists to the women's movement makes the study of individual insider activists necessary.

Finally, I contend that creating a theory of the intersection of social movements and the state requires an examination of different theories of the state and the development of state interests. States are complex institutions, and their many parts have varying capacities to enforce a single set of interests or policies, resulting in internal conflicts and contradictions. Moreover, democratic states offer numerous opportunities for intersections with social movements because representing societal interests and encouraging at least some level of participation by civil society is one of the state's fundamental functions. Although some areas of the state – such as the bureaucracy – are not considered part of this function, these areas are nevertheless affected by these democratic functions.

After creating the theoretical rationale for this study, I then place the empirical analyses in the book in context by discussing the aspects of women's movements and states that influenced the intersection of these two entities. Because some women are better able to enter the state than others, the part of the women's movement that intersects the state is not representative of the whole movement. This has consequences for the types of policies that ultimately are adopted. I also maintain that the demands of the women's movement can be addressed in multiple locations in the state, allowing feminist activists working in many different parts of the state to utilize their positions to further the movement – even in agencies and departments that had little explicit focus on women. Finally, I emphasize that the state is not static but changes in form and function over time, and organizational changes provide new opportunities for movements that intersect with the state.

I conclude this chapter by discussing the sources of evidence that I use – archival research and in-depth interviews with forty "insider" feminist activists – and outlining the rest of the book. I argue that networks of movement activists within the state played important roles in mobilizing and organizing the movement, altering the political opportunities available to the movement, and creating concrete policy changes that altered the social landscape in the United States.

UNDERSTANDING INTERSECTIONS BETWEEN SOCIAL
MOVEMENTS AND THE STATE

Social movements have traditionally been viewed as outsiders to the state (Birnbaum 1988; Burstein, Einwohner, and Hollander 1995; Diani 1992; Flam 1994; Jenkins and Klandermans 1995; Tarrow 1998; Tilly 1978). For example, Diani (1992: 7) notes that definitions of social movements include an emphasis on actions "largely outside the institutional sphere." Such definitions focus on either a movement's existence outside the realm of the state or the use of confrontational political actions such as protest to distinguish movements from other political actors (Burstein et al. 1995; Goldstone 2003; Katzenstein 1998). Increasingly, though, social movement scholars are examining movements within existing institutions (Meyerson 2003; Moore 1999; Raeburn 2004; Zald and Berger 1987[1978]), and specifically within the state itself (Binder 2002; Goldstone 2003; McAdam, Tarrow, and Tilly 2001; Santoro 1999; Santoro and McGuire 1997; Skrentny 2006, 2002; Smith and Lipsky 1993; Wald and Corey 2002; Werum and Winders 2001; Wolfson 2001; Zald 2000).[2]

Women's movement scholars have recognized the intersection between women's movements and the state for much longer, both in the form of women's policy agencies – that is bureaucratic structures that focus on women or women's movement goals (Mazur 1995, 2001, 2002; Pringle and Watson 1992; Sawer 1995; Stetson and Mazur 1995) – and in terms of individual women located within the state, even coining the term "femocrats" to denote such women (see for example Chappell 2002; Eisenstein 1996, 1990; Katzenstein 1998; Outshoorn 1997, 1994; Sawer 1990; Vargas and Wieringa 1998).[3] However, even those works concentrating on individuals often separate feminists inside the state from the movement outside using concepts of iron or velvet triangles (Vargas and Wieringa 1998; Woodward 2003) or focus only on those women in women's policy agencies (Outshoorn 1994; Sawer 1990; Watson 1990).

Taken together, such analyses raise the question of how social movements can be outsiders when they exist inside the halls of power. In this section, I will explain why the intersection between movements and state needs to be reconceptualized and develop the concept as a *variable*

---

[2] Interest group scholars have also long recognized the interconnectiveness of traditional interest groups and the U.S. government, both through the capture of governmental offices by interest groups (e.g., McConnell 1970; Stigler 1975) and through the career paths of individuals who move from the bureaucracy to lobbying organizations and vice versa (see, for example, Heinz et al 1993 and Salisbury and Johnson 1989).

[3] The definition of "femocrat," used outside the United States, varies quite widely by author and some definitions do not require a connection to the women's movement. Here the feminist activists that I delineate are activists in an autonomous movement; we know this because comparatively we know that a strong women's movement has existed independent of the government in the United States, and the criteria for the feminist activists in this study is that they were an active part of that independent movement.

that can characterize every movement. ⌐I argue that outsider status is not determined by location or by tactics but by the degree of *inclusion* in institutions.⌐Extending the logic of Katzenstein (1998) and Zald and Berger (1987), I argue that it is important to separate a movement's goals from its strategies or tactics, and from its location vis-à-vis the state. I then challenge traditional assumptions that movement–state intersections necessarily derive from movement institutionalization.

Why It Matters: Movement–State Intersection and Political Opportunity

Social movement scholarship has traditionally identified state actors who advocate for movements as political allies. These allies are viewed as part of the larger set of political opportunities that movements face (e.g., McAdam 1982; Tarrow 1998). Even scholars of "femocrats," who have gone the furthest in recognizing the existence of feminists in the state, have tended to implicitly separate femocrats from the women's movement. For example, in her analysis of feminists in women's policy positions, Outshoorn (1994) divides femocrats into allies of the movement and professionals. Yet several of the feminist bureaucrats she interviewed "denied the implicit dichotomy of my question by pointing out resolutely that they themselves were part of the movement (or by saying 'you belong to both')" (Outshoorn 1994: 152). Similarly, Vargas and Wieringa (1998) note that feminists have become both politicians and civil servants; nevertheless, their use of the concept "iron triangle" has the effect of analytically separating feminist politicians and femocrats from the women's movement.

"allies"   Labeling feminist activists within the state as "allies" can be misleading and consequential for several reasons. Feminist activists inside the state and state allies of the women's movement differ in several key respects. First, "allies" who advocate a movement's agenda may do so for reasons other than those held by movement activists. For example, in discussing why President Kennedy created a President's Commission on the Status of Women, many have noted the importance of women voters to his 1960 election and a desire among Democrats to avoid the issue of the Equal Rights Amendment, which would antagonize their labor constituencies (Pedriana 2004; Zelman 1982: 25).

Allies can therefore be expected to make very different decisions from movement activists and base these decisions on concerns that may be unrelated or even opposed to movement concerns.

②Second, while allies often provide a movement with political sup- *differences* port, important information or tangible resources – the transfer of such support or resources will occur only when it serves the interests of that ally – interests that are probably unrelated to the goals of the movement itself. On the other hand, support, information, or resources are likely to flow more freely _within_ the movement because movement actors are committed to at least some movement goals. Intersections with the state thus improve movement resources and capabilities even when (perhaps especially when) the state itself may be hostile to the movement. For example, movements are likely to have more complete information about state actions and policies through intersections with the state. While allies of a movement might encourage coordination of efforts between themselves and the movement, that coordination is *actors have* likely to be negotiated and partial. However, actors who are part of *more power* the movement are likely to be in a position to coordinate actions with *within* the movement more completely and effortlessly.

Most importantly, from the standpoint of explaining the causes of movement mobilization, development or outcomes, the degree to which external factors, such as political opportunities, influence the movement will be overstated if the movement's intersection with the state is defined as outside of the movement. Such a misclassification reduces social movements' agency vis-à-vis the state. In this book, I show that women's movement activists within the state played a key role in the movement both acting as a part of the movement that was located in the state and by creating lasting political opportunities that aided the future development of the movement.[4] Thus, identifying movement–state intersections as part of a movement's political opportunities underestimates movement agency and overstates the importance of external factors.

---

[4] The effect of political opportunities on movement outcomes is well established (Amenta and Zylan 1991; Banaszak 1996; Costain 1992; Giugni 1999), but I believe that one key mechanism by which social movements can alter their political opportunities themselves (cf. McAdam 1996) is through movement–state intersections.

The Intersection of Movements and States

I define the movement–state intersection as occurring when a network of movement actors or organizations is located within the state. These networks operate within the constraints of state institutions, and describing how they manipulate those institutions can clarify the role of interests versus the role of institutional rules. These collective actors are also constrained by their positions within both the state and the movement, which may shape appropriate behavior, interests, and goals.

The intersection of movements with the state varies across movements and across time for the same movement. At one extreme, a movement may exist completely within the state. For example, Katzenstein (1998, 1998a) analyzes women's activists within the military as a separate movement completely within this institution. More commonly, movements intersect only partially with the state. For example, the creationists that Binder (2002) analyzes captured school boards in a number of communities in Kansas; yet, creationism as a movement occurred mostly outside the state and the intersection of the movement within the state was both small and temporary (see also Wolfson 2001). In Chapter 2 I argue that during the 1960s the U.S. women's movement's intersection with the state involved more movement activists than did the Civil Rights movement's intersection. This was because African Americans' exclusion from society kept them largely out of the ranks of government. While both were outsiders to the political process, the nature of their "outsider" status was quite different.

Even when located inside the state, social movements maintain their outsider status because *exclusion* from the polity is not completely synonymous with *location.* Instead, I argue that there are several forms of exclusion, which can occur separately or jointly, and some of these occur even when actors are located inside the state. These varying types of exclusion are illustrated in Table 1.1.[5]

---

[5] The different types of marginalization and exclusion described in Table 1.1 are not mutually exclusive. Some movements may be characterized by multiple layers of exclusion, while others may face a single form of exclusion. Although not the focus of this book, examining the different forms of exclusion that social movements face would go far in elucidating the "outsider" status social movements have and how this varies from movement to movement.

TABLE 1.1. *Theorizing the Types of Outsider Movement Status in Democratic States*

Type of Exclusion	Movement Example	Descriptive Examples
Rights or Repression Based	Civil Rights Immigrants	Dahl (1971)
Societal Norms	Welfare Rights Civil Rights	Bachrach and Baratz (1962); Lukes (1974)
Minority Size or Institutional Exclusion	Environmental	Rohrschneider (1993)
Marginalization by Devaluation	Creationists in Kansas, U.S. Women's Movement	Binder (2002) Skrentny (2006)
Intra-institutional Marginalization	French Femocrats	Mazur (1995a)

One form of exclusion occurs by limiting the rights available to a *example 1↑* particular portion of the population by, for example, law or physical repression (Dahl 1971). After Reconstruction, for example, America's southern states excluded African Americans from legal rights by physical repression, poll taxes, and segregation laws. Immigrants to most countries also face legal or rights-based exclusion from the state. While these individuals are subject to the state's power, they are excluded from most possibilities of state influence.

A second form of exclusion may result from society's norms and *ex. 2* practices. Here, exclusion comes, not from legal exclusions or from the state's use of force, but from the ways that society excludes groups by not recognizing their existence or the issues that they face (Bachrach and Baratz 1962; Lukes 1974). For example, grievances of poor people in the United States have largely been invisible because of the expectation that equal opportunity allows economic advancement for all. As a result, issues of poverty may not be seen as a societal problem and the economic claims of poor people may not be considered. Similarly, even outside of the South, African Americans were excluded by societal practices of segregation that tended to keep them out of networks with their white counterparts.

Even where groups' interests are recognized, a third form of exclusion occurs when institutions allowing representation of interests within the state prohibit or limit the representation of a group (Gaventa 1980; Schattschneider 1960). For example, Rohrschneider (1993) argues that early environmental or green movements faced this type of exclusion. Legally, movement activists could vote and hold office. Yet, the nature of the electoral system and of established political parties influenced whether their issue concerns were incorporated into party positions. Institutional characteristics of some states assured that movement goals were not discussed by government actors. Thus, the environmental movement remained outside government not because of societal norms or legal rights but because institutional arrangements excluded them wholesale from the state.

Even when individuals are included in the state, they may still be excluded internally if they "lack effective opportunity to influence the thinking of others even when they have access to forums and procedures of decision-making" (Young 2000: 55). There are at least two forms that this internal exclusion may take. One is described by Young (2000) who notes that even when people are part of a conversation they may still be excluded if their arguments are not taken seriously, devalued as silly or simple, or dismissed out of hand (see Ferree 2003, 2005 on how such practices are used to marginalize or exclude feminists). This form of internal exclusion occurs because of social practices and shaming but also because of informal norms on who has a legitimate voice. In the early 1960s, even within the Equal Employment Opportunity Commission, feminists experienced this form of internal exclusion because their concerns were devalued compared to the claims of African Americans and other nonwhite ethnic groups (Skrentny 2006; see also Chapter 4). Similarly, Binder (2002: 228) notes that although creationists controlled the school board in her Kansas example, they were unable to influence science curriculum despite their positions of power because they "could reach the inside of the institution and, yet, still not have what was defined as a legitimate voice there."[6]

---

[6] Indeed, some feminist scholars (Kathlene 1994; Weldon 2002) argue that gender reduces the political power women have been able to obtain, creating a form of exclusion even with inclusion.

ex. 5   Another form of internal exclusion results more from institutional marginalization. For example, in France, offices representing feminist interests and incorporating femocrats have rarely been located centrally in the bureaucratic structure or been in position to influence presidents or prime ministers (Mazur 1995a). This kind of marginalization occurs when individuals' place within institutional hierarchies give them little power, and are far from where policy debates are decided.

These examples suggest that even when movements are found inside the state they may still face important forms of exclusion that merit the challenger status defining social movements. The intersection with the state is therefore a *variable* for social movements that, in order to analyzed, must be clearly conceptualized. One purpose of this book is to more clearly define the dimensions of this variable by carefully examining an important example of movement–state intersection.

Defining "Insiders" and "Outsiders"

Social movement scholars and many activists are highly skeptical about movements acting within the state, given the state's monopoly on legitimate force and its control over policy. Scholars tend to associate movement activists within the state with specific ideological perspectives and tactical choices (as Katzenstein 1998: 39–41 has noted).[7] While other social movement scholars have long argued that each of these aspects – strategies, ideology or goals, and location – are relatively independent (Katzenstein 1998; Zald and Ash 1966; Zald and Berger 1987 among others), the term "insiders" is often used loosely to delineate not just location inside the state, but a combination of a conventional tactics and goals of limited reforms.

Another purpose of this book is to explore how location inside the state influences the choice of goals (Chapter 3) and tactics or strategies (Chapter 5). Hence, the distinction between location, tactics/strategies, and ideology is important. I will show that feminist activists in the federal bureaucracy did not always employ "insider" tactics; nor were their goals always reformist or incremental. Indeed, the linkage among

---

[7] See for example Eisenstein 1990; Ferguson 1984; Outshoorn 1997. Outshoorn (1994: 144) is an exception in recognizing that insider tactics may be separate from the position of femocrat. She notes that it is unreasonable to assume that "activists who take on government or state-subsidized positions adjust to its culture and jettison the more radical part of their ideology."

location, goals (or ideology), and strategy (or tactics) was more complex than that. Feminist activists inside the bureaucracy occasionally encouraged confrontational tactics by outside activists because they knew conventional tactics would be ineffective. They also found ways of turning conventional tactics to radical aims. Finally, many feminist activists located inside the state had (and have) revolutionary views of change, particularly in the latter years of the movement.

To differentiate among these three characteristics of "insiders" I utilize different terms for each. I reserve the term "insiders" for actors (either collective or individual) located inside institutions of the state. In this book, the movement activists that I label "insiders" are individuals who identify themselves with the movement during their government service and are activists in one or more women's movement organizations.[8] When groups of insider activists organize for change, the resulting organization is not necessarily "inside" the state as well. Rather whether organizations are inside or outside the state depends on the role they play vis-à-vis the state. I define an "insider" organization as one that is incorporated officially within the specific functions of the state. For example, Smith and Lipsky (1993) describe nonprofit organizations that contract with the state to carry out state functions; these groups would qualify as insider organizations (see also Banaszak, Beckwith, and Rucht 2003 on "offloading"). The importance of this distinction is developed in Chapter 4 where I discuss movement organizations created by insider activists that occasionally focused on changing state behavior toward employees of the federal government. Although these movement organizations targeted the state, were run by feminist activists located inside the state, and served to further the goals of women inside the state, they had no official connection with the state and were therefore not "insider" organizations.

Strategies and tactics that are considered part of the normal political repertoire are usually designated as insider. These conventional

---

[8] Here activists are identified largely by having held positions in women's movement organizations. While some held these positions in women's movement organizations during their tenure in office, for many, that was not possible. In these cases, the feminist activists were identified by numerous other individuals as activists during their tenure in office and held positions in women's movement organizations prior to or after their tenure as "insiders." As I shall show in Chapter 3, some insider feminist activists were working for the government before they became feminist, in which case I am careful to only discuss their activities after their entrée into the women's movement.

institutional tactics include trying to elect sympathetic individuals, lobbying public officials, and the use of litigation. Scholars have usually contrasted these tactics with extrainstitutional tactics such as protest, demonstrations, or building alternative communities (for examples of the difference between the two strategies see Amenta 2005; Banaszak 1996, chap. 7; Bernstein 2001; Rochon and Mazmanian 1993 among others).[9] Here I use the designations *conventional* and *confrontational* rather than "insider" or "outsider." I argue in Chapter 5 that the decision to utilize conventional or confrontational tactics is separate from the overlap in groups and individuals of movements and states,[10] and I also show that institutional tactics may occasionally be confrontational.

Lastly, I am also concerned with the goals that motivate movement activists' actions. Most authors draw a distinction between goals that seek *revolutionary change* of societal institutions (including the state) and goals of *incremental or limited reform*. While revolutionary views of feminism do not focus solely on altering the state, they do include the belief that patriarchy is inherently incorporated in the structure of state institutions and these continue to result in the oppression of women (see Connell 1990). On the other side, those who advocate incremental reform do not see state institutions as inherently problematic and believe that limited change is sufficient to solve the problems women face. Scholars who view movement–state intersections as the result of movement institutionalization often believe that location inside the state makes movement activists inherently reformist.

While some scholars have characterized these variables as dichotomous (see, for example, Outshoorn 1994: 5) I believe it is more useful to view them as continua. Individuals may hold primarily radical beliefs even while believing some institutions to be less patriarchal than others, while others may reject all of society's institutions. Only rarely are such tensions forced into dichotomous categories, such as when individuals find themselves forced to exist in state structures antithetical to their movement positions. In that case, regardless of the

---

9 I admit the dimension from conventional to confrontational does not do justice to the wide array of tactics and strategies that exist under it; yet, my purpose here is to differentiate tactics and strategies (what Katzenstein 1998 calls "form") from other types of "insider" designations.

10 Katzenstein (1998) also finds locations and tactics to be separate dimensions in her study of women in the church and military.

underlying continuum individuals may be forced into strictly dichotomous choices of remaining in state institutions or exiting the state to continue movement activism. However, as I will show in Chapter 7, the conditions that force dichotomous decisions are rare because variability within the state permits a wide variety of activities and roles even when presidential administrations are hostile to movement goals.

Institutionalization and Development of Movement–State Intersections

When scholars have recognized significant movement–state intersections, they have typically attributed them to social movement success or the institutionalization of the movement. If movements entered the state at all, it was because of state acquiescence either in the face of overwhelming mobilization (Santoro 1999; Weldon 2002) or because important state actors were allies who provided opportunities for entrée (Piven and Cloward 1978; Wald and Corey 2002). By and large, when social movement scholars recognize the existence of activists in the state, they are assumed to enter *after* the initial mobilization of the movement and the entry is taken to be a sign of movement success (Burnstein, Einwohner, and Hollander 1995; Gamson 1990; Reinelt 1995; Santoro 1999). Thus, Katzenstein sees feminist protest as having "moved inside institutions" of the military and church (1998: 3), and Santoro (1999) sees institutional activists as a sign of the movement's ability to achieve desired outcomes. The literature on comparative women's movements has, in most cases, also argued that women's movements open spaces for "femocrats" to act (Eisenstein 1996; Watson 1990: 5; Stetson and Mazur 1995), although it also recognizes the possibility that states adopt feminist policies without a movement at all (Hatem 1994; Mazur 2001: 298). In this literature, feminist insiders owe their positions or power to pressure and support from the women's movement (Weldon 2002), entering the state only after the movement has mobilized and organized; their entrance into the state is viewed as one of the movement's achievements.[11]

---

[11] The connection between feminist policies and the women's movement is less direct, in part because other state characteristics may intervene. For example, states' responses may be influenced by external pressures (see for example Towns 2003).

Movement–state intersections are also seen as a sign of the institutionalization of the movement toward normal politics, as, for example, when environmental movements form political parties and enter government (Desali 2003; Glenn 2003; Meyer and Tarrow 1998). Institutionalization is characterized not just by changing location of the movement but also by deradicalization of movement goals and a move toward employing mostly conventional tactics (Costain 1998; Costain and Lester 1998; Piven and Cloward; Walker N.d., but see Ferree 1996). Institutionalization also implies greater professionalization of movement organizations (Walker N.d.: 8). Hence, one reason that many scholars conflate location, goals, and strategies is that all are seen to be part of the larger process of institutionalization (see for example Walker N.d.).

I will demonstrate that movement success and sympathetic allies are not the only means by which such movement–state intersections occur. The multifaceted and varied nature of both states and movements allows intersections at any stage of movement mobilization. As Chapter 4 shows, the intersection between the U.S. women's movement and the state was not a result of second wave mobilization but existed from the very beginnings of the movement. Several characteristics of both the women's movement and the state made such an intersection possible (see Chapter 2). On the side of the state, the characteristics of state bureaucracy, including its extensive growth during wartime and lack of partisan patronage, created opportunities for women to enter the state. On the movement side, the continued activity of first-wave women's groups as well as an early emphasis on lifting educational barriers created incentives for as yet unmobilized feminists to enter the state. Thus, when the women's movement arose in the 1960s, feminists within the state mobilized themselves and were instrumental in mobilizing feminists outside the state. This initial mobilization transformed other women – both inside and outside the state – into feminists as well.

Moreover, as Chapter 3 shows, although "insider" feminist activists were never representative of the movement as a whole – most were drawn from the many variants of liberal feminism – the ideology of feminist insiders inside the state was not uniformly accepting of the political system. More radical views of social change and social justice could be found among insider feminist activists in every era. Early insider feminists – some of whom were converted to the cause after already being employed by the U.S. government – were only slightly less radical in their ideology than those who came later. But ideologies that judged political institutions as patriarchial or felt the need for more radical change could be found among insider feminist activists at any time-point. Thus, if a change occurred at all among the nature of feminist activists inside the state it was not in a direction typical of institutionalization narratives.

UNDERSTANDING THE STATE AS A LOCATION
FOR MOVEMENTS

The liberal state has unique features that distinguish it from other institutions. These include a monopoly on the legitimate use of force and legal authority, its regulatory authority and its mechanisms for direct societal influence such as elections (Moore 1999: 100; Poggi 1990; Rockman 1990). These distinguish the state from other institutions, such as the church and corporations, where the existence of movements inside institutions have been analyzed (Katzenstein 1998, 1998a; Raeburn 2004). The state is a complex institution, composed of many organizations. This means its capacity for internal control and the imposition of uniform norms varies across locations within the state. Moreover, while the state as a whole has specific interests, many of the organizations that comprise the state have additional interests, resulting in "a set of pluralistic goals" (Zald and Berger 1987[1978]: 218). The plurality of goals can lead state actors to act in opposition to each other (Rockman 1990). While examinations of the state have focused mainly on its institutions and interests, the individuals who occupy positions within the state also bring with them interests that shape policies and their implementation. In the next three sections I discuss these three aspects of the state – organizations, interests, and individuals – that affect what movements may achieve when they intersect with the state.[12]

---

[12] This typology draws on thoughts from Tilly (1978: 9) on the definition of a social movement (see Figure 1.1). Like the social movements we study, the state also takes on a very fuzzy quality. The state occurs on multiple levels for analysis, includes a variety of types of units, and its boundaries are blurred. All of this makes it difficult to subdivide the state or clarify its components. The typology presented here does so in ways that are relevant to social movements.

Organization and Bureaucracy

One way to deconstruct the state is to recognize the wide array of organizations that comprise it. A few, like the president's cabinet, are relatively informal and operate almost exclusively on norms and informal rules. Most, however are formal organizations that change with the introduction of new interests and issues (Baumgartner and Jones 1993) and with larger developments of the state itself (Skorownek 1982). Changes in the organization or rules of the bureaucracy are important in determining both the character and the influence of movement–state intersections because change creates opportunities for movements even if they do not already intersect the state. Periods of change within an organization offer opportunities to rewrite the rules, alter the focus, or create new organizational forms that may benefit (or hinder) social movements. However, such opportunities are better utilized if movement personnel are strategically located to take advantage of them – either by already being ensconced in the office or by entering the organization during its initial development.

Favorable location within the bureaucracy of the state is especially powerful in its ability to create lasting influences on policy and praxis. As Binder (2002: 228) notes: "Certain insider positions have greater capacity to advance challenges and draft revisions than do others." In her study, creationists were unable to create lasting policy even though they controlled school boards because they were not among the teachers and administrators who implemented policy changes. Rules and procedures once implemented may help maintain the movement; Laughlin (2000), for example, argues the Women's Bureau helped maintain a latent women's movement through the period labeled by Rupp and Taylor (1987) as "the doldrums." These same rules and procedures create changes in the way that society deals with certain issues – changes that are hard to reverse. As Chapter 6 shows, even small changes in the implementation of policy can have big effects on movements.[13]

At particular moments of organizational change within the bureaucracy, when new agencies are created or responsibilities combined under a single roof, individuals within the state have greater

---

[13] Meyerson (2003) makes the same argument about changes inside of corporations.

opportunities to mold and alter state policy than at other times. Thus, Ware (1981: 117) notes that women in the New Deal had more opportunities to affect policy because women "have tended to achieve success in newer government agencies, or during periods of government expansion." In Chapter 6 I demonstrate how the creation of the Equal Employment Opportunity Commission provided similar opportunities for feminist actors in the state to influence policy, although they did not always use conventional strategies or act as bureaucrats to do so.

The State's Varied Interests

The existence of movement–state intersections is predicated on the fact that numerous, often competing, interests exist within the state as a result of two processes. As many authors have pointed out, state actors develop their own interests; primary among them is the maintenance of the state as a whole and of the particular part of the state they inhabit (Carpenter 2001; Evans, Reuschemeyer, and Skocpol 1975). In the United States, like many democracies, the state also responds more or less to societal interests depending on the specific array of electoral and political institutional arrangements. Moreover, these interests develop in a historical process where they are redefined, refined, augmented, or combined through continual contestation within society, between state and society and between different constituent parts of the state (Pierson 1993; Rockman 1990). Thus, any particular state agency, department, bureau or office has a specific set of historically defined interests that may be closer or farther away from the interests of a social movement. Moreover, specific policies are constantly altering both the interests of that specific arm of the bureaucracy as well as influencing – in direct and indirect ways – larger societal interests.

For this reason, a movement–state intersection is likely to appear with differential probabilities at different locations within the state and the location of a movement–state intersection within the state will affect the movement's ability to alter state policy. The degree to which a movement–state intersection occurs in any particular organizational entity within the state depends in large part on the degree of congruity between the movement's interest on the one hand and those of the state organization on the other. One advantage enjoyed by the U.S. women's movement was the wide array of locations within the government bureaucracy where the interests of feminists could be incorporated. While many analyses have focused specifically on the Women's Bureau (Duerst-Lahti 1989; McBride Stetson 1995), I show that feminist activists found many locations within the state where they could influence policy outputs, suggesting the importance of not overlooking activists outside of agencies focused on "women's issues." However, different locations provide varying opportunities to have a lasting influence on policy. For example, Bonastia (2000) finds that the Equal Employment Opportunity Commission was a better "institutional home" for affirmative action than the Department of Housing and Urban Development although both received mandates to create such policies. The ability to influence policy also depends on the existing practices of the organization, and the degree to which it is subject to presidential or public scrutiny.

The Changing Personnel of the State

While discussions of the state center around its interests and organizational capacity, the individuals who occupy positions within the state are relevant as well. The state is larger than the individuals who occupy it; in almost all cases it is impossible for an individual or a set of individuals to alter the fundamental interests of the state, or even those of a department, agency, or office as most presidents sadly acknowledge. Any particular part of a state is too constrained by its existing institutions, historical development, and by the characteristics of the state writ large to be fundamentally altered by even the most dedicated group of individuals.

Yet, a set of individuals can have relatively small effects on the policies of the state – effects which, while small in comparison to the compelling interests of the state, may be fundamentally important in creating and maintaining social change (Skrentny 2006, 2002; see also Meyerson 2003). For example, Title IX, a law requiring equity in education, and the rules that implemented this law, have had almost no fundamental effect on the character of the state. Yet, the specific provisions of the law and the rules that implemented it are vitally important in fundamentally altering not only intercollegiate sports, but the sports industry and our gendered conceptions of athleticism.[14] As Zald and

---

[14] Although as McDonagh and Pappano (2007) suggest Title IX did not completely eliminate gendered stereotypes in sports and even reinforce some.

Berger (1987[1978]: 200) note in discussing movements within other bureaucracies: "Often... insurgency operates in gray areas where organizational behavior has not been explicitly prescribed," allowing the movement activists to "establish their own definition of the situation or shift the weighting of priorities." Movement activists in the federal bureaucracy often operated "under the radar" – in ways that never attracted the attention of their supervisors, the media, or opponents and occasionally even went unnoticed by other feminists – but their actions did alter public policy in ways that aided movement goals. Thus, social movement personnel within the state bureaucracy, by the nature of their position, are able to effect some social movement goals.

Moreover, the individuals who occupy the state's bureaucracy are not isolated from larger social influences; they experience the same forces that influence civil society outside the state, although state institutions and norms also act to influence and constrain their actions as state actors. Hence, I find in Chapter 3, that some of my insider feminist activists were state actors before they became feminist activists. As the women's movement increasingly mobilized, these women within the state converted to feminism and became inside feminist activists because they were already inside the state. As such, the story of insider feminist activists is not one of a group within civil society capturing the bureaucracy but of a more synergistic relationship between state and civil society where the state is not immune to large scale social forces.

An important factor in determining whether, when, and which movement actors will enter the state is the recruitment processes used in various parts of government. The state's willingness to hire movement activists will vary across location; in some parts of the bureaucracy, for example, movement activity may be seen as a qualification. Yet, because selection procedures reflect state interests, it is unlikely that the social movement activists who enter the state will mirror the movement as a whole.[15] In almost every movement, the poor and members of excluded minority groups, are unlikely to be among the members of

---

[15] State personnel also self-select into the state (that is they choose to work there). Hence, in some social movements it is less likely that social movement actors will choose to work for the state. However, because employment and activism decisions may be separated, activists could work a day job in the state even as they seek to overthrow it during non-work hours.

the movement who enter the state. I show in Chapter 3 that this was also true of the U.S. women's movement. The selection of movement actors who can move inside the state, combined with the opportunities presented by the privileges of this location, mean that insider activists are likely to press for some types of social change over others.

The willingness of the state to permit movement activists will not only vary across movements and locations within the state, it will also vary across time. State change provides opportunities or constraints for movement activists to enter the state. As Ware (1981: 61) notes in the case of women, "in times of expansion or emergency, the usual inhibitions against hiring women are dropped, and women as a group make important, albeit temporary, progress. Women generally do better in the formative periods of organizations. . . . Conversely, when the sense of emergency or newness recedes and the bureaucratic structure stabilizes or tightens, the situation for women deteriorates." Changes in the nature of the state itself, particularly an increased tendency to shift its responsibilities to nonstate actors, also increases the intersection between movements and states (Banaszak, Beckwith, and Rucht 2003; Smith and Lipsky 1993).

Democratic States

Democratic states also act as intermediaries, taking input from society to define policies (Rockman 1990). The process of representing societal interests in policy creates expectations of bureaucratic responsiveness to changes in government, although researchers have generally found that such responsiveness is limited (Carpenter 2001; Golden 2000; Wilson 1989; but see Aberbach and Rockman 2000). Indeed, U.S. presidents are generally able to alter bureaucracies in only a few areas where they concentrate their policy focus. Even when political appointees completely represent a new government's policy preferences (and often they do not since reasons for their appointment varies), they often find it difficult to mold an entrenched bureaucracy. As we shall see in Chapter 7, the limits of bureaucratic responsiveness can become an opportunity for social movements when an intersection between the movement and the state is already in place. Thus, feminist insiders within the Reagan and Bush administrations were able to continue to fight for feminist goals in some state locations because presidential policies were unable to always reach all locations and levels of the bureaucracy.

Scholars have long recognized that societal interests may capture individual agencies and departments, allowing them to influence the activities of that particular arm of the state (McConnell 1970; Stigler 1975; but see Carpenter 2002). As clients' interests come to define also a particular section of the bureaucracy's interests, this can both open and close opportunities for those parts of the movement inside the state. For example, although the Women's Bureau may have helped to maintain parts of the women's movement between 1920 and 1960, others have found the Women's Bureau's ties to organized labor during the same period limited what the women's movement could achieve, particularly by rejecting an Equal Rights Amendment (Rupp and Taylor 1987: 146–8). Because such established interests can constrain policy, new movements can achieve the most if their policy goals are not limited to a single part of the bureaucracy or if bureaucratic change allows them to capture new organizations within the bureaucracy.

THE U.S. WOMEN'S MOVEMENT
IN THE FEDERAL BUREAUCRACY

The U.S. women's movement is a counterexample to traditional assumptions that movements begin outside the state, moving in only as they succeed, after which they deradicalize and adopt conventional tactics. Indeed, one of the interesting characteristics of the U.S. women's movement has been its ability to achieve policies relatively early without either extensive protest (Tarrow 1998, 172) or a single state bureaucracy devoted to women's interests ("state feminism"). Because many historical accounts of the U.S. women's movement note the presence of the feminist underground within the U.S. bureaucracy (see for example, Friedan 1998: 95),[16] the U.S. women's movement is an important case for examining movement–state intersections.

To say that the U.S. women's movement intersected with the state, however, is not to say that either the movement or the state was

---

[16] Few authors have analyzed the feminist underground in the U.S. bureaucracy but see Duerst-Lahti 1989 and Pedriana 2004.

delimited by the other. The U.S. women's movement encompassed a wide range of ideologies, tactics, and locations. Most movement activists and movement organizations were not part of this movement–state intersection although they may have been affected by it. Moreover, the movement activists who permeated the state were not a random sample of movement activists as a whole – they were a select group in terms of race, profession, and education – and this had implications for the movement–state intersection. Within the wide array of feminisms existing within the movement, the feminist activists in the federal bureaucracy were drawn from a narrower range, yet they were not all liberal feminists who strongly supported existing institutions.

Similarly, the wide goals of the women's movement also allowed feminist activists within the state to pursue movement goals in many different locations within the state. Whether those goals were equality in employment or changing the gendered nature of institutions, pursuit of those goals was not limited to a single governmental agency. Thus, feminist activists in the State Department could hope to change the state in ways that furthered feminist goals just as feminists located in the Women's Bureau and the Equal Employment Opportunity Commission could do the same.

Thus, characteristics of movements also affect both the intersection between movements and states and the effect these intersections will have. Not all movement goals can be easily achieved from within the state, or from every location within the state. Antiwar activists within the Women's Bureau and the Equal Employment Opportunity Commission would be unlikely to affect the peace movement or policy outcomes, and even those within the Department of State would be highly constrained in what they could achieve. The story of feminist activists within the state and their effects is a tale of a confluence of factors – the nature of the U.S. women's movement, historical social trends, and the nature of the state itself were all important in these feminists' ultimate effects.

STUDYING THE U.S. BUREAUCRACY

I choose the federal bureaucracy as my focus for a number of reason, recognizing that as I do so I examine only a small part of the state. Several studies already explore how elected officials represent

movements in democracies (Binder 2002; Goldstone 2003; Santoro
and McGuire 1997) and there are extensive studies of the intercon-
nection of interest groups with the state (see for example, Aberbach
and Rockman 2000; Carpenter 2001; Heinz et al. 1993; McConnell
1970). Most of the exploration of the intersections of states and movements has come in the form of examining intermediary organizations
and their role as part of the delivery system of state goods (Banaszak,
Beckwith, and Rucht 2003a; Smith and Lipsky 1993). Similarly, in
democratic systems elected representatives – in the executive or legislative branch – officially represent constituents in society. Within the
literature on women and politics, many authors have examined the
degree to which women elected into office represent the demands of
the women's movement (Center for American Women and Politics
1991, 1978; Freeman 1987; Swers 2002; Wolbrecht 2000). Given
the nature of elected officials, interest groups, and political parties
as the official institutions of intermediation between civil society and
democratic states, this focus is not surprising. However, although such
intersections can occur within the bureaucracy, only a few women
and politics scholars have examined the U.S. bureaucracy and they
largely focus on the numbers of women and not the representation of
the women's movement specifically (these exceptions include Borrelli
1997; Naff 2001; Martin 2003, 1989).[17]

   There are also a number of reasons that the intersection of movement and state within the bureaucracy is of particular interest. The
bureaucracy has a particularly strong influence on policy and as such
may allow for movement activists to have considerable influence.
For example, Binder (2002) argues that "power in institutions (like
schools) is frequently more diffuse than power in political institutions,
insofar as authority is spread among professional bureaucrats, which
insulates them from direct pressure" (p. 221). For that reason, the intersection of movement and state is examined here in the form of individuals who identify with and act as part of the feminist movement but
who also work within the organization of the federal government
bureaucracy. The bureaucracy also represents the institution thought
to most strongly represent state interests. In a democratic state the

---

[17] There is also a fairly large amount of literature on the gendered nature of the bureaucracy (Ferguson 1984; Savage and Witz 1992).

bureaucracy is perhaps the most likely point of pure state autonomy and the furthest from being an intermediary organization.[18]

I chose to focus on individuals at all policy-making levels of the bureaucracy because ultimately I am interested in whether movement activists at these levels bring state power and policy to bear in the aid of movement goals. Contrary to those who focus on policy elites, I delve relatively deep into the bureaucracy – looking not just at the top layer of policy makers, but also at their subordinates who do not get to determine the general policies of a particular government. Many of the people I interviewed are in some sense "faceless bureaucrats": they have not appeared on the nightly news, been named the author of a new policy directive, or led an agency, department, or bureau. They toil in relative obscurity, yet they are able to influence the course the state takes.[19] They help to create the minor course corrections that are important to the path the state takes even as they do not determine the destination or goal. However, as I will argue throughout this book, those minor course corrections are vitally important to outside movements trying to get their voices heard and their policies instituted.

Most authors who have written about feminists in government limit their analysis to feminists in specific locations within the state. For example, Duerst-Lahti (1989) and Stetson (1995) focus on the Women's Bureau. Yet, I draw on women in a wide variety of locations within the government bureaucracy. Like Eisenstein (1990), I prefer not to identify, a priori, the locations within the state that movement activists must occupy. Rather the movement–state intersection (in the form of movement activists within the state) may be located in multiple locations within the state, not just in those agencies that are considered primary policy makers in the area of interest to a particular movement.[20] Indeed, as I show in Chapter 6, feminist activists have

---

[18] The judiciary might also fit these qualifications. Yet the judiciary is indirectly or directly elected in the United States, allowing interests to be represented, although this representation is heavily limited by the constraints of the institution of the law (see, for example, Kenney 2008, 2004).

[19] As Meyerson (2003: 16) notes in examining corporations, those who seek to change the institutions in which they are situated and who can have large effects on those institutions, are often not situated at the highest levels of the institution.

[20] One reason for not preidentifying particular locations associated with the movement is that the identification of particular agencies with particular issues is often the result

influenced policies important to the women's movement from many locations within the state.

Data Sources

The data in this book are drawn from a combination of archival research and in-depth interviews (see Appendix A for more information about the research design).[21] The archival work and interviews provide information on a wide array of feminist activists employed by the federal government during different periods of the second wave of the women's movement. Archival research provided both primary documents and oral histories. The primary documents consisted of personal papers of feminist activists who worked within the federal bureaucracy as well as the papers of several feminist organizations (a list of sources is provided in Appendix A).

As part of the research on feminist activists within the state, I conducted interviews between March 2002 and July 2004 with forty women's movement activists who held positions in the U.S. bureaucracy between 1960 and 2000 where they could potentially influence policy. All were either political appointees, women in the Senior Executive Service, or women holding a civil service job at the level of GS-14 or above. Feminist activists employed in the White House were included, despite the clearly political nature of this position, because they had ties to the federal bureaucratic machinery and because I wanted to examine how political control by the administration created differences between political appointees and civil servants. Each individual was interviewed once and the semistructured interviews lasted from forty minutes to two and one-half hours; all but one were tape-recorded.

To locate the activists I interviewed, I used a modified snowball design. I started with an initial list of feminist activists in government provided by Jo Freeman, and supplemented this list with people

---

of considerable conflict and even if seemingly stable in the short-term may undergo rapid change in some periods (Baumgartner and Jones 1993).

[21] In a few cases, quotations are also drawn from interactions with these feminist activists on other occasions. I had the opportunity to meet with a few of the women on multiple occasions, including a dinner party organized by Jo Freeman. I note the context when such comments occur outside of an interview.

I identified in historical archives and secondary literature. In the course of my interviews, I also asked people to identify feminist activists who were in the federal government. To qualify as an activist, an individual had to have a clear record of activism within feminist organizations. However, how they came to be feminist activists within the state differed substantially. Some were already feminist activists when they became employed by the federal government; others were converted into feminist activists after they were already bureaucrats. Interviewees' activism ranged from major organizations like the National Organization for Women to participation in smaller or more radical groups like rape crisis centers, women's peace groups, and antipornography actions.

This methodology no doubt has several limitations. One consequence of limiting my sample to high-level bureaucrats is to restrict the education and socioeconomic status of my sample (see Chapter 3). Moreover, I do not know whether these activists are a representative sample of the women's movement or even of the population of feminist activists meeting the selection criteria. I sought unsuccessfully both lists of feminist activists and lists of bureaucrats with membership in feminist organizations from which I might pull samples but could find neither. In selecting participants, I focused on maximizing variation in location within different branches of the bureaucracy and obtaining a mix of political appointees and civil servants. I also interviewed both women who entered the bureaucracy already feminists and those who were converted within the state. I feel confident therefore that the forty women provide a sense of the range of feminist activism within the mid- to upper-levels of the federal bureaucracy, but I cannot speak to the interviewees' representativeness of feminist activists within the U.S. federal bureaucracy.

THE PLAN OF THE BOOK

This book follows the movement–state intersection through its founding and then examines its effects on both the women's movement and on the policy-making process of the state. Chapter 2 begins the story by discussing the factors that led to feminist activists being in the state as the women's movement remobilized in the 1960s. To provide some context, I compare the women's movement's ability to create such an intersection with the absence of civil rights activists in the state during the same period. Chapter 3 looks at the biographies of feminist activists in the federal bureaucracy, focusing on their representativeness of the movement as a whole. Although these feminist activists were an elite group demographically, I find that ideologically these feminists were not easily pegged as simply liberal feminists interested in reforming an existing system.

Chapters 4 and 5 focus on the effect that feminist activists inside the federal bureaucracy had on the women's movement. In Chapter 4 I show how insider activists played an important role in mobilizing "the second wave" of the women's movement in the 1960s. Chapter 5 examines the tactics used by feminist activists employed by the federal government, showing that feminist insiders chose both confrontational and conventional tactics often depending on the openings that existed within government. Thus, at several crucial points within the history of the women's movement, feminist insiders initiated confrontational action precisely because they knew that the government was closed to certain types of issues. I also show how feminist activists inside the state were heavily involved in changing legal precedent through external lawsuits. Some of their litigation was a tactical form that represented a fundamental challenge to the state although scholars usually characterize legal strategies as a conventional tactic. Hence, the assumption that location inside the state necessarily leads to conventional activity is both false and ignores the strategic considerations of these activists.

Chapters 6 and 7 examine the relationship of feminist activists within the federal bureaucracy to the state and policy making. Chapter 6 focuses on whether feminist insiders were able to change state policy in ways consistent with the feminist agenda, and to what degree these have influenced society. In each of three case studies –Title IX, equal pay, and women in development – I find that feminist activists were effective in changing policy in ways consistent with women's movement goals. Chapter 7 asks what happens to feminist activists within the state when a presidential administration is opposed to feminist goals. This question becomes particularly important as the women's movement goal of social change collides with the desire that the bureaucracy be responsive to elected officials. I show that feminist activists can and do continue to exist and work during hostile administrations, often using subtler tactics to maintain previously gained policies, but that much depends on where they are located within the state. Finally, the concluding chapter discusses the implications of this case for social movement scholarship and gender studies.

2

Moving Feminist Activists Inside the State

The Context of the Second Wave

As the women's movement mobilized during the mid-1960s, feminists were already located within the federal government. The existence of this intersection between the women's movement and the state from the very beginning of the second wave was advantageous for the U.S. women's movement. Its supporters were already well placed to take advantage of the burgeoning interest in feminist policies and the increasing mobilization of women and allies both within and outside of government that accompanied the rise of the second wave. Understanding how and why these feminist activists came to be inside the state and how they formed a feminist network within government is essential to understanding their impact on the women's movement.

The presence of feminist activists in the state during the initial phases of mobilization as well as in later years is a result of a confluence of factors. However, three factors were crucial to these women[1] entering government service and developing the social networks that allowed them to mobilize as feminists. First, large scale changes in women's education and employment created a pool of working professional women that chose government service in pursuit of the careers they desired. Second, changes in the nature of the U.S. bureaucracy – both

---

[1] Although I will focus on women feminists in this chapter, it is important to note that several of the feminist activists I will discuss in later chapters are men. However, because the overwhelming number of them were women, I focus here on understanding the contextual factors that opened up government service to women.

permanent as in the move toward a civil service and temporary as when government burgeoned during wartime – created opportunities for professional women within the state. Third, the continued activity of women's organizations throughout the 1920s, 1930s, 1940s, and 1950s sustained extensive networks of women activists, allowing feminist bureaucrats to participate in networks of activism even before the mobilization of the second wave in the 1960s. Feminist organizations also lobbied for many of the changes in the federal bureaucracy that provided opportunities for women as a whole to enter the state.

While women were still very few in number, particularly at the upper ranks of the civil service, this confluence of factors created sufficient critical mass to allow the development of a small network of feminist professionals that crossed departments and agencies within the federal government. Indeed, this insider network set the women's movement apart from some other movements, like the civil rights movement, that lacked the structural opportunities for a network inside the state during its initial mobilization. The network of insider feminists allowed the passing of information and the development of collective identity across the federal bureaucracy, and as I show in later chapters, played an important role in the initial phase of the women's movement.

THE CHANGING NATURE OF WOMEN'S EDUCATION AND EMPLOYMENT

Feminists could not have achieved a significant presence inside the state had there not been overall increases in the number of women in the federal bureaucracy. These numbers were a result of societal increases in the number of women achieving a college education or moving into the work force. Of particular importance was women's experience within the legal profession because many feminist activists within the state are lawyers. One reason for the concentration of women lawyers within government bureaucracy was their experiences with discrimination in the legal profession. Although women entered law school in increasingly large numbers in the 1940s and 1950s, few outlets in private practice were open to them. The result was (and continues to be) a large movement of women lawyers into government. In comparison, the federal bureaucracy was almost completely closed to African American lawyers at the policy-making levels in the 1940s and 1950s, reducing the numbers of black civil rights activists, especially those in the law, within the federal bureaucracy.

Women's Education and Employment[2]

stereotypes

Betty Friedan's *The Feminine Mystique* noted that although the media usually portrayed white women as happy homemakers who spent their time attentively attending to the house and children, women's true social experience did not fit that stereotype. For one thing, the long-term changes in women's education and employment made women more active outside of the home. Even when the proportion of women among students receiving college and graduate degrees dropped in the 1950s and 1960s, the actual number of women in postsecondary education climbed, outstripped only by the flood of veterans taking advantage of the G.I. bill (Sapiro 1994: 129; Ware 1981: 22). By the mid-1970s, female high school graduates were attending college at the same rate as their male counterparts (Ford 2002: 183).

stats

Women's employment statistics heading into the 1960s also showed that women continued to work in increasing numbers even as the stereotype of women as housewives remained. In 1950, one-third of all women over the age of sixteen were in the paid labor force (U.S. Bureau of the Census 1975: 128). In 1960, as the second wave movement began, almost one-third of married women were working outside the home and the proportion of widowed, divorced, or separated women who were working was even higher (Ries and Stone 1992: 320).

---

[2] In this chapter, I often use the term women to discuss the status of women of all racial categories both in society and within the bureaucracy. Similarly, when discussing African Americans, I am referring to both black men and black women. I do not intentionally ignore the existence of the intersection of race and sex, nor the unique conditions that black women faced. However, I find myself faced with scant historical and empirical evidence of how the effects of race and sex intersect, making it difficult to trace changes over time. For example, labor force statistics were not collected by race prior to 1972. Even studies conducted by feminists within the state (e.g., U.S. Civil Service Commission 1968) do not acknowledge race as dividing women and simultaneous studies examining race within the federal bureaucracy do not look at men and women of color separately. This is itself an indicator of the lack of attention paid to the specific situation of black women.

Between 1960 and 2000, the percentage of married women in the labor force doubled, giving rise to political concerns about family and maternity leave and the quality of child care facilities (U.S. Bureau of the Census 2002: 372). By 1999 almost 60% of all preschool children attended some sort of child-care center (Office of Educational Research and Improvement 2001: 61).

It is worth noting that these statistics hide huge disparities by race. African American women were always part of the paid labor force. In 1972 (the first year statistics were available by race), African American women's labor force participation exceeded that of their white counterparts by over 10%. On the other hand, African American women did not receive the same benefits from the expansion of women's educational opportunities in the nineteenth and twentieth centuries. In 1957 only 2.9% of black women over twenty-five years of age had completed four years of college, less than half that of white women. In comparison, 10.1% of white men over twenty-five years of age had completed four years of college (U.S. Bureau of the Census 1957).

Nonetheless, the overall changes in women's employment and education rates have implications for two specific aspects of our story. First, as women's education and employment increased, more and more women began to work for the federal government, including more feminist activists. Indeed, as I shall show shortly, even though the federal government discriminated against women, even reducing its female work force in times of depression or after World War II, it was nevertheless more open to women employees than the private sector. Second, women's employment and education also created an increasing need for action on many feminist issues. These demographic changes spurred much of the activism on issues of women's employment throughout the 1920s–1950s, and even influenced feminist organizing of the 1960s.

The Rise of Women in the Law

Among the structural changes that occurred in women's employment, the transformation of women's place in the legal profession deserves special attention for two reasons. First, evidence suggests that as a

TABLE 2.1. *The Number of Women in the Legal
Profession, 1910–1990*

Year	Number	% of all Lawyers
1910	558	0.4
1920	1,738	1.4
1930	3,385	2.1
1940	4,447	2.4
1950	6,348	3.5
1960	7,543	3.3
1970	13,000	4.7
1980	72,312	13.8
1990	190,145	24.4

Sources: 1910: U.S. Bureau of the Census. **1940:** *16th Census of the
United States: Population: The Labor Force (Sample Statistics): Usual
Occupation.* Table 9 and Table 10. **1920–1970:** Epstein (1993): 4 See
also Drachman (1998): 253. **1980:** Calculated from 1980 Census of the
Population. Vol. 1. Characteristics of the Population. Individual State
Reports. Table 219. **1990:** 1990 *Census of Population Table 2.*

group women lawyers were particularly attracted to federal employment and constituted a large number of the women at the more senior
ranks of the bureaucracy in the movement's early years. Second, as
future chapters demonstrate, the legal training of these feminist activists influenced their ability to pursue lawsuits on behalf of feminist
causes – something they were able to do largely because they were
located within the state.[3]

Having
legal training
benefitted the
movement

While law schools were relatively closed to women, there was some
growth in the number and proportion of women in the profession of
law between 1920 and 1970. In 1920, women constituted 1.4% of
the legal profession while by 1970 that number had risen to 4.7% (see
Table 2.1). However, this rise occurred as the number of men in the
legal profession was also expanding. While the proportion of women
in the legal profession rose relatively slowly, the number of women
lawyers increased almost tenfold between 1920 and 1970.

Despite this expansion, discrimination against women in the law
remained strong. Most law schools had informal quotas that limited

---

[3] While these women qualify as cause lawyers, their employment by the state means
that they existed in a location that is not usually considered in the study of cause
lawyers (see for example Jones 1999; Marshall 2006: 175–179).

the number of women in the entering class (Epstein 1993: chapter 3). As one graduate of an Ivy League law school noted:

Every single...class had had 6 [women] or under until our class, which had 13 out of 180. And people said that our class was like the sky was falling. That it was an accident because there were a couple of people in our class who had men's names. So they said that those people had been accidentally admitted. At the time people were alarmed. And the class after us had 6. And then it continued that way until there was this sudden increase in the number of women that came to law school. (Interview, June 25, 2004)

Marguerite Rawalt, a long-time Internal Revenue Service attorney, noted that she was one of only three or four women in her class at George Washington University (Chester 1985: 75). Moreover some elite law schools did not admit any women until the 1950s. When Pauli Murray applied for graduate work at Harvard Law School in 1944, for example, she was told "You are not of the sex entitled to be admitted" (Hartmann 1998: 180). Harvard Law School admitted its first women law students in 1953, and was followed by Notre Dame and Washington and Lee (Epstein 1993: 50). Even when women gained admission to law schools they were told that they should not be there, and that they were unlikely to have careers in the law (Epstein 1993: 52).

Part-time law schools were particularly important for women, who often lacked the resources to study full-time and needed to work while they were enrolled (Chester 1985: 9), and also for government employees in Washington, DC, who studied law at night to advance their employment opportunities (Drachmann 1998: 119 and 153). Women employed by the federal government in the DC area who wished to acquire a law degree required the ability to study law part-time. In the pre-World War II period, Howard University was the first DC law school to accept women[4] (Drachmann 1998: 152). The Washington College of Law, which later became American University's Law School, opened in 1898 originally to offer white women an alternative to Howard (Drachmann 1998: 150–152; Chester 1985), but many

---

4 Women at Howard (including black women) experienced the same hostile environment as elsewhere. For example, Pauli Murray noted that her cohort of women students at Howard also faced discrimination (Kerber 1999: 188; Smith 1993: 55).

of the other part-time law schools remained closed to women either officially or by maintaining stringent quotas.

Moreover, women law school graduates faced enormous discrimination when trying to find a position. Sonia Fuentes, one of the first women lawyers in the Equal Employment Opportunity Commission, in describing her quest to gain a position in a law firm, noted that two interviewers offered positions as secretary or receptionist, another asked her point blank how he would know she wouldn't get pregnant, and a third suggested that she marry him and become copartner in the firm in that way (1999:119–122). Fellow women law students told Marguerite Rawalt: "you'll never make a lot of money hanging up a shingle by yourself. There isn't a law firm in the city that would employ you as a partner. They might employ you as a ghostwriter and a researcher, but you would not be a member of the firm" (Chester 1985: 76).

Overt discrimination meant that women who considered joining a law firm or opening up their own practices faced many problems. They were excluded from the kinds of networks that might bring in high paying customers and from activities, such as appearing in court, that aided career paths in the law (Epstein 1993: 103). When they did open their own practices or join firms, they largely ended up in lower-paying areas of matrimonial law, real estate, and estate law (Epstein 1993: 102).

In part as a result of these obstacles, women lawyers tended to move into government employment more often than men. Table 2.2 reports U.S. census data that classifies all lawyers and judges by sex and by the economic sector in which they worked.[5] It shows that women lawyers and judges were twice as likely to work for the government as their male counterparts. Numerically, these proportions translate into roughly 1,700 women lawyers in government in the 1950s and over 4,800 women lawyers employed in government bureaucracies in 1970. Indeed, by 1970 government was the primary employer of women lawyers – more than either private firms or individual law practices. By

[5] I am unable to provide comparable information by race because these data were not reported in the census reports, and the small number of African American lawyers nationwide prior to 1970 makes it impossible to use the 1% samples that are publicly available.

TABLE 2.2. *Type of Employment for Male and Female Lawyers and Judges, 1950–1990 in Percentages by Sex*

Year	Private Firms	Government	Self-Employed
1950			
Men	24.9	14.2	61.0
Women	31.0	27.7	41.1
1960			
Men	20.6	14.3	65.0
Women	31.2	28.1	40.0
1970			
Men	27.5	18.3	54.1
Women	30.0	36.7	32.8
1980			
Men	38.8	18.8	42.4
Women	51.1	33.7	14.9
1990			
Men	37.9	17.3	44.7
Women	55.1	26.0	18.5

Sources: **1950–1970:** Epstein (1993): 97. **1980:** U.S. Bureau of the Census. 1980. *Census of the Population: Characteristics of the Population:* Vol. 1–50 [50 State publications], Table 220. **1990:** Calculated by author using Ruggles et al. (2004). SPSS code and output available upon request.

1980 women lawyers' employment patterns began to change; employment in government was outstripped by private practice for the first time. Yet, even as late as 1990, women lawyers were still more likely than their male counterparts to enter government.

African Americans in the Legal Profession

To understand the role that women lawyers[6] played in the existence of feminist activists inside the state, I compare their situation with that of African Americans. Discrimination had a very different effect on African American lawyers than it did on women. Because the legal system was so imbued with racial discrimination, the law was one

[6] Women lawyers, both inside and outside government, were overwhelmingly white; few African American women became lawyers at that time. In 1940 for example, blacks constituted less than 1% of all women lawyers (Smith 1993: Appendix 2), although they constituted a higher proportion of black lawyers (3.7%) than the percentage of women among all lawyers (Smith 1993: 636 taken from the 1940 Census).

of the last professions that blacks sought (Smith 1993: 4). Excluded from most white law schools, the number of black law students even declined starting in the early 1920s as changes in credentialing by the American Bar Association (such as requiring some college experience from incoming students) hurt many black law schools (Smith 1993: 43). As late as 1960, the U.S. census counted only 2,180 black lawyers nationwide (Shuman 1971: 230). Moreover the color bar in the American Bar Association fell only in 1943, long after white women had already been admitted (Shuman 1971: 230). Careers in the law were even more limited for African Americans; many ended up leaving the profession because it was impossible to practice law in any form. When they did remain in the law, African American lawyers were largely confined to criminal law because even other blacks were more likely to turn to "white lawyers in the more lucrative civil cases" (Smith 1993: 4).

While sex discrimination propelled women lawyers into government, racial discrimination kept black lawyers largely out of the federal government. In 1942, for example, "the number of black lawyers in the federal government could be counted on two hands" (Smith 1993: 548). Although black lawyers in the DC area often worked for the federal government, discrimination was so strong that they ended up in nonlegal or even menial government jobs (King 1995). For example, a National Bar Association study found that there were 225 black lawyers in Washington DC – half of whom "worked at government jobs during the day and practiced law in the evening" (Smith 1993: 565).

Thus, the patterns of discrimination against women lawyers created a pool of highly educated women in the federal government, 99% of whom were white (Smith 1993: appendix 2). A network of feminist lawyers along with other feminists in government would play a large role in the women's movement. But discrimination did not have the same effect on the civil rights movement. While black lawyers were also important to the civil rights movement, they largely remained excluded from the higher ranks of the civil service until after the civil rights movement was in full force, creating quite a different relationship between the civil rights movement and the state.

CHANGES IN THE FEDERAL BUREAUCRACY

Rising education and employment, especially in the professions, influenced women's entry into the federal government. But changes in the nature of the federal government such as the development of civil service procedures and expansions of the bureaucracy during the New Deal and wartime also helped to speed the movement of women into civil service positions. Part of the integration of women into civil service arose from the needs of the state, particularly a constant need for cheap labor but also a need for civil servants that waxed and waned with wars and economic cycles. Civil service reform and government reorganization also encouraged women's incorporation into the federal bureaucracy. Thus, despite continued discrimination and limits on women's occupational life, the federal government had a long history of employing women, allowing a network of professional women to thrive within the ranks of the state before the advent of the women's movement in the 1960s.

Women had been in government service since the founding of the federal government, although largely in lower paying jobs (Morgan 1913). Indeed, the first attempted uniform pay scale in 1853 included a separate class for women (McMillin 1941). In these early years, women entered the federal government as low-paid wage workers (such as money counters in the Department of Treasury) or through the patronage system (Claussen 1996; McMillin 1941). The latter were often widows of party loyalists who got their jobs by pleading economic hardship to party leaders (Aron 1987; Claussen 1996). An 1870 law allowed women to be appointed to clerkships and, because women did not receive the same compensation as male clerks, department heads attempted to increase productivity by replacing male clerks with lower paid women. The result was that by 1880 women accounted for 29% of those employed in executive departments in Washington, DC (Claussen 1996: 236).

In 1883 when the Civil Service Commission and a competitive examination system were created, women were allowed to compete for the same positions as men (Morgan 1913). However, the Civil Service Commission interpreted the new law as allowing agency heads to "specify the preferred sex of a worker," which resulted in women largely receiving the lower paying jobs (Harrison 1988: 142).[7] Moreover, civil service examinations could be limited to men if the agency whose vacancy inspired the examination asked for male applicants. Because agencies seeking to hire the same category of worker later were required to draw from the same examination for their pool of eligible workers, this policy limited women's government employment (McMillin 1941: 18–19). A 1919 Women's Bureau report showed that this process excluded women from 60% of all examinations, leaving them largely limited to the clerical, teaching, nursing, and office service areas (Nienburg 1920: 11). Pressure resulting from this report forced the Civil Service Commission to allow women and men to attend all examinations, although agencies could still request candidates of a particular sex (Harrison 1988: 143, see also Aron 1987). With a brief exception between 1932 and 1934, agencies continued to be able to limit their positions to men until 1962, when President Kennedy implemented new regulations prohibiting this practice (Harrison 1988: 143–145).

Until 1920, departments were also authorized to pay women considerably less than men (Claussen 1996: 238). The Classification Act of 1923, which instituted pay grades for government workers to reduce pay inequities among those performing the same jobs, also included a clause that required that men and women employees in the same positions be given equal compensation. A 1925 survey of women in the Federal Service conducted by the Women's Bureau found that this change did help equalize the pay imbalance for women compared to men in the same grade (McMillin 1941: 21), although women continued to be concentrated in lower end jobs.

Women's representation in the federal government also waxed and waned with the supply of male labor and the demands of the state. Not surprisingly, war provided major opportunities for women to enter the federal government in even greater numbers. This is illustrated by a graph created by McMillin in her 1941 Civil Service Commission report (see Figure 2.1). War created both a shortfall of male labor and

---

[7] Agencies generally asked for male candidates only. Indeed, in 1902, when the Civil Service was unable to supply agencies with enough qualified male stenographers, it sent a memorandum to the agencies calling attention to the quality applicants on the female list (McMillin 1941: 15–16).

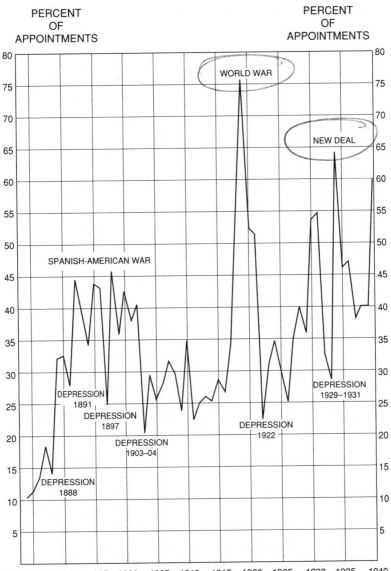

FIGURE 2.1. The Percentage of Women among Civil Service Appointments, 1883–1940. *Source:* McMillan (1941: 13)

at the same time increased the responsibilities of the state, increasing the size of the bureaucracy. The great demand during war often led the government to bypass normal civil service procedures in order to simply keep itself running (Ingraham 1995: 61). While war was the major stimulus of increased demand for women in the federal government, it was not the only one. State expansion during the New Deal also increased the number of women in the federal government (Ware 1981). Ware (1981: 61) argues that women's entry was helped by the creation of new agencies in the bureaucracy, because these had "less prejudice against using female talent."

If war and government expansion provided an opportunity for women to enter the federal government, economic downturns and returning veterans constrained their entry. Often women's employment was reduced by prohibitions against employing a number of people from the same family. In the 1870s, many departments forbid hiring "more than one family member" (Claussen 1996: 234). Even when that was not law, married women were often dismissed or not hired because of the assumption that husbands should be the breadwinner (Aron 1987; Claussen 1996). The 1932 National Economy Act, adopted after the 1929 economic collapse, included Section 213 prohibiting both husband and wife to be employed by the federal government. While the law did not explicitly exclude women, they largely suffered its consequences. Thus, McMillin (1941: 30) showed that about 75% of those dismissed under Section 213 were women. Between 1932 and the repeal of Section 213 in 1937, Ware (1981: 79) estimates that approximately 1,600 female government employees were dismissed.

The onset of peace also resulted in sharp reductions in women entering the federal government (see Figure 2.1), particularly after WWI and WWII. With the onset of peace the extra demands on the state created by war disappeared, and at the same time the supply of men who could fill civil service jobs increased. The Veterans' Preference Act of 1944 also reduced the number of women entering the federal government. Between 1945 and 1949, the percentage of federal employees who received preference in employment because they were a veteran went from 16% to 47% (Ingraham 1995: 49). Women's absence from the military reduced their ability to get hired and to advance up the career ladder.

TABLE 2.3. *Women's Employment in the Federal Government*

Year	% of Employed in General Population Who Are Women[a]	% of Federal Government Employees Who Are Women	% Washington, DC Government Employees Who Are Women
1870	13.1		16.4[b]
1880	14.7		22.5[b]
1890	17.4		
1893			32.6[b]
1900	18.8		
1903			26.6[b]
1920	21.0		
1923		14.9[e]	41.4[e]
1930	22.0	14.6[e]	41.1[e]
1939		18.8[e]	40.0[e]
1940	25.4		
1941		19.6[d]	42.3[d]
1966	40.3	26[c]	41[c]
1997		42.8	

[a] All of the numbers in this column come from U.S. Bureau of the Census. *Historical Statistics of the United States: Colonial Times to 1970*; Series D11–25 (p. 127–8).
[b] Calculated from Aron 1987: 5.
[c] *Statistical Abstract of the United States 1967* Table No. 570 (p. 407).
[d] Calculated from McMillin 1943: 6–7.
[e] Nyswander and Hooks 1941: 8–9.

Even with the large variation caused by war and depression, the proportion of women employed in the federal government grew steadily. For example, from 1930 to 1939 – a period that encompasses the passage and then repeal of the National Recovery Act – the percentage of federal government employees who were women grew from 14.6 to 18.8% (see Table 2.3). Women were an even larger part of the federal work force within the nation's capital. As early as 1923, women constituted fully 40% of federal employees within the District of Columbia, and that number rose as women became concentrated in the secretarial positions that keep a modern state working (Claussen 1996: 242). Once in the federal government, most women were then protected by civil service rules about hiring and firing, allowing them long careers in the bureaucracy. Catherine East, working in the Civil Service Commission at the end of World War II noted for example:

After the war, there were a lot of agencies that wanted to fire the women wholesale ... [T]here was a memorandum that went out from the Civil Service

Commission saying that although the law was that you could hire by sex, there was nothing in the law that said you could fire by sex . . . the agency heads were advised to separate employees in an orderly fashion, but reminded . . . that once they started to hire, they could then hire only men if they wanted to. (East 1982: 56)

Overall, from the late 1930s to the mid-1960s women were more likely to be employed by the private sector than by the federal government. However, many of those private sector jobs were low-level manufacturing jobs. Moreover, the lack of women in the federal government nationwide reflected a lack of women in the branches of the federal government outside the nation's capital. The percentage of women employed in the federal government in Washington, DC, outstripped the national average. In the final analysis, the federal government in Washington, DC, was a haven for women seeking full-time employment.

Race and Federal Employment

A comparison to the opportunities for African Americans to gain federal employment is useful in understanding white women's position of simultaneous privilege and discrimination.[8] Women constituted a much larger percentage of the civil service than blacks, and women could be found in midlevel and even some administrative positions. As King (1995) documents, blacks were largely relegated to custodial or manual labor positions within the federal government prior to the civil rights movement, and particularly after the election of Woodrow Wilson. Discrimination against blacks in the hiring process was aided by the requirement of photographs on job applications between 1914 and 1940 (King 1995: 48–49). Washington DC's location in the South meant that much of the capital's white population supported segregationist policies. Highly trained African Americans often ended up taking jobs as manual laborers or were given the more menial tasks within a civil service grade, which in turn made it difficult to be promoted.[9]

---

[8] See Chafe (1977) for an extended discussion of the similarity and differences between the women's and civil rights movements and their causes. I focus here only on their insider activism.

[9] Moreover, looking only at grades and promotion does not give us much of a sense of the level of integration into the workplace on a social and cultural level. Aron (1987,

For example, King (1995: 72) notes that when the Department of Commerce hired an African American messenger in 1937 he had both a BA and a law degree.

Comparable federal government employment statistics for African Americans as a group and women as a whole are impossible to find. However, two separate studies both conducted in 1938 provide a fairly clear picture of the employment differences. L.J.W. Hayes, studying African Americans in the District of Columbia employed by the federal government, found that 90% were employed in custodial positions (Davis and Golightly 1945: 340, see also King 1999: 349); in contrast Nyswander and Hooks (1941: 52) examining all women within the federal service within the same year found that only 3,200 out of the more than 145,500 women employed in the federal government (slightly more than 2%) worked as "janitors, charmen and charwomen." In contrast, the data in Nyswander and Hooks suggest that only 1.3% of all men – not distinguished by race – held these custodial positions. At the upper levels, Hayes found only .5% of African Americans in federal employment in the district could be classified as subprofessional (Davis and Golightly 1945: 340, see also King 1999: 349)[10] while the Nyswander and Hooks data show that nationwide 7.9% of women (and 6.9% of all men) fall into that category. Combined, these two studies suggest that African Americans in the 1930s were largely concentrated in unskilled government occupations, while women (both white and black) were concentrated at secretarial and clerk levels and could even be found in administrative positions.[11]

While discrimination and harassment still made most workplaces uncomfortable for many women, by the 1930s women were an accepted part of the federal workplace even as they were held back from

[margin note: Studies comparing AA + women]

Chapters 6–7) discusses how offices in the federal government changed to integrate women into their work spaces as early as the late 1800s. Despite problems in fully incorporating women, it is likely that even stronger interpersonal problems occurred for African Americans.

[10] The remainder of African Americans – 9.5% – were categorized as clerical, administrative, fiscal, or clerical-mechanical.

[11] As was the case for women, King (1995: 75) notes that there were a higher percentage of African American civil servants in higher grade levels in Washington, DC, offices compared to the field offices – although the numbers were still quite miniscule.

the highest positions. For blacks integration into the federal workplace
came much later, long after the end of WWII (King 1995). The consequences for the movement are important. When civil rights organizations mobilized in the 1940s around the war and in the 1950s, the
few black activists within the state were largely political appointees –
beholden to the president that had appointed them for their continued
presence within the state. Thus, it appears that the civil rights movement lacked a network of mid-level policy makers who could serve the
cause. The women's movement, however, had a network of activists,
which though small in number, were spread throughout government:
a few as political appointees, a few in Congress, and the few in the
mid- to upper levels of the civil service that I examine in this book. The
existence of this network and the ties among congressional women,
bureaucratic women, and the political appointees were an important
part of the mobilization of the movement.

WOMEN'S ORGANIZATIONS BETWEEN THE FIRST AND SECOND WAVES

Although the period between 1920 and 1960 is largely considered one
of demobilization and inactivity within the women's movement, continued activism for feminist causes during this period was important to
the existence of a network of feminist activists within the state as the
second wave arose.[12] The activism of women outside the state during
these years contributed to the rise of second-wave feminism within the
state in two ways. First and foremost, the network of feminist activists inside the state was developed through ties made within women's
organizations that existed outside the state. As Taylor (1989) shows,
even organizations with declining membership could help maintain
connections and collective identity among feminist activists. Second,
women's organizations during this period also consciously shaped
policies in the federal government that affected the overall numbers
of women in government, thereby creating future political opportunities for later feminists.

---

[12] Rupp and Taylor (1987) and Taylor (1989) chronicle continued activity within the
women's movement during this time point and show that these "abeyance structures"
shaped the second wave of the women's movement. Here I focus specifically on the
influence of these groups on feminists inside the state, although Hartmann (1998)
also chronicles their influence on feminist networks in other organizations.

Women's Organizational Strength

Many expected that women's organizations would wield considerable power after women's enfranchisement, and indeed, women's organizations were crucial to the passage of the Sheppard-Towner Act, which provided social welfare for destitute mothers in 1921 (Skocpol 1992). Yet, by 1927, women's organizations were unable to halt the repeal of this act, and feminism entered a period of retrenchment that lasted until the 1960s (Harvey 1998; Rupp and Taylor 1987; Skocpol 1992). Major women's organizations split over whether to pursue protective legislation for women or an Equal Rights Amendment, significantly weakening the movement (Banaszak 1996a; Ryan 1992; Ware 1981). Moreover, the red scares of the 1920s hurt many women's organizations as they were linked with communist organizations through a "spider's web" of organizational connections (Banaszak 1996a; Talbot and Rosenberry 1931).

weakened movement bc couldn't decide on goals

Despite the decline in mobilization that occurred during the 1920s, a strong network of women's organizations and activism continued throughout the 1930s, 1940s, and 1950s (Anderson 1996; Mathews-Gardner 2005). This wide range of women's organizations included women's rights groups, professional associations, and a number of other types of associations. The National American Woman Suffrage Association reformed itself as the League of Women Voters (LWV) in 1920, focusing on supporting women candidates and encouraging women voters to serve as a force for progress (Young 1989). The National Woman's Party focused its energies on an Equal Rights Amendment but also encouraged women into elective office (Rupp and Taylor 1987). Additional women's organizations that fought for women's interests after 1920 included the General Federation of Women's Clubs (Wells 1953), the National Association of Colored Women (White 1999), the Women's Christian Temperance Union; the Women's Trade Union League, the National Association of Women Lawyers (Smith 1999), and the American Association of University Women[13] to name but a few. In addition, in the period after suffrage, a number of women's professional organizations appeared as

women's organizations

---

[13] The AAUW began its life as the Association of Collegiate Alumnae. In 1903 a parallel organization was formed in the South – the Southern Association of College Women. In 1921, the two groups merged to form the American Association of University Women.

well, including the National Business and Professional Women (1919), Financial Women International (1921), the National Federation of Press Women (1937), and the American College of Nurse-Midwives (1955).[14]

These organizations enjoyed a very healthy membership; for example, in 1969, the LWV had over 156,000 members, while the National Federation of Business and Professional Women's Clubs (BPW) more than doubled its membership from 79,332 in 1944 to 175,274 in 1960 (Rawalt 1969: 341).[15] The National Association of Colored Women's Clubs attracted large numbers of African American women – more than 1% of the entire black female population according to Matthews-Gardner (2005: 551).

Specific women's organizations appealed to distinctive groups of women, although their membership base also changed over time. The League of Women Voters, for example, while attracting highly educated young women represented largely full-time homemakers; even in the early 1970s, only 25% of LWV members had a full time job (Young, L. 1989). On the other hand, through World War II the American Association of University Women was dominated by single professional women, many of whom had graduate or professional education, although afterwards it increasingly attracted younger members, the vast majority of whom were married and housewives (Levine 1995: 84–85).

Even as different women's organizations attracted distinct types of members, there was also overlapping membership among the women's organizations. A survey conducted of the American Association of University Women in 1955 indicated that a large percentage of members said they belonged to other women's organizations particularly the LWV, BPW, and GFWC (Levine 1995: 85). At least one-third of the membership up through 1980 participated in other women's organizations (Levine 1995: 142–143, see also Talbot and Rosenberry 1931: 342, 355). The overlapping membership was also evident in the biographies of organizational leaders. Presidents of the General

---

[14] For a complete list of organizations and their founding dates see Barakso (2005, Appendix B).

[15] Membership in the National Federation of Business and Professional Women's Clubs exceeded that of the League of Women Voters throughout the postwar period (cf. Rawalt 1969: 341 and Young 1989: 3).

Federation of Women's Clubs had also been presidents of the WTUL and the Association of Collegiate Alumnae (later the AAUW) (Wells 1953). The leadership of BPW had extensive overlap with the YWCA, which had encouraged its creation (Bowman and White 1944: 117 and 12–14).

Marguerite Rawalt, one of the feminist activists in the bureaucracy whom I discuss later, is a good example of this overlapping membership. When she became a member of the Kennedy's President's Commission on the Status of Women in 1961, she was a long-time member of the National Woman's Party; and had already served as president of the National Federation of Business and Professional Women's Clubs (BPW) and the National Association of Women Lawyers (Paterson 1986). She went on to become a founding member of the National Organization for Women's Legal Defense and Education Fund, and later became president of the Women's Equity Action League's Educational and Legal Defense Fund (Women's Equity Action League Educational and Legal Defense Fund 1980). Rawalt was not the only activist within the BPW to work within the state; of the eighteen BPW Presidents from 1919 to 1960, three worked for the federal government, one for state government, and one served as a judge.

Many of these organizations were particularly strong in the Washington DC area, which greatly contributed to the building of a feminist network within government. Two organizations illustrate this point: the Business and Professional Women's Club and the National Woman's Party. Between 1941 and 1949 – when a decision was made to create sister organizations and a state federation – the DC club of the BPW was the largest local club in an already large and active national association (Rawalt 1969: 285). The DC group played a large role in the national BPW because an office focusing on lobbying was located in DC starting in 1946, and in 1956 their national headquarters moved there. Similarly, the National Woman's Party (NWP) was small but played an important role among Washington's feminists. Although the NWP had only 627 active members in 1947, and only 200 in 1952, they were largely concentrated in Washington, DC, and "most of the activity took place in Washington" (Rupp and Taylor 1987: 26). Moreover, feminists within the federal bureaucracy were a significant part of the National Woman's Party membership; as one member observed, "we had women in every department in

Washington" (Rupp and Taylor 1987:40). While these feminist activists were already within government when the movement mobilized
in the 1960s, they contributed to the strengthening of this feminist
network by converting women within government to feminism and
recruiting them into women's organizations.

Pursuing Feminist Government Policies

Women's organizations pursued a wide agenda between 1920 and
1966. I focus here on two aspects of their agenda – the pursuit of
equality for women in the workplace and the increased representation of women in government – because these issues played a large
role in the story that follows. But these goals were only two of a wide
array of policies pursued by an active women's community throughout
these years (Anderson 1996; Matthews-Gardner 2003, 2005; Skocpol
1992). While descriptions of this period note the divisions between
women's organizations over whether to pursue protective legislation
or an Equal Rights Amendment, there was also considerable agreement
on such issues as increasing women's representation. Even those organizations primarily concerned with charitable works or serving religious
communities occasionally engaged themselves on these feminist issues.

The Equal Rights Amendment vs. Protective Legislation
The most controversial item pursued during this period was the Equal
Rights Amendment (ERA). While the National Woman's Party and
women's professional organizations like the National Federation of
Business and Professional Women (BPW), the National Association
of Women Lawyers and the American Medical Women's Association
focused their energies on pursuing an Equal Rights Amendment, other
organizations like the League of Women Voters (LWV), the Women's
Trade Union League (WTUL), and General Federation of Women's
Clubs (GFWC) sought protective legislation for women (Banaszak
1996a; Bowman and White 1944: 74; Rupp and Taylor 1987).[16] Many

---

[16] The GFWC was one of the first organizations to reverse its position on the ERA.
In 1934, the organization instigated a study program to review its stand against the
Equal Rights Amendment and a decade later reversed its position and supported
the ERA (Wells 1953: 202). In that same year, the organization sent delegates to
both national party conventions to ask that support for the ERA be included in the

women's organizations suffered from internal conflict about the ERA. For example, while the American Association of University Women remained officially against the ERA until 1971 and was the last major women's organization to endorse the ERA (Levine 1995: 162), several prominent individuals within the AAUW publicly endorsed the amendment much earlier. Other women's organizations like the National Council of Women, and the National Association of Colored Women included the ERA only sporadically on their agenda (Rupp and Taylor 1987).

In addition to the ERA, a number of organizations – including the GFWC and the BPW – endorsed a national equal pay bill through the 1940s and 1950s (Matthews-Gardner 2005: 558; Rawalt 1969). Although they were unable to get Congress to consider it, thirteen states passed similar legislation during this period. For the BPW, equal pay was an important long-term issue. For example, in 1930, BPW raised $1,000 to conduct "a Study on Discriminations Against Women in Business and the Professions" (Bowman and White 1944: 60) and the organization published a number of studies showing women suffered from pay discrimination in the 1930s and 1940s. Thus, although there was not agreement on whether protective legislation or an Equal Rights Amendment would best advance women's causes, between 1920 and 1960 women's organizations actively pursued whichever policy they thought best furthered women's interests.

Electing and Appointing Women to the Federal Government

While women's organizations were divided by the Equal Rights Amendment, they were unified on the issue of increasing women's representation in the federal bureaucracy. Even those organizations whose primary purpose was charitable works or serving religious communities occasionally engaged themselves on the issue of increasing women's representation in the federal government,[17] either individually or in umbrella organizations like the Committee on the

platform; they continued this type of lobbying in other election years (Wells 1953: 202). In 1953, when Wells wrote her history of the GFWC, it listed the ERA as one of the top eight legislative priorities.

[17] On the AAUW see Talbot and Rosenberry 1931; Levine 1995; on the National Association of Women Lawyers see Smith 1999; see also Rupp and Taylor 1987: 77–78.

Participation of Women in Postwar Planning. At the forefront of this battle was the BPW, which continually pushed "the election and appointment of qualified women to city, state, and national office (Bowman and White 1944: 88; see also Rawalt 1969: 26).

However, many other women's organizations were actively engaged in increasing women's representation in appointed office as well. The National Association of Women Lawyers devoted considerable attention to getting women into judgeships[18] (Smith 1999). The General Federation of Women's Clubs pushed for women's inclusion in the diplomatic service and the U.S. delegation to the United Nations (Wells 1953: 221). From the 1920s to the 1960s, the AAUW nominated qualified women to public service commissions and boards (Levine 1995; Talbot and Rosenberry 1931).

Increasing Women's Representation in the Civil Service

In addition to trying to increase the number of women in elected and appointed office, women's organizations turned their attention to discrimination within the federal bureaucracy between 1920 and 1960. Because the federal government was a major employer of women, especially in the capital, civil service reform was important to the women's organizations that represented professional women, such as the AAUW and BPW. These organizations devoted considerable energy to the situation of female federal employees. The AAUW's Washington, DC, branch, dominated by a large number of government employees, focused extensively on women in the civil service (Talbot and Rosenberry 1931: 207–210) At its first convention in 1919, the BPW passed a resolution demanding that all civil service examinations be open to women and calling for the collection of statistics on women in government service (Bowman and White 1944: 21). Advocacy of civil service reform by the League of Women Voters, the Women's Trade Union League, the Women's Christian Temperance Union, and the GFWC (among others) in the early 1900s contributed to the adoption of the Classification Act of 1923 (Claussen 1996: 241).

The adoption of Section 213 of the Economy Act of 1932 stimulated substantial activism among women's organizations. Beyond its direct impact, Section 213 also inspired the passage of similar laws

---

[18] They were also on the forefront of the fight to include women on juries.

in the states that forced many school teachers to resign (Claussen 1996: 245; Rung 2002: 64–66). Women's organizations including the LWV, NWP, WTUL, the Women's Joint Congressional Committee, and NAWL fought hard to have Section 213 removed from the Economy Act. In 1935, the president of BPW, Geline Bowman, met with President Roosevelt to argue the injustice of Section 213; "she had also asked frankly for Presidential support to bring about the amendment of the Civil Service Act so as to render discriminations against women impossible" (Bowman and White 1944: 68). Even the LWV took on civil service reform in 1935 by actively encouraging President Roosevelt to send the Reorganization Bill to Congress although it ultimately failed (Young, L. 1989: 113). Only in 1937 was Section 213 repealed.

The BPW took a particularly strong stand on the treatment of women within the civil service. In addition to supporting changes in merit reform that would make the civil service less biased against women, the BPW opposed the attempt "to drive women out of the upper bracket jobs in government" after WWII (*Independent Women* cited in Rawalt 1969: 23). For example, Margaret Hickey, president of the BPW in 1946, argued that "there are grade cuts, demotions, firings, all to reduce women from the technical, professional and administrative classifications in Civil Service. In the matter of new appointments, most jobs paying more than $2400 are tagged 'Men Only' although Civil Service policy claims to be nondiscriminatory." (Rawalt 1969: 23).

These historical accounts show that, especially in the nation's capital, women's groups remained active during the period that Rupp and Taylor (1987) label "the doldrums." Women's organizations outside the state pursued women's representation within the civil service as well as in elected and appointed positions, often shaping the political opportunities that determined whether women could enter the civil service at high ranks as I show later.[19] Perhaps most importantly, the existence of vibrant women's organizations outside the state facilitated the networking of feminist activists within the bureaucracy during the

---

[19] In achieving some of these changes, women's organizations were no doubt aided by activist Democratic administrations, such as those of Franklin Delano Roosevelt, Harry Truman, and Democratic majorities in Congress.

1930s, 1940s, and 1950s – well before the rise of the second wave. Many of the early feminist activists in the federal bureaucracy were members of one or more of these organizations, and would play an important role in recruiting and mobilizing a wider network of insider activists who pursued feminist policies inside the state in the early 1960s.

Race and Feminist Networks in the 'Doldrums'

It is important to note that the network created by *these* women's organizations in the 1930s through the 1950s was one that excluded almost all African American women. Most women's groups were slow to integrate black women into their networks, and many explicitly excluded black women, particularly in the DC area where Southern segregation played a strong role. Rupp (1985: 719) notes that Mary Church Terrell was the only black member of the National Woman's Party that she could identify. The AAUW, although it always *allowed* national membership for black women, permitted local branches to choose whether to accept black women into their ranks. This policy remained until the end of WWII[20] when Mary Church Terrell's application for branch membership moved the organization to a national policy of nondiscrimination (although not all branches welcomed black women).[21] While the YWCA also integrated black women into its ranks in the post-WW II years, the National Federation of Business and Professional Women, the League of Women Voters, and the General Federation of Women's Clubs were slower to do so (Levine 1995: 107; Wells 1953: 362–368). The few networks that existed between white and black women were tenuous at best; even when African American women were included in white women's organizations, racial discrimination limited the strength of the ties between individuals (White 1999).

---

[20] Interestingly, the International Federation of University Women, which the AAUW had initially helped found, began pressuring the AAUW to eliminate its racial barriers during WWII, in part as a response to Germany's discriminatory policies (Levine 1995: 111).

[21] Levine (1995: 135) argued that the conflict over desegregation both within the AAUW but also in the larger society helped to push the AAUW away from taking issue positions and towards more research and "abstract study."

Black women developed their own strong network through black sororities like Alpha Kappa Alpha and Delta Sigma Theta (both founded before 1920), women's church organizations, and organizations like the National Association of Colored Women and the National Council of Negro Women. Both of the latter organizations actively fought for the cause of African American women during the period of the doldrums. The National Council of Negro Women, for example, engaged in lobbying during this period on a wide range of policies designed to increase black women's employment such as the inclusion of blacks in New Deal programs, and the elimination of photographs from civil service job applications (White 1999: 150). They also organized local grassroots self-help actions designed to aid the African American community, particularly black women and children (White 1999: 52).

Still, black women's organizations faced a highly closed political opportunity structure after suffrage was adopted and, despite their activism, many of these organizations remained largely unnoticed in (white) national politics (White 1999: 173–174). The Depression reduced opportunities for blacks in general as high unemployment in the white population created dire conditions among African Americans, and most New Deal policies discriminated heavily against blacks. Even as political opportunities began to loosen slightly for black men on the national level in the 1940s, black women's organizations did not gain greater governmental access. For example, as presidents after Hoover began to react to the rising call for equality from the black community they increasingly took in black advisors, but most of them were men. Only one black woman was appointed in FDR's administration – Mary McLeod Bethune as director of African American Affairs in the National Youth Administration (Smith 1999: 148).

Thus, while women's organizations were active across the racial divide during the 1920s through 1960s, the networks created were heavily divided by race. When the state responded to women's demands, they were largely the demands posed by middle class, white women. Although there were some gains in the integration of women's networks, the networks of feminist activists inside the state as the movement arose in the 1960s were largely white and middle class (Jones 1982).

Women's Organizations and Insider Feminist Activists

The activism of women's organizations provided three types of context for feminist activists in government. First, women's organizations helped to shape the openness of the federal bureaucracy to hiring and promoting women as a group. These women's groups helped to create the structural conditions that allowed women to move into mid-level policy-making positions. Second, many of the insider feminist activists who were part of the initial group that existed in 1960 were active in these organizations and for women's causes. For these first feminist activists in government their networks with each other were strengthened by connections forged in women's organizations outside of government; they knew not only other women in government but feminists who supported and fought for women's rights.[22] The few black feminists in the federal government participated in many of these largely white middle class women's organizations even as they also worked in organizations for black women as well. This made them part of the network of activists within government. Third, women's organizations had been actively fighting for a number of feminist policies during the years before 1960. Thus, as the President's Commission on the Status of Women's 1963 report, *American Women*, publicized these issues to the general public, they were already well known to the women activists who had been fighting for the policies for years.

FEMINIST NETWORKS AND THE PRESIDENT'S COMMISSION
ON THE STATUS OF WOMEN

The continued activity of women's organizations outside of government from the 1920s into the 1960s combined with women's modest presence in the bureaucracy to create conditions that fostered a feminist network within the state. This occurred well before the formation of the President's Commission on the Status of Women (PCSW) in 1961, an event often identified as the step that initiated the second wave of the women's movement. Rather than understanding the President's Commission on the Status of Women as a political opportunity that

---

[22] Hartmann (1998) finds that similar networks within the Ford Foundation, ACLU, and other organizations also played a role in the development of policy.

gave rise to the women's movement, attention to the role of insider feminists shows that the creation of the PCSW is an example of the movement shaping its own political opportunities from inside the federal bureaucracy.

Preexisting Feminist Networks within Government

As various authors have highlighted, there were several networks of women at the professional levels of government, often a result of the relative scarcity of women at these levels. Chester (1985: 56), for example, describes "a small, but relatively effective, informal network of female government attorneys" during the 1920s and 1930s. Ware (1981) follows another network of social reformers that came to prominence as political appointees in the New Deal. While she sees this network disappearing after 1945, she also notes that new networks arose around the wartime hiring of women and around agencies such as the Women's Bureau (Ware 1981: 128).[23]

A number of conditions encouraged the existence of such networks. First, professional women in the bureaucracy tended to get to know other women in the civil service who shared their interests. For example, one of my interviewees noted that: "There was a small cadre of women... who met periodically to talk about women's issues" (Interview 14, October 16, 2003). Second, professional women also found like-minded women through their involvement in women's organizations and professional organizations in the DC area. Federal employees active in women's organizations such as the National Woman's Party (e.g., Caruthers Berger), the National Federation of Business and Professional Women's Clubs (e.g., Marguerite Rawalt) or in professional organizations, developed networks with other women concerned with issues of women's equality.

In some ways the state itself encouraged these networks by increasing the focus on women in the federal government around 1960. The first way the federal government increased network opportunities and the salience of women's equality was with the introduction of the Federal Woman's Award in November 1960. Begun by an Eisenhower

---

[23] Although Ware (1981) denies the existence of postwar networks, she focuses on the highest level of policy makers and so misses those at the lower levels.

appointee to the Civil Service Commission, Barbara Bates Gunderson, the award was given to the top career women in the federal bureaucracy. The presentation of the Federal Woman's Award was intended to highlight the accomplishments of professional women in government who were largely ignored in the awarding of other prizes for meritorious service. It had the unintended consequence of forging ties among the highest levels of professional women even as it highlighted the lack of opportunities for these women to receive recognition and promotion. Indeed, in 1966, Lyndon Johnson brought a group of the awards' recipients together to study careers for women, and their report on March 3, 1967 eventually led to Executive Order 11375, which prohibited sex discrimination in the federal service (Federal Woman's Award Study Group on Careers for Women 1967).

Professional women also networked in the few places where they could receive additional training to further their careers. While Executive Leadership Training was available for civil servants at the higher GS levels (around GS11 and above), women in these grades were not sent for leadership training in the late 1950s and early 1960s. When the Federal Woman's Award Study Group on Careers for Women examined leadership training in 1966, they found that fewer than half the management training courses served women at the GS12 level or above. (Federal Woman's Award Study Group on Careers for Women 1967: 9). One of the few opportunities for women at these levels to receive training was a three-day seminar run by Helen Dudley within the Department of Agriculture's Graduate school[24] entitled "Seminar for Executive Women." In 1968, the feminist organization Federally Employed Women (FEW) was formed by participants in this seminar.

The Women's Bureau also served as a networking point for a subset of feminist professional women. As Laughlin (2000: 4) notes, civil servants within the Women's Bureau after 1945 often worked toward a feminist agenda through the "strategic use of resources, such as national conferences...and a research and public relations staff." Because the Women's Bureau's main constituency – labor women – supported protective legislation for women, however, these insider activities were limited. Yet, feminists within the Bureau were linked

---

[24] The Graduate School of the U.S. Department of Agriculture provides continuing education to adults associated with the federal government.

to other feminists through women's organizations and informal networks.

The President's Commission on the Status of Women

Scholars of the U.S. women's movement note the importance of President Kennedy's Commission on the Status of Women (PCSW) in the revival of the U.S. women's movement (Duerst-Lahti 1989; Freeman 1975; Harrison 1988; Rupp and Taylor 1987). I will argue in Chapter 4 that the PCSW's effect on the early women's movement was mediated in large part by feminist activists in the federal government. While Chapter 4 discusses the role of the PCSW in encouraging the women's movement, here it is worth noting how the PCSW altered the network of feminist activists within the federal government.

Executive Order 10980, which created the PCSW, authorized the hiring of an executive secretary for the commission as well as the use of other personnel as "may be found necessary" (EO 10980, sec. 105). Even before the commission had issued its report, professional women from around the federal bureaucracy were mobilized to aid in the work of the PCSW. The staff members were temporarily assigned from different parts of the bureaucracy: Mary Eastwood was a lawyer in the Department of Justice and Catherine East came from the Civil Service Commission.[25] Esther Peterson, and Marguerite Rawalt were the only federal government employees who served as members of the commission.

The PCSW played two roles in these women's development as feminist activists within government. First, the PCSW allowed them to engage in feminist activity *as government employees* – an opportunity that was provided to few women within government prior to 1963. Thus, Catherine East, Mary Eastwood, and a number of other women describe the PCSW as a chance to engage in full-time, active research into and advocacy of women's rights by nature of their assignment to the PCSW. Working for the PCSW provided the opportunity to devote time from their official activities to the issues of women's status and women's rights.

---

[25] The PCSW also had male staffers, but it was particularly the women who were affected by serving on the PCSW. Interestingly, East (1982: 137) noted that the male staff all held GS15 positions while the women were appointed to work at GS14.

Second, while some of the government employees involved in the commission – like Marguerite Rawalt– were already strong feminists, others – like Catherine East and Mary Eastwood – were not. Working with the PCSW gave these women a chance to gather systematic information about women's civil, economic, and political rights, increasing their consciousness about the issues and transforming their thinking about women's rights. For example, Mary Eastwood noted that although she had experienced direct discrimination while seeking employment in the federal government: "my consciousness was not raised about discrimination until I started working with the President's Commission on the Status of Women, and started researching those Fourteenth Amendment cases" (Eastwood 1990–1993: 80). Thus, the PCSW played the role of expanding existing feminist networks by bringing existing feminists together with others who were not strong feminists in a context where women's inequality was the major focus.

The connections created by working on the PCSW were important for the future women's movement. For example, Mary Eastwood, Catherine East, and Marguerite Rawalt, who met through their work on the commission, later became important members in the network of feminist civil servants that helped to mobilize the women's movement. If the PCSW provided these women with information and resources, these women's wider network of feminist women in government allowed them to play a key role at the beginning of the second wave. The research and discussion from the PCSW reached this wider group of professional women within the federal government, increasing the motivations for action among those who were already feminists. As feminist consciousness spread across the existing network of women in government, it created a core group of feminist activists who would play key roles in the rise of the second wave of the women's movement.

CONCLUSION: FEMINIST NETWORKS
WITHIN THE BUREAUCRACY

As the women's movement began its upward trajectory in the early 1960s, feminists in the federal government were already poised to play an important role *as activists*. Their position in the bureaucracy was a result of general changes in employment and education that had occurred for women everywhere, as well as specific changes to the American state that encouraged the hiring of women as a class. Their sensitivity to women's social and political inequality resulted from the continued activism of women's organizations since the 1920s. The feminist activists within government were members of these organizations, which carried the feminist agenda through a period when there was little receptivity for it in government.

But most of all, the federal employment of women helped create a network of feminists that was uniquely poised to mobilize when the second wave started. Comparisons to African Americans in the federal government are telling here. While the federal government was more welcoming for women lawyers than private practice, African American lawyers found few opportunities to practice law within the federal government before 1960. Even though black lawyers would play an important role in the burgeoning civil rights movement, these lawyers remained largely outside the state. On the other hand, as I demonstrate below, feminist lawyers were located both inside and outside the state and at times their position within the federal government provided important information and access to plaintiffs for landmark cases. African Americans were confined to the lower levels of the civil service regardless of their level of education or experience. While women also faced discrimination, there were always some (mostly white) women who broke the barrier into the positions of GS12 and above.

Not all of these women were feminists, but there were many factors that allowed feminists within the federal government to form networks. Their connections outside of work in women's organizations – through activism in existing women's organizations – helped forge networks across departmental or agency boundaries. There were also places within government such as the Women's Bureau, the Department of Agriculture's Seminar for Executive Women, and the President's Commission on the Status of Women (PCSW) where feminist women could discuss feminist issues. The PCSW was particularly important for extending the networks that crossed agency lines because it brought a number of civil servants together to work specifically on the status of women. That work not only reverberated among women on the outside, but also altered the network of feminist women in the bureaucracy.

This part of the movement inside the state made the women's movement different from the civil rights movement. While the civil rights movement developed outside the state as is traditionally expected of social movements, the existence of a part of the women's movement inside the state, although only a small part of the movement, altered the initial mobilization of the movement, as well as its ability to achieve certain policies. Like other movements, the women's movement blossomed largely outside the state. Yet because part of the women's movement was focused on changing state policy, the small network of feminists within the state had a larger effect on some of those policies than would be expected based on their relative number. To understand how they did so, I must first discuss how this network of feminists fit into the larger women's movement.

3

Who Are Movement Insiders?

Actually, I was working 10 or 12 hours a day, [so] that I didn't feel a
need to be engaged in another organization because I was lucky enough
to be able to do feminist work inside the federal government. If I had
been an employee of the U.S. Department of Defense doing budget and
accounting work that would have been different, but I was working 12
hours a day for the feminist revolution so why would I do it elsewhere?

Interview with feminist activist about being employed
by the federal government, September 25, 2003

So it was really a dreadful personal . . . situation during that time [in my
office]. But I was just determined that these were issues that I wanted
to work on and I felt very fortunate during the time that my volunteer
activities became something that I was able to do professionally.

Interview with feminist activist employed by the federal
government, July 19, 2004

This chapter examines the characteristics of insider feminist activists
vis-à-vis the movement and the government bureaucracy with the goal
of better understanding the role that insider feminist activists played
within the women's movement and in changing public policy. To
appreciate these activists' role in the women's movement, it is important to know whether they were drawn from a particular section of
the movement, and how important their activism was to their activities as government employees. Understanding their reasons for choosing government service, the relationship between their activism and

their decisions to work for the federal bureaucracy, and their career trajectories is also a crucial step in analyzing the degree of movement institutionalization. These characteristics influence the role that insider feminists might play within the state and the degree to which we might expect them to challenge the institution within which they are imbedded. As the quotations above suggest, many (if not most) feminist activists are as motivated by their activism as their careers. While some develop this activism in the course of existing careers in the federal bureaucracy, for others a job in the federal bureaucracy is part of a career trajectory created by a desire to be active on feminist issues.[1]

The literature on women's movements and on social movements generally creates five expectations about the feminist activists who work inside the federal government. First, feminist activists inside the state will generally be middle class and highly educated, which will heavily influence their ideology and activism. Freeman (1975: 55), examining the rise of the second wave of the women's movement, noted that founding members of many of the organizations from the older branch of the women's movement "were primarily from the professions, labor, government and the communications industry" (Freeman 1975: 55). By examining feminist activists at the mid or high levels of the federal bureaucracy, I have already limited the population to individuals who earn more than the median income and fall into the higher educational categories. Nonetheless, I examine activists' education and the economic background of their parents and find that feminist activists are drawn from the middle and upper class ranks of the women's movement.

Second, scholars of the early women's liberation movement note that the racial composition was almost entirely white (Barakso 2005; Freeman 1975; Ryan 1992). While Roth (2004) has clearly shown that feminist organizations of women of color existed from the very emergence of the second wave, she argues that women of color were active in separate organizations, largely ignored in studies of the feminist movement, and worked on issues at the intersection of race and gender. Given discrimination and the problems of obtaining the high education levels that faced many women of color, I would expect to

---

[1] Meyerson (2003: 32) argues that external commitments and networks are important to individuals seeking change in institutions.

find few women of color among my sample of feminist activists within the bureaucracy. Below I look explicitly at those women of color that I did interview to ascertain the kinds of feminist activism that they engaged in and their effect within the bureaucracy.

Third, the location of feminist activists inside the government bureaucracy creates the expectation that they will be more moderate in their ideology, both because they are drawn from a middle-class, highly educated population of women, and because their location is taken to indicate an actor's preference for reform over more radical change. Oftentimes, scholars and feminists assume that only those who are more moderate feminists and therefore support existing institutions will enter the state or that individuals who take such jobs are completely molded by bureaucracies.[2] Following these assumptions, the expectation is that feminist activists are working for incremental changes that are easily incorporated in liberal politics, rather than adopting more radical ideological perspectives that are also present in the women's movement (see, for example, Ferree and Hess 2000; Gelb 1989; Ryan 1992). While there are numerous ways to define radical feminist ideology, I focus specifically on the degree to which these feminist activists saw sex oppression tied into the structure of political and social institutions. Such radicalism includes a belief that minor reforms will not be sufficient to eliminate sex discrimination. It also sees connections between gender oppression and race and class oppression. More liberal variants of feminism believe that the elimination of sex discrimination can be achieved through political and legal reform and through socialization changes that can be achieved on an individual level. In short, liberal feminists believe institutions like the family or the bureaucracy are gender neutral. If feminists inside the bureaucracy really are more reformist, the connection of feminist activists within the state to specific wings or factions within the movement may be one reason that the resulting government policies have concentrated in some areas more than others. I will show that although many of the feminist insiders were liberal feminists, a wide range of feminist activists existed inside the state including many who held more radical beliefs. In particular, among feminist activists within the state we find those who believe that

---

[2] Outshoorn (1994: 144) is an exception in recognizing this underlying assumption.

gender bias is deeply embedded in societal and political institutions, and who sought extensive social and institutional change.

Fourth, and in relation, feminist activists inside the state might be expected to be more career oriented than movement oriented because existing within the state is often conflated with support for existing institutions and a belief in institutional mobilization (see, for example, Eisenstein 1990; Outshoorn 1994, 1997). Individuals working within the state can be distinguished by their identity, specifically the degree to which they see their location as influencing their activism or vice-versa. Some insider feminist activists are unwilling to see their location inside the state as limiting what they voice about movement activism or altering their ability to act for the movement. Others are much more willing to allow their job to limit how they act for the movement. Such activists are therefore likely to be more concerned about their careers than furthering the movement.

Fifth, the literature on institutionalization of movements leads us to expect that the ideology of these feminist activists will become more moderate over time (Meyer and Tarrow 1998; Walker 2005, but see Zald and Ash 1966). Many people have argued that the U.S. women's movement changed over time with strong calls for revolutionary social, economic, and political change disappearing in the later years of the women's movement, particularly in the face of political conservatism (Ferree and Hess 2000; Ryan 1992). I argue below that looking at insider feminist activists over time suggests that there has been no moderation of the feminist activists within the federal bureaucracy. Indeed, feminists who entered the state in the later years of the movement tend to have stronger views regarding the need for revolutionary change than those who were part of the state from the very beginning.

This chapter examines these expectations in greater depth, using primary and secondary historical sources, in-depth interviews with feminist activists in the federal government, and a survey of women activists conducted at the National Women's Conference in November 1977. I begin by examining the number of feminist activists within government, and follow with sections exploring each of the five hypotheses – that feminist activists within the state are white and well-off, ideologically moderate, career oriented, and have become more moderate and career oriented over time.

HOW MANY FEMINIST ACTIVISTS WERE THERE WITHIN GOVERNMENT?

Before I examine these hypotheses, however, I ask how extensive the intersection between the women's movement and the state is. There are two ways to examine this question: The first, focused on the degree to which the state has penetrated the movement, asks what percentage of the feminist movement is inside the state. The second, focused on the degree to which the movement has penetrated the state, asks what percentage of state actors are part of the social movement. My in-depth interviews cannot speak to either question, based as they are, on purposive sampling. However, two pieces of previous research suggest that "insider activists" were consistently a significant part of the larger women's movement. Leila Rupp and Verta Taylor (1987: 51) provide evidence of the existence of feminist activists inside the federal bureaucracy before the rise of the second wave. Analyzing 108 core members of the women's movement between 1945 and the 1960s, they found that 11% of these activists who were employed listed their occupations as "politicians or civil servants[3]" (Rupp and Taylor 1987: 51). In 1977 and 1978, Alice Rossi (1982) also surveyed activists who attended the National Women's Conference in Houston that was organized as part of the International Year of the Woman. She finds that government employees were an even higher percentage of this select group of activists: 9.5% were employed by the federal government and an additional 34.7% were employed by state or local governments (Rossi 1982: 81).[4]

---

[3] In 1950, government employees constituted 13.3% of all nonfarm employees (U.S. Census Bureau 2003: 55). Given potential error of a small sample and the fact that the criteria for joining the sample was notoriety – a condition government employees generally avoid – it is unlikely that government employees were either over or under represented in the pre–second-wave women's movement.

[4] There are a number of reasons why the National Women's Conference survey might inflate the number of government workers in the feminist movement. First, attendees at the National Women's Conference included a number of antifeminists, who could not be separated from other participants. The National Women's Conference was also limited to representatives selected by state governments, which may explain the high number of state government employees at the conference. Finally, it is likely that some types of feminist groups – particularly local radical feminist groups – would be less likely to participate in the selection process that would allow them to be part of

The data on the penetration of feminist activists into the state are also slim. The Center for American Women and Politics (1978) surveyed all women appointees to the federal executive in 1977. That survey suggests that during the Carter administration, women's movement activists were quite common in this group. Of the twenty-two women who completed the survey and answered this question, 36% stated that they were members of feminist social action organizations such as the National Organization for Women (NOW) or Women's Equity Action League (WEAL). More than half of the respondents reported that they belonged to other sorts of women's organizations, including groups like the National Federation of Business and Professional Women that sought greater opportunities for women. However, a low response rate both for the entire survey (only 40% returned the questionnaires) and for the particular question (of the thirty-five individuals who answered the survey, only twenty-two – 62% – completed this question) means that there is information for only 25% of the total female federal appointees surveyed. Nonetheless, the numbers suggest that the percentage of activists at the highest levels of the bureaucracy may be fairly high under the right circumstances. Even if we assume that all non-respondents are nonfeminists, at least 9% of the women appointees were members of feminist organizations.

While the data presented here can only provide rough parameters on the numbers of feminist activists in the federal bureaucracy and only during the late 1970s, it is clear that insider activists never dominated the feminist movement in numbers. But neither did they represent a trivial number. Feminist activists were a part of the federal bureaucracy just as they were a part of other occupations as well. Where then do they fit into the larger movement? Were feminist activists within the federal bureaucracy typical of activists generally? It is to this question that I now turn.

THE CHARACTERISTICS OF INSIDER FEMINIST ACTIVISTS

Looking at the social characteristics of feminist activists inside the bureaucracy, I focus specifically on social class and race. Because

the Houston conference, which might lead to an overrepresentation of the "older" branch, which is more likely to include professionals and civil servants.

TABLE 3.1. *Educational Level of Feminist Activists Inside the Federal Bureaucracy* (N = 40)

	High School Only	B.A. Only[b]	M.A.[a]	J.D.	Ph.D.	Row Total
Highest degree obtained before entering U.S. bureaucracy	2	11	5	12	3	33
Highest degree obtained during employment in U.S. bureaucracy	0	0	1	2	2	5
Unknown when highest degree was obtained	0	1	1	0	0	2
Total number in degree	2	12	7	14	5	40
%	5%	29%	17%	34%	12%	

[a] One individual had both a J.D. and master's degrees. In this case I coded her as a J.D.

[b] Two individuals with a BA eventually left the government to pursue different careers in the course of which they obtained another degree. In the coding above, these individuals are coded as having a BA only.

the feminist insiders I interviewed were at the higher levels of the civil service pay scale (GS14 or above), they are also by definition middle class.[5] Nonetheless, two additional elements tell us something about the social class of these activists: their post-secondary education, and their descriptions of their parents' economic status. Table 3.1 presents the educational level obtained by the respondents I interviewed. Given that the people interviewed have obtained the rank of GS14 or above or were political appointees, it is not surprising that thirty-eight of the forty feminist activists had a college diploma, and 63% of these feminist activists had achieved a graduate degree of some sort (seven had master's degrees, fourteen had a law degree, and five had a PhD). Five of the women with these advanced degrees acquired them after they had joined the federal bureaucracy, typically returning to law school for a law degree.

[5] Although this does not necessarily mean that they were always middle class. For example, two respondents mentioned that they took their government jobs because they had become divorced and had small children to support.

TABLE 3.2. *Economic Status of the Parents of Feminist Activists Inside the Federal Bureaucracy* (N = 40)

	Exact Info. Available	Proximate Info. Available	Total	%[a]
Middle or upper class	3	13	16	70%
Working class or in poverty	0	7	7	30%
Total	3	20	23	100%

Notes: Proximate information on parents' class was determined by parents' occupation or other information about the interviewees, early life that implied class background.
[a] % of all individuals with information on parents' background.

A second indicator of social class is the economic background of the home in which these individuals were raised. From an economic perspective the feminist activists within the federal government reflected a much more privileged background than the population at large.[6] As Table 3.2 shows, of those who provided a direct or indirect measure of class, about 70% indicated that they came from middle or upper-class backgrounds. In many cases, the feminist activists indicated that their parents were professionals. Where respondents mentioned their parent's occupations, the most commonly mentioned jobs were lawyer, teacher, or professor. Although there are no comparable statistics on "outsider" feminist activists, it is likely that these insider feminist activists were also more privileged than movement activists generally.

Race

My sample of forty activists included three African Americans and one Latina. These women represent 10% of my sample, which is slightly

---

[6] I did not ask individuals about their economic background during their youth because this was tangential to the major focus of the interview. Nor was this information specifically volunteered; only three individuals mentioned their economic class specifically – in all cases mentioning that they came from well-off families. Nonetheless, half of the individuals interviewed talked enough about their background growing up to allow me to classify their background as either middle/upper class or working class/in poverty. This classification is based on the respondents' parents' occupations or on statements about their economic situation during their youth. For example, one respondent mentioned that her father had died at a young age, throwing the family into a dire economic situation.

less than the percentage of African Americans and Latinas in the population during this time period.[7] In comparison, Alice Rossi found that African Americans and Hispanics represented over 23% of the elected delegates at the National Women's Conference in Houston (Rossi 1982: 32). The fact that racial minorities were underrepresented in my sample of feminist insiders is important because several studies have suggested that the specific character of black and Latina women's gender oppression (and its connection to race oppression) meant that their needs were not addressed by the white women's movement (Strolovich 2007) and that they largely organized separately from their white counterparts in order to address the racism in white middle-class organizations and to critically engage white feminists (see Roth 2004; Springer 2005).

Compared to the white women interviewed for the study, the women of color who spoke to me were no less likely to participate in the national feminist organizations. Of these four women, all but one were active in either the National Organization for Women, Women's Equity Action League, or Federally Employed Women – three of the overarching women's organizations often characterized as being overwhelmingly white.[8] Indeed, all three played important roles in these organizations – either being part of the initial founding or holding important offices. Three of the four women also mentioned involvement in organizations representing women of color, ranging from the National Council of Negro Women to second-wave black feminist organizations, while the fourth discussed her extensive involvement in the civil rights movement during the fifties and sixties. This suggests that women of color who were also insider feminist activists participated actively both in what have been traditionally considered white middle-class organizations (like the National Organization for Women) but also organized separately along lines of racial identity.

A good example of one such feminist insider is Aileen Hernandez, an early president of the National Organization for Women (NOW).

---

[7] In the United States in 1970, women of color constituted 12.7% of the female population and in 1960, 11.6% of the female population (U.S. Bureau of the Census 1972: table 48: 262).

[8] Of course, this could be an artifact of the snowball sample design, which was heavily influenced by the white women who dominated the sample.

Hernandez worked for the International Ladies' Garment Workers' Union until she entered government service to work on equal employment issues – first for the state of California and then as one of the first commissioners at the Equal Employment Opportunity Commission (EEOC). When she resigned from the EEOC in November 1966, members of the founding group of NOW had already appointed her to the governing board of the organization. She went on to become president of the National Organization for Women in 1970–1971, and also helped to organize the National Women's Political Caucus. In 1973, Hernandez helped found Black Women Organized for Action, and continued her activism both among women of color and for feminism for many years.

The dual activism of the black and Latina feminists inside the bureaucracy mirrors what others have found among feminist women of color who were activists generally: that they actively participated in the leadership of what have traditionally been considered "white" feminist organizations even as they also recognized the importance of separate organizations for women of color. One respondent explained her dual organizational life in this way:

I felt that it [NOW] was an elitist group, and even the Board... Betty Friedan ... Gene Boyer, Anna Hedgeman... Pauli Murray. These are people of the movement who are inclusive... but the other women who were more elitist... I got along with them, they never knew I thought they were elitist, because I felt they had a role. And that's my sense of the movement, of any movement, that you've got to look at what they're doing positive to forward the agenda, the objectives for the public. (Interview, June 25th, 2004)

Summary

The feminist activists inside the bureaucracy who I interviewed were substantially different from the general population. I have no sample of outsider feminist activists with which to compare them, but Rossi's study suggests they differ from this population as well. It is no surprise, given their positions within the bureaucracy, that they were highly educated and above average in socioeconomic status; they were also slightly more likely to be white than the average population. Although it is difficult to generalize from the few women of color in my sample, these women were active both in organizations for women of color and in the larger national organizations as well.[9] At least among the few women of color in my sample, that dual activism reflects the fact that even as women of color experienced racism within the larger movement, they also continued organizing across racial lines for larger feminist issues (Springer 2005; Thompson 2002).[10]

WHAT DO INSIDER FEMINIST ACTIVISTS STAND FOR?

The ideological views of feminist activists inside the state are also important for understanding their role in the movement and in influencing government policy. If feminist activists inside the bureaucracy were especially well placed to influence government policy, what parts of the larger movement's ideological tenets did they represent? Most of the literature on the institutionalization of social movements presumes that activists inside the state should accept established institutions and be more moderate in their beliefs. I explore that issue here by describing the ideology of the feminist activists within the government bureaucracy whom I interviewed.[11] Although ideology was not the central topic of these interviews, most of the feminist activists I interviewed discussed their beliefs and values. Supplemented by primary and secondary historical sources, the interviews permit an assessment of how insider activists may have differed from those outside the state.

I look at the ideology of feminist activists in three ways. First, I examine the degree to which feminists inside the state focused only on the achievement of equality with men based on individual rights (liberal feminism), and eschewed wider social change and social justice that might require more fundamental changes in society, the economy,

---

9 My conclusions here mirror those of Hartmann (1998: 197) who, in looking at African American feminists in the Ford Foundation and National Council of Churches, also found African American feminists working with white feminists even while maintaining independent organizations.

10 However, I cannot exclude the possibility that my sample is biased toward feminist activists of color who work in both types of organizations, because I rely on a snowball sample that begins with members in the larger women's organizations.

11 It is difficult to define existent feminist ideologies; while scholars have developed categorizations of the ideologies that are present within feminism – such as the distinction between liberal, socialist, radical, and cultural feminism – these often result in artificial categories that may not reflect the complexity and intersections that exist among these beliefs. Moreover, the ideologies in the movement shift over time as activists react to the political events and societal change (Whittier 1995).

or political institutions. Second, because liberal feminists also vary greatly both in terms of their partisan attachments and in their beliefs on social issues, I also discuss the variety of opinions that existed among those that focused on achieving equality through political and legal reform. Third, a major issue within feminism is how widely or narrowly to constitute the feminist agenda; those who advocate a narrow focus often exclude other groups of feminists, particularly those at the intersection of other movements or who are part of underrepresented groups such as women of color, women in poverty, and lesbians. A belief in the structural nature of poverty is also part of many radical ideologies. And so I focus on the degree to which these feminists' view of feminist activism included a wide agenda versus those who believed in focusing on a more limited set of feminist issues such as violence against women, abortion or the Equal Rights Amendment.

Advocating Equal Rights vs. Social Justice and Social Change

In trying to identify the degree to which the ideology of the feminist activists I interviewed expands beyond liberal feminism, I used two criteria. First, some people were very explicit about whether they viewed themselves as pushing for radical social change or as pursuing women's equality through the existing system of individual rights within liberal democracy. These people's ideology could be unambiguously categorized. For example, one political appointee during a Democratic administration said:

[Sarah Evans] ... put us in 2 categories; the liberationists and the legalists. And I was on the legalist side, but I must say the liberationists made us look respectable and really gave us more attention. (Interview, December 18, 2003)

On the other hand, a long-time activist who also pursued a lengthy career within the federal government said:

Women have to empower themselves. . . . For example, I have always felt, and by the way, the founders felt, that this was a liberation of women. . . . (Interview, June 25, 2004)

Second, the activists I interviewed could also indicate their beliefs in equal rights in the context of discussing specific issues or policies on which they were active. For example, one individual framed her activism on the issue of violence against women in terms of individual rights in democracies:

I think that what remains to be done is that we need to understand the civil rights implications of stopping violence against women. We understood it with respect to African Americans, we've understood it with respect to people with disabilities... but on this very broad spectrum of issues regarding the equality of women there's probably more resistance than on any of these other issues. It's the last great civil rights frontier we have to fight... nobody says the obvious... which is to me that women cannot participate fully in this democracy or any other democracy if they are not living free from violence. How can I worry about equal pay if I can not guarantee my own safety or the safety of my children on a daily basis? (Interview, July 30, 2004)

It is important in this case to note that while some issues are normally associated with liberal feminism and some with radical feminism, there were important variants. Radical feminists, particularly those who were active at the start of the women's movement, also pushed for laws ending employment discrimination, although their agenda for social change went much deeper. Similarly, in later years, issues like violence against women attracted both those feminists seeking equality through individual rights as well as those seeking more radical change in society. For example, a feminist activist who worked for the federal government describes her activism in a local shelter:

We had a huge discussion... [on] the question... how do we take it [government money] without letting it ruin us.... Initially, the money came in only on the counseling side, which was fine because then we would use that money for the counselors and support groups and use all our other money for social change, radical agenda.... I've always said that you can be extremely radical in your analysis of your work if you, quote, look more respectable. (Interview, June 26, 2002)

Overall, feminist activists who worked inside the bureaucracy were more likely to advocate for equality through individual rights, but there were also many advocates of more fundamental change. Of the thirty-six activists whose ideology I could categorize on the basis of the interview, thirteen (or more than one-third) viewed themselves as seeking radical social change or social justice. Interestingly, although radical feminism is often considered to be a phenomenon of the early years of the U.S. women's movement, the group of insider feminists who were categorized as radical feminists is evenly split between those whose activism began prior to 1970 (six) and those who became active afterward (seven). Moreover, those who supported radical social change or social justice entered government at different times. Several entered government before the rise of the second wave of feminism and were converted to feminism from within; while others entered government after 1966, and were usually already strong feminists when they entered government. Most of the insider feminists who believed in radical social change or social justice remained in government through the early 1980s.

Divisions among Liberal Feminists

Among the "insider" feminist activists who held a worldview that centered on achieving equality through individual rights, there also exists considerable variation. On the one hand, these individuals differ in their party affiliation. Although most indicated either directly or indirectly that they were Democrats, two were strong Republican partisans and a few others indicated that they began their activism as Republicans and only later switched to the Democratic party. While feminism now is identified almost exclusively with the Democratic Party (see for example, Freeman 1987; Freeman 1993), these Republican feminists remind us of the earlier era when feminism clearly bridged both parties, and of the continuing disagreement among Republicans over issues related to feminism.

One Republican woman described herself as a Rockefeller Republican and talked extensively of her advocacy for both child care and the Equal Rights Amendment. Describing the 1972 Republican Convention, for example, she stated:

We went down to Miami [in 1972] with the goal of changing the platform to include child care for women. And Peggy Heckler had a bill in the House which basically mandated federal money going into childcare. I remember that bill. That was the issue. ERA was never an issue to be taken off [the agenda]. (Interview, January 9, 2004)

She ended the conversation by proudly noting that her daughters continued to be Republicans but also highlighting their liberal feminist ideals:

[My daughters] . . . don't define themselves by the fact that they are women and they have a different viewpoint at all. They define themselves as thinking X or Y in policy, or they're a moderate or a conservative . . . and that has nothing to do with their sex. Absolutely nothing, except when you talk about choice. And that is very personal to them. And they are very pro-choice, all three of them. (Interview, January 9, 2004)

The other strong Republican in the sample also had been very active in the early National Organization for Women. She was also pro-choice, and was proud of her work forcing television stations to create a more balanced portrayal of women in their programming:

We challenged the licenses of television stations on the grounds that they were day in and day out violating the Fairness Doctrine because they were taking a position on the controversial issue of public importance . . . – the role of women in society – by only showing women in one role. (Interview, October 18, 2003)

While both Republican women still felt strongly about the issues that had motivated them in the 1970s, neither used the term "feminism" to describe their ideology by the time I talked with them in 2003–2004. It did not appear that their ideology had changed from the earlier years, but that the political context around them had. On the one hand, it was probably difficult to label oneself a feminist within the Republican Party given the greater dominance of social conservatives and the Republican Party's greater emphasis on discipline (although neither woman said this). On the other hand, both did mention that feminism itself had changed, encompassing now many things that they firmly opposed. For example, one of these women argued that

Feminists got a dirty name with NOW in the 70s when it became extreme. It was a problem we always face. Women had a really good explanation of what the word meant, which was not threatening at all, but it was hard to overcome a lot of extremism that got all the publicity. (Interview, October 18, 2003)

As a result, neither used the label of feminism in today's context.

National Organization for Women vs. WEAL
Another division among the liberal feminists in the group was their stance with regard to the National Organization for Women (NOW) versus the Women's Equity Action League (WEAL). WEAL was

formed in 1968 by those members of NOW that thought the organization should only focus on educational and economic discrimination
and should avoid social issues, particularly abortion (Freeman 1975:
81). While some individuals became active in both groups, WEAL's
membership generally held a less expansive view of what feminism
should seek to change. The two organizations also differed in tactics
as WEAL was the consummate insider organization – focusing exclusively on lobbying and influence in Washington (Marx Ferree and Hess
2000: 110). Although WEAL disbanded in the 1980s, its presence until
then helps to further differentiate among the liberal feminists in my
sample. If feminist activists inside the state are more conservative and
likely to work inside the system, I would expect them to be more likely
to join WEAL than NOW.

Of the twenty feminist activists within the federal bureaucracy who
belonged to one of these two organizations,[12] only five were exclusively WEAL members. Fourteen were NOW members, and one individual belonged to both organizations. However, among the fifteen
who indicated that they were members of NOW, four mentioned they
had left NOW over the years for ideological reasons. Two indicated
they left because the organization had gotten too radical while two
indicated they left because the organization was not radical enough.
The preponderance of NOW members compared to WEAL members,
and the fact that NOW members who left were evenly split between
those dissatisfied with its conservative bent and those who saw it as
too radical contradicts the expectation that feminist activists inside the
bureaucracy would be more conservative in their ideology.

Overall, I find meaningful variation among these insider feminist
activists. Feminist activists inside the state could hold radical views
about the necessity of extensive social, political, or economic change
or they could be highly conservative, believing only in the need for
individual rights to build a fair playing field for women. Even among
those that might be labeled liberal feminists, there was considerable

---

[12] Half the sample belonged to neither group or was missing information. It is not
surprising that half of the sample was not a member of either organization given
the wide variety of groups and organizations that make up the women's movement.
What is impressive is the large number of NOW activists in the sample, probably
indicating the relative importance of Washington activists, particularly in the early
years.

variation in their beliefs, ranging from strong fiscal conservatives fully vested in the Republican Party to those that thought NOW should be a more radical organization.

Inclusiveness of Feminism

A third ideological dimension differentiating feminist insiders is the degree to which they viewed feminism as including a wide range of issues. For some, feminism was concerned only with issues that were specific to women only; while feminists might be interested in other issues, these were not *feminist* issues. Alternatively, other feminists viewed feminism as taking a stand on a whole host of issues, arguing that women themselves had special interests or worldviews that might provide a better perspective on issues like ecology, war, and civil rights. These ideological differences often played out in debates about the appropriate agenda for feminist organizations like NOW. Attempts to concentrate on a small set of issues were seen by some as creating exclusivity within the organization. For example, as one respondent explained her reasons for quitting the National Organization for Women:

In the early '70s, NOW was very different than it is now. It was very diverse. We had national councils on every possible feminist issue you could think of, which is not the case today. I was involved in a big struggle with Ellie Smeal over that and that's when I quit NOW. My issue organization versus an organization that focuses only on the ERA and abortion and as you know now [in] NOW, that's the primary concern. They do do something on employment and stuff. But they still do not do anything on poverty or art or all the other wonderful things.... They just don't do that anymore. That was one of the reasons that I quit the organization. (Interview, March 11, 2004)

The belief that feminism includes some issues not specifically related to women is not exclusively connected to radical feminism.[13] In my sample of feminist activists working inside the state, both radical feminists and liberal feminists reflected a belief in inclusivity. As one liberal feminist noted:

[13] Indeed, as Freeman (1975) and Ryan (1992) have indicated, exclusivity can be equally strong among radicals as well.

Feminism, to me at least, is not monolithic. Within the term there are all sorts of different degrees and strategies that one can employ in being a feminist. And I think being a feminist lawyer – which means to me working within society and established institutions – gave me certain opportunities. (Interview, June 15, 2004)

Similarly, an activist in a community rape crisis center, who strongly supported radical social change noted:

We were questioning everything. You know, all the hierarchies of gender and race and class. At the rape crisis center in '76, I mean, one of my contributions was, we had this enormously wonderful complex heated debate about race and class and gender issues, and gay/straight and, you know, inclusivity and exclusivity. (Interview, June 26, 2002)

The "insider" feminist activists I interviewed manifested their inclusivity or exclusivity in a number of different ways. A few talked explicitly about their view of feminism – as the above quotations show. Others indicated their opinions on how inclusive feminism should be when discussing specific issues. On the other hand, participation in other movements was not an indicator that the individual believed in inclusive feminism[14]; much more important was whether the individual saw her actions on issues to be inspired by her feminism or by simply being concerned with a number of issues.

Racial discrimination was by far, the issue most often mentioned by insider feminist activists. In addition to the women of color mentioned earlier, six of the thirty-six white feminist activists volunteered that they had been active on the issue of civil rights. Many viewed this activism as part of an ideological commitment to political advocacy, as the following activist suggests:

I have always felt and thought that it was important to make a social contribution, in part, because of the issues that were important at that time, the influence of my parents, [and] what I saw in law school. And I also think because I've always been socially concerned. (Interview, June 15, 2004)

Several insider activists felt their feminism was tied to racism. Certainly, racism and feminism were inextricably linked for those insider

---

[14] Actually, almost all of the respondents indicated they were active on a wide variety of issues and in a number of movements.

feminists who were women of color. For two of the six white women in my sample working on civil rights, issues of racism were also tied to their feminist beliefs. As one of these woman stated as she talked about her feminist achievements within the government:

> We were really focused a lot on the double discrimination issue that faced women of color. And I have carried that to this very moment... we were looking at racism and sexism and we saw the two forces and the two areas of oppression as being tightly linked with each other. And we saw women of color as the fulcrum, I used to say – actually I still do – 30 years later I still say the same thing, if you add race discrimination and sex discrimination together, race + sex, it's not 1 + 1 = 2, it's 1 + 1 = 2000. And so we were very focused in that direction. (Interview, September 25, 2003)

A second issue where the debate about inclusivity and exclusivity played out was the issue of poverty. At least four of the women I interviewed mentioned that issues of poverty were also part and parcel of their feminism. Three of these women had begun their activism working on issues of women in poverty: one in the National Welfare Rights Association and the other two in local grassroots groups. The fourth woman had largely been active in international issues (and had come to her feminist activism more recently) but saw poverty as broadly affecting other feminist issues. For example, she spent some time discussing how issues surrounding incarceration in the United States, such as public transportation to and from prisons, should also be considered a feminist issue (Interview, March 8, 2004).

Feminists inside the government were also split on whether the Vietnam War was a feminist issue or not. Two of the insider feminist activists I interviewed noted disagreements about the place of the war within their feminist circles. One mentioned being disappointed that her paper on equality in the draft had been rejected by other feminists in her group because they "felt it would look like [we] wanted to send women to Vietnam (a bad war) and they wouldn't have it" (Interview, March 25, 2002). A second interviewee mentioned quitting the National Women's Political Caucus during "the Ford administration, because instead of being an organization that was going to open up the political process to women, they wound up taking sides in Vietnam and on all sorts of issues" (Interview, January 9, 2004). But feminist activists who worked for the federal bureaucracy could also be found supporting the idea that antiwar activism was feminist activism. Aileen Hernandez, former commissioner at the Equal Employment Opportunity Commission, found herself defending anti-war activism within NOW by saying that:

> I would find it impossible to decide that all my energies had to go to NOW... especially if NOW viewed its own interests so narrowly that it did not see a relevance in the struggle against racism and war. (Letter to Eve Norman dated April 29, 1971)

She goes on to say that a NOW resolution condemning the war

> permits NOW members, already active in the movement for peace, to speak to feminist concerns within that movement and to do so as NOW members. In order to do this effectively it becomes important for the proponents of the resolution... [to] produce the supporting rationale that will address the feminist viewpoint on war. (Letter to Eve Norman dated April 29, 1971)

Issues of sexuality also divided the women's movement, particularly in the early years. Catherine East, often labeled a founder of the second wave from within the federal bureaucracy, was one feminist insider whose definition of feminism excluded issues of lesbian rights:

> My feeling was that lesbianism and sexual preference is not a sex discrimination issue.... I certainly agree that there should not be any discrimination because of sexual preference and I thoroughly approve of the fact that there are organizations that are tackling that issue. But I felt that it was separate from the women's movement. (East 1982: 256)

Using statements about how inclusive feminism should be, and about which issues are included in their definition of feminism, I was able to code thirty-two feminist activists inside the federal bureaucracy for the inclusivity or exclusivity of their feminism. A little more than half of them (eighteen of thirty two) held a more inclusive view of feminism.[15]

In all, then, while I cannot say that this sample of "insider" feminist activists was more inclusive or radical than feminist activists as a whole, they did hold a wide range of viewpoints. Although the

---

[15] When I used a stricter coding scheme, one where inclusivity and exclusivity were coded as existing based only on ideological statements and not on a discussion of issues, twelve out of the twenty individuals that could be unambiguously coded held inclusive views of feminism.

majority were liberal feminists, a range of feminist activists from pro-choice Republicans to those seeking radical change in society existed within the federal bureaucracy. Moreover, a large proportion of these "insider" feminists held very inclusive views of feminism, believing that a range of issues should be included under the banner of feminist politics. These findings suggest that assumptions that feminist activists inside the state represent only less radical feminist ideologies, or that they hold a narrow view of feminism can be rejected.

Comparing Insider Feminist Activists to Feminist Activists Outside the State

Additional evidence about the ideology of insider feminists is provided by a survey of those attending the 1977 National Women's Confer-ence in Houston conducted by Alice Rossi. Unfortunately, Rossi's ori-ginal survey data have been lost and so I rely here on tables from her book, *Feminists in Politics* (1982), focusing specifically on the tables that distinguish whether the individual surveyed was a deleg-ate to the convention, a commissioner of the International Women's Year (IWY), or on the IWY secretariat staff. The secretariat staff were the federal employees responsible for helping the International Women's Year Commission with their duties, which included writ-ing several reports and organizing the national women's conference in Houston.[16]

To examine how feminist activists inside the state compare to those outside, I compare the secretariat staff to the delegates at the conven-tion. While the secretariat staff need not be feminist activists, I used a staffing plan that provided short biographies of the anticipated hires to determine how many of the secretariat staff fit my existing defini-tion of insider feminist activist.[17] These biographies indicated that at least half of those suggested for positions at the upper levels fit the

---

[16] The secretariat staff constituted less than one fifth of the total sample of federal employees (23 out of 117) surveyed. Although 9.5% of all the women interviewed in Alice Rossi's survey worked for the federal government, Rossi does not break down ideological beliefs by employer. The loss of the original survey data means that we can examine only the Secretariat staff separately.

[17] The staffing plan can be found in a memo to Mr. Ingersoll from Mildred Marcy dated February 25, 1975 (papers of Catherine East [MC477], Schlesinger Library, Box 19, Folder 26). Catherine East was one of those who made the move to the IWY secretariat office.

definition of feminist activists. Moreover, as a group, the secretariat staff was similar to the other participants in the National Women's Conference in terms of their membership in feminist organizations (Rossi 1982: 128).[18] While it would be better to have more exact information about the secretariat staff, or more information on all of the federal employees who were part of Rossi's sample, the data on the secretariat staff provides the only opportunity to compare the ideology of insider and outsider activists.

Rossi, herself, examined the feminist attitudes of individuals at the National Women's Conference, categorizing them as strongly, moderately, or slightly/not feminist. More than two-thirds of the administrative and professional staff in the secretariat office were characterized by Rossi as either strongly or moderately feminist (1982: 71). Indeed, the secretariat staff members were among the strongest supporters of resolutions for reproductive freedom and lesbian rights – issues that represented fairly radical views in 1977 (Rossi 1982: 132). In addition, compared to other individuals in attendance at the Houston conference, the secretariat staff was much more likely to be classified as radical in general political orientation, and the nonradicals were much more likely to be labeled very liberal as opposed to liberal/moderate or conservative (1982: 126). The picture painted by Rossi's analysis suggests that the insider feminists of the secretariat staff were more radical than the delegates at the National Women's Conference.[19] This provides additional evidence contradicting the assumption that federal bureaucrats will be more reform oriented than outside activists.

ENTERING THE STATE

This chapter's final question focuses on insider feminist activists from the perspective of their employment in the federal government. I have already discussed the question of their ideology, challenging the

[18] However, the secretariat staff was much less likely than other attendees to be a member of any type of nonpolitical or political organization including traditional women's organization.

[19] While I cannot directly look only at those among the secretariat staff who fit the definition of feminist activists, the fact that some of the secretariat staff are not feminist activists should make the secretariat staff as a group less feminist and less supportive of lesbian rights and abortion. So in this case any error that comes from comparing secretariat staff to the delegates should work against Rossi's finding that staff were more feminist.

assumption that they are ideologically moderate and accepting of existing institutions. In this section I examine the relationship of their feminist activism to their public service, focusing on three specific questions.
First, did these women enter the federal bureaucracy as feminists or
did they become active during their government employment? Second,
I ask whether feminist activists were employed within the offices of the
federal bureaucracy devoted to issues important to feminist activists.
Finally, I examine the degree to which insiders activists were motivated
more by their activism or by their careers. While Chapter 7 investig-
ates what feminist activists chose to do when faced with actual choices
between pursuing their activism and keeping their job, here I explore
which aspect of their lives motivated them more generally.

Feminist Activism: Moving into the State or Developing Within?

Traditionally, social movement scholars have presumed that feminist
activists move inside government only after the movement is mobilized.
However, as I argued in Chapter 2, there were many reasons why
feminist activists could be found within the state at the rise of the
second wave. Moreover, it is also possible for civil servants to become
feminist activists after entering the federal government. What, then, is
the relationship between their activism and their employment within
the federal bureaucracy for these insider feminist activists?

One way of examining this question is to ask when, vis-à-vis their
employment, these individuals became feminist activists. I make three
distinctions among feminist activists inside the state.[20] First, feminist
activists may *infiltrate* the state after they are already fully involved in
the women's movement. In this case, entrée into the federal government
follows their activism in second-wave organizations. A second alternative is possible for others who were already in the state before the second
wave began. They may have been ideologically feminists or members
in first-wave women's organizations such as the National Woman's
Party or the National Federation of Business and Professional Women.
What distinguishes this group of feminist activists is that they already
were feminists and were in the state before the second wave occurred.
These women within the state were *mobilized* into newer second-wave

---

[20] I thank Francis Chen for pointing out these three types of insider feminist activists
to me.

TABLE 3.3. *The Relationship of Feminist Activism to Employment within the Bureaucracy*

	Number	Percent of Coded
Active feminist infiltrating the federal bureaucracy	20	50%
Feminist federal employee mobilized by second wave	6	15%
Converted to feminism when already federal employee	9	23%
Could not be classified	5	12%
Total	40	

organizations as they arose. A third group of women within the state may not have been feminists – either ideologically or by their participation in first-wave organizations – when the second wave arose. These women became feminist activists because they were *converted* into the feminist cause and became active in feminist organizations, after the second wave began.

Table 3.3 shows that only half of the women I interviewed were already feminist activists when they entered the federal government. However, not all of these feminist activists expressly took jobs in the federal government so that they could continue their activism; some activists chose the civil service for other reasons but continued their activism outside work. Fifteen other women that I interviewed were already in the federal government when they were either converted to feminism or were mobilized by the second wave. Except for one, all of these women became active in the initial years of the second wave as new feminist organizations formed and new issues mobilized women to protest.

Where Insider Feminist Activists Work

Table 3.3 suggests that while half of the insider feminist activists I studied entered the bureaucracy as feminist activists, many also entered the bureaucracy first and only later turned to activism. Yet not all feminist activists entering the bureaucracy sought jobs related to their movement activism. Table 3.4 focuses on where the insider feminist activists I interviewed worked during their careers in the federal bureaucracy. I find that two-thirds of the activists I interviewed worked in offices

TABLE 3.4. *Feminist Activists in the Federal Bureaucracy by Substantive Focus of Location*

	Number	Percent
Entire career outside of women's policy offices	13	33%
Worked part of their careers in women's policy offices	14	35%
Worked exclusively in women's policy offices	13	33%
Total	40	

that dealt with policies related specifically to women (here termed women's policy offices, see Stetson and Mazur 1995: 2–5). In making this determination, I utilized a wide definition of women's policy offices including any agency, bureau, office, or commission that clearly identified women as a client; these offices included the Women's Bureau, the Violence against Women Office, the Equal Employment Opportunity Commission, and the Office of Women in Development among others. However, among women who worked in women's policy offices, only half limited their careers in the federal government to women's policy offices. The other half moved into other parts of the federal government at some point in their careers. This finding suggests that those who have studied feminists inside the state by focusing only on women's policy offices may be seeing only part of the picture. Indeed, as Chapter 6 shows, one strength of insider feminist activism was the myriad of locations within the state from which it occurred.

The Orientation of Feminist Activists

Finally, I examine whether insider feminist activists talked about their employment in terms of activism or building a career. In this case, the discerning factor is whether, in discussing their lives, they emphasized their career track or whether they emphasized a specific issue (or set of issues) or feminism generally, and indicated that the job they were in was less important. The group of activists I interviewed contained both feminist activists who chose their positions largely for career reasons and those who thought mostly about their activism. One of the feminist activists I talked to described the others in her office in those terms:

There's a group of people who stay at the Women's Bureau because they're committed to making change for women, to improve the status of women.

There's another large group of women, people, who stay at the Bureau because it's a good job and because they also offer benefits they like, and I think they sometimes get comfortable there. And it's very difficult to get them to give up, even when they really should move on. And I would say that both kinds of people are in jobs that have . . . a lot of impact on women. . . . The Bureau has always been blessed with people, with a majority of people who are committed to women. It's getting now to the point where that's going to be difficult because there's so many, there's so much movement right now in the Bureau. But the people who are committed to doing something for women, I mean, you're not going to stop them. They don't stop just because they're not at the Bureau. Most of them continue to work on women outside of their positions and with more spring because they expanded their knowledge and contacts and what not. (Interview, October 10, 2002)

Indeed, of the thirty-seven individuals who could be identified as career oriented or activism oriented, nineteen seemed more focused on their activism, and eighteen emphasized their career. One example of the career-oriented activist can be found in a woman who decided because of her beliefs that she wished to work in the field of equal employment opportunity. She talked about her jobs often in terms of building a career in that particular field:

I had this strategy, which was to get out of teaching and into full-time civil rights work. . . . It took me four jobs to do that. . . . When I was in the Bureau of Training at the Civil Service Commission, I was in the content area of civil rights, but I was doing 100% training. When I moved to the Community Relations Service as the Training Officer, I was in a civil rights agency. . . . There in addition to training, I was doing some program analysis work, and some survey compilations, so I was doing maybe . . . 80% training, and 20% program analysis. When I moved to the General Services Administration as the Equal Employment Opportunity Coordinator, I was working full-time in equal employment opportunity but I was also training EEO Officers, and EEO counselors. I always did a number of workshops for FEW [Federally Employed Women] during that time . . . so I call that position my "75% civil rights" job. . . . When I went over to the Equal Employment Opportunity Commission [EEOC], that was a full-time civil rights: it was in a civil rights agency, and I was the supervisor of an investigatory team. . . . After [name removed] left . . . the EEOC, I thought it was time to move on. I had been there for four years – the longest I'd been anywhere. . . . I really didn't like being a supervisor that much, and as I had gotten that aspect of my career taken care of, I thought I could do something else. (Interview, May 10, 2002)

Even though this individual talked about her career in fairly strategic terms, underlying that strategy is a deeply held belief that she could make a difference by having a career in the area of equal employment opportunity.

On the other hand, some of the individuals I interviewed clearly expressed the idea that they were willing to lose or leave their jobs inside the federal bureaucracy to be true to their feminist activism. For example, one feminist activist responded to a question about how constraining a job within the federal government was by noting she was motivated more by whether the job would help her to achieve feminist goals:

I was not constrained, which is why I did not last more than a year and one half.... I knew my time was limited.... If you had interviewed 1 or 2 people around me when I got this position, I turned to them and I said, 'I will not be in this job more than 2 years.' They said 'Why?' I said, 'Because I am taking it to get something done.' (Interview, March 15, 2004)

Yet others who viewed themselves as focusing on a career were sometimes placed in situations that led to them having to make a choice between their career and activism. For example, one individual who talked about her career aspirations quite openly noted that there was a point in her career where she chose to take an activist stance over her career, although as a political appointee she risked losing her job.[21] In this case, it involved protesting Carter's antiabortion stance:

The next job I wanted was to be on the Supreme Court.... Most of the things that I didn't agree with [the administration position], I'd concede the government side when I didn't feel strongly. But this was one that I felt like even if I got fired for doing it, this was something that I had to do – to protest on this issue. I had to be there. (Interview, June 25, 2004)

The even split between those feminist activists in the federal bureaucracy who were career oriented and those who emphasized their

[21] For most of the "insider" feminist activists that I talked to, the contradiction between career and activism was not so stark. Few insider feminist activists – either career oriented or activism oriented – were forced to choose between their careers or their activism (although there were exceptions, as I show in Chapter 7). Many others had jobs that allowed them to be active but did not see their careers and their activism as strongly intertwined. For example, one feminist activist talked about her series of jobs in the federal government, which often were not focused on women: "Through most of my career, even when I didn't have gender equity as my primary responsibility . . . I was able, in general, to take whatever I was doing and figure out a gender equity component to it and a way I could help influence or encourage people to pay attention to gender equity" (Interview, March 8, 2004).

activism suggests that not all insiders are motivated by career aspirations within the bureaucracy.[22] While some were focused on their careers, others were only willing to serve in the bureaucracy as long as they could achieve what they wished.

Moreover, the importance of activism to the insider feminist activists I interviewed is confirmed by the jobs these individuals took upon leaving the federal bureaucracy. While two women were still employed by the federal government when the interviews were conducted, and eleven had retired from the federal government and pursued no other occupation, ten of the remaining twenty-seven women (more than one-third) left government for feminist organizations. Many of the remaining feminist activists continued in jobs that were related to their activism, such as university teaching on women. Hence, insider feminist activists in the federal bureaucracy were not primarily motivated by their careers. Nor were they always willing to conform to the constraints of government regardless of the consequences for the women's movement.

CONCLUSIONS

Feminist activists inside the state were positioned to have a disproportionate impact on public policy. For that reason, it matters how representative these women were of feminist activists generally. This chapter explored the demographic and ideological characteristics of feminist activists who were employed in the U.S. bureaucracy. I focus particularly on the assumptions made about insider activists within the literature on women's movements, and social movements more generally, showing that many of these assumptions do not describe most of these women.

Achieving a political appointment or a GS14 position in the civil service signals membership in an elite group, and, as this suggests, these women certainly were more educated and better off than the general population, if not than feminists in general. Moreover, compared to the general population, slightly fewer women of color could be

---

[22] Although, again, I cannot state that they were as activism oriented as "outsider" feminists in the women's movement as I have no sample of outsiders to compare with my group.

found among the feminist activists within the bureaucracy. This finding corresponds to the expectations of insider feminist activists within the literatures on women's movements and social movements. Yet, in other ways these "insider" feminist activists differed considerably from these expectations.

In ideology, the feminist activists within the government bureaucracy were a varied lot – ranging from Republicans to radical feminists. Given the assumption that "insiders" are more moderate, it is perhaps surprising that I found the entire feminist ideological spectrum represented within the state. Indeed, Alice Rossi's data suggest that at least in the late 1970s, insider feminists may have been even more radical than feminist activists outside the state in some respects.[23] Moreover, feminist activists working in the federal bureaucracy also vary from expectations in their pathways to being insider feminist activists and in their commitment to activism. A large minority of feminist activists did not enter the bureaucracy as activists in an already successful women's movement, but were first-wave activists mobilized in the new wave or were already inside the bureaucracy when they were converted to feminist activism. Moreover, roughly half of these insider feminists indicated a willingness to sacrifice their jobs in the bureaucracy for their activism. Indeed, an impressive number of these women made activism their careers – leaving jobs in the federal bureaucracy for other positions that allowed them to be active (see McAdam 1988: chapter 6).

Altogether, these descriptions of feminist activists inside the federal bureaucracy suggest that insiders and outsiders may differ less in their orientation to the movement and in their activism than theories that distinguish between insiders and outsiders might lead us to believe. Moreover, they also suggest that in looking at what feminist "insiders" achieved within government, the types of individuals that become insiders matters less than the political constraints (or opportunities) that characterize the state at any particular time.

---

[23] Although given the inability to do secondary analysis and develop clear samples of insider feminist activists, we cannot make any firm conclusions.

4

Mobilizing and Organizing the Second Wave

Given the significant number of feminist activists inside the federal government at the rise of the second wave, how did they influence the mobilization and organization of the women's movement in the 1960s and 1970s? In this chapter I show that insider feminist activists were crucial to the initial mobilization of a significant part of the U.S. women's movement.[1] Responding to the unwillingness or inability of existing women's organizations to deal with emerging issues, these insiders encouraged the formation of movement organizations – some specifically for insider feminists but also organizations to mobilize all feminists. Some of these organizations are very well known, such as the National Organization for Women; others, like Human Rights for Women, are smaller and less well documented. While many of these groups reflect what Freeman (1975) labels the older wing of the movement, the wing that developed from more established women rather than out of the New Left, they nonetheless reflect a wide array of interests, organizational forms, and tactics. The role that insider feminist activists played in the women's movement's mobilization contradicts the idea that activists enter the state only after movements succeed.

In this chapter, I provide five case studies of women's movement organizations that feminist activists within the state helped establish.

[1] According to Minkoff (1995: 66), the number of women's organizations founded began climbing after 1960 and peaked in the early 1970s.

The five cases highlight a range of actions undertaken by feminist activists in government bureaucracies. Some of the movement organizations discussed below are national in scope, others are local. In all five cases, feminist activists within the state played an important role in the initial mobilization and organization. They are illustrative of a larger number of organizations that feminist activists in government helped to mobilize. Even though much of the mobilization of the women's movement takes place outside of organizations, I focus here largely on organizations because it is easier to document the role that feminist activists played. Nonetheless, I will also provide evidence from my interviews that some feminist activists employed in the federal bureaucracy played significant roles in the movement's informal feminist networks as well.

I begin this chapter by discussing the formation of two feminist action organizations – the National Organization for Women and Human Rights for Women – that were designed to be general feminist organizations. In both cases, feminist activists inside the state acted in concert with other feminist activists located outside of the state to mobilize both inside and outside feminists. I then focus on three organizations for feminists inside the federal bureaucracy, emphasizing their relationship with the larger women's movement. Finally, I discuss the implications of the mobilization and organization by insider feminists for the women's movement.

ORGANIZING AND MOBILIZING INSIDE AND OUTSIDE FEMINISTS

Feminist insiders were active in mobilizing and organizing a number of women's movement organizations whose focus and primary constituency lay outside the state. In the case of the National Organization for Women, their role was not particularly visible but it was decisive in determining the course of events. Insider feminist activists also played a role in the creation of feminist legal defense organizations, many of which helped to determine important cases in the first years of the movement. Although insider feminist activists worked within strictly bureaucratic organizations, the types of movement organizations they founded reflected a range of movement organizational forms as the example of the Human Rights for Women illustrates.

The National Organization for Women

The story of the founding of the National Organization for Women (NOW) – one of the biggest women's movement organizations – is rife with the influence of feminist activists within the state. Although this story has already been told in numerous places (Carabillo, Meuli and Csida 1993; Ferree and Hess 1985; Freeman 1975; Friedan 1998; Harrison 1988; Wolbrecht 2000), many accounts slight the role that feminist activists within government played in the creation of the organization.[2] Here I highlight the pivotal role they played in the creation of this organization.

NOW was created in reaction to a number of events occurring within government. As many scholars have noted, one important event was President Kennedy's creation of the President's Commission on the Status of Women (see, for example, Duerst-Lahti 1989). Encouraged by Esther Peterson, Kennedy established the commission to review women's status and to make recommendations on necessary changes (Harrison 1988: 114). The commission and its report, *American Women*, mobilized many existing women's organizations to think about women's status and encouraged, with the aid of the Women's Bureau, the formation of state-level commissions as well. While the commission was disbanded in 1963, there was a push among the commission members to make sure that some organization continued: The result was two committees: the Interdepartmental Committee on the Status of Women composed of individuals from government agencies, and the Citizen's Advisory Council on the Status of Women. The latter monitored activities in the federal government and supported conferences of the state commissions on the status of women (Harrison 1988: 184–185).

As these two organizations were getting established, the Equal Employment Opportunity Commission (EEOC) came into being in July 1965 with the task of enforcing the Title VII of the Civil Rights Act of 1964. The EEOC's initial actions and public statements by government officials showed that most commissioners had very little interest in pursuing the sex clause of Title VII. For example, in August 1965, the commissioners of the EEOC voted 3–2 to allow sex-segregated job

---

[2] Friedan (1998), Harrison (1988), and Carabillo et al. (1993) are among the few publicized versions that discuss the role of feminist insiders.

advertisements in newspapers (Harrison 1988: 188). Rumors among government officials suggested that one of the supporters of equal opportunity for women, Richard Graham, a Republican commissioner with only a one-year appointment, was not going to be reappointed by President Johnson.[3]

The EEOC's hostility to the sex clause of Title VII received little to no publicity, and existing women's organizations showed little interest in monitoring the new agency. Feminists in government who were familiar with the EEOC's actions tried unsuccessfully to organize existing women's organizations. Marguerite Rawalt, an attorney for the Internal Revenue Service and past president of the National Federation of Business and Professional Women's Clubs, wrote letters to different organizations, without success, urging them to pressure the EEOC (Paterson 1986: 162–163). Instead, concern about the issue grew among a small group of women within government who were informed about the problems within the new agency and then engaged in a campaign to inform and mobilize women's organizations:

We wrote up a one page flyer and used Rawalt's connections to women's clubs to try and get the organizations to adopt resolutions asking them [the EEOC] to enforce this law, especially concerning sex-segregated advertisement. From East's basement... we sent several hundred envelopes out but nothing happened because the women's organizations took too long to function. (Interview, March 22, 2002)

After realizing that existing women's organizations were not going to take up the battle, several women employed by government then turned their attention to the creation of a new organization to pursue women's equality.[4] Especially important were Catherine East, the civil servant serving as the executive secretary for the Interdepartmental Committee on the Status of Women, the Citizen's Advisory Council on the Status of Women, and the earlier President's Commission on the Status of Women, and Mary Eastwood, a lawyer from the Department of Justice. East and Eastwood met with Betty Friedan several times

---

[3] Indeed, Graham was not reappointed when his term expired.
[4] There is disagreement about who had the original idea to form a new organization. Friedan (1998: 100) and Fuentes (1999: 135) state the idea came from Sonia Pressman Fuentes, a lawyer in the General Counsel's office of the EEOC. On the other hand, several others attribute the idea to Richard Graham (East 1982: 171; Interview, March 22, 2002; Paterson 1986: 160).

to encourage her to form a new organization because she was "the only woman with the public recognition who was capable of doing that" (East 1982: 172). Friedan initially rejected the idea, but sought instead to get the League of Women Voters involved (East 1982: 171). Eventually, she became increasingly open to the idea.

The issue came to a head in 1966 at the Third Annual Conference of Commissions on the Status of Women sponsored by the Women's Bureau – in large part because of behind the scenes work of insider feminist activists. Prior to the meeting, Catherine East distributed copies of a speech by Congresswoman Martha Griffiths lambasting the EEOC to attendees as part of the materials delivered by the Women's Bureau (Harrison 1988: 191).[5] It was Catherine East who included Betty Friedan's name on the list of attendees to the conference. Although Mary Keyserling, head of the Women's Bureau, was not a strong feminist and did not approve of including Friedan at the conference, the bureau eventually allowed her to participate (East 1982: 173–174). Catherine East and Mary Eastwood further encouraged Friedan to organize by providing her with lists of names of potential supporters (Harrison 1988: 193). When Friedan brought these women together to discuss a new organization, they initially rejected the idea, arguing that they should instead use the conference to pass resolutions calling for more action by the EEOC and the retention of Richard Graham. It was only when their resolutions were rejected because the conference was sponsored by the government that the women, huddled around one of the tables at the conference, agreed on the necessity of starting a civil rights organization for women.

The organizing conference of NOW was held in October 1966 in Washington, DC. Mary Eastwood, the Department of Justice lawyer, arranged the conference, securing meeting space in the Washington Post's office building. Although from its beginnings NOW included many feminists outside the state, the group photograph taken at the organizing conference shows the strong initial influence of governmental employees. Of the twenty-five people included in the group picture (see Figure 4.1), five were employed by the federal government

[5] East (1982: 172–173) claims that she and Mary Eastwood were asked to draft the speech for Martha Griffith with the help of Phineas Indritz in part because they had the best information about the problems with current government programs.

FIGURE 4.1. **Founding Members of the National Organization for Women at the Organizing Conference (October 30, 1966).** Photograph by Vincent J. Graas; copy courtesy of the Schlesinger Library, Radcliffe Institute, Harvard University. **Front row** (left to right): Inez Casiano (NY, Community Activist, Program and Research); Clara Wells (NY, Community Development Human Relations, Resources Committee); Inka O'Hanrahan (CA, California Comm. Status of Women); Alice Rossi (IL, Sociologist, University of Chicago); Lucille Kapplinger (MI, Legal Assistant to Governor, Governors Commission); Ruth Gober (WI, Academic); Caruthers Berger (Washington, D.C., Attorney, U.S. Dept. of Labor); Sonia Pressman (Washington, D.C., Attorney, EEOC); Amy Robinson (IN, Governors Commission; UAW); Betty Friedan (NY, Author, *The Feminine Mystique*). **Back row** (left to right): Morag Simchak (Washington, D.C., Equal Pay for Equal Work, U.S. Dept. of Labor); Mary Esther Gauldin (TX, Univ. of Texas Southwestern Medical School); Dr. Pauli Murray (Washington, D.C., Poet, Attorney, EEOC Consultant); Mary Eastwood (Washington, D.C., Attorney, U.S. Dept. of Justice); Dr. Caroline Ware (VA, Consultant, U.N.); Sister Mary Joel Read (WI, Alverno College); Unidentified; Dorothy Haener (MI, UAW, Women's Department); Unidentified; Anna Arnold Hedgeman (NY, National Council of Churches); Robert Gray; Muriel Fox (NY, Carl Byoir & Associates); Pat Perry Gray, (Washington, D.C., Carl Byoir & Associates); Colleen Boland (IL, President, Steward & Stewardesses of Airline Pilots Association); Charlotte Roe (NY, Project Director, National Affairs Assoc. U.S. Youth Council).

and three by state governments. At least two of those not in the federal government when the picture was taken would go on to become government employees in future years.

The history of the founding of NOW provides an interesting example of the role that activists inside government can play in mobilizing and organizing a social movement. In this example, feminist activists *inside* the state were vital to the initial mobilization and organization of the National Organization for Women – an organization *outside* of government. Activist insiders were among the first to conceive of the necessity for such an independent organization, in large part because they had access to information about the behavior of state institutions and because they understood the significance of government actions. Because the hostility of the EEOC toward equal opportunity for women was not a major news item, it otherwise might have completely escaped public notice. As insiders, these feminists understood the importance of an outside organization that could influence the federal bureaucracy, so they actively mobilized outside women. Finally, their positions in the federal government provided them with both information and material resources that helped to build the initial organization for NOW. Although NOW's membership was always dominated by outsider feminists, insider activists played a crucial role during this period of initial mobilization.

The Informal Networks of the Washington Underground

Activists inside the federal bureaucracy also played important roles in the informal networks of feminists that were important to the mobilization of the women's movement. While undoubtedly these insider feminists constituted a small portion of the women in such networks and were not the only (or even the major) factor that determined the nature of these networks, location inside the state provided feminist activists with the information and contacts that were important to the mobilization of the nascent movement. The role that such insider feminist activists played can be seen by examining one central node within the informal networks of the early second wave – Catherine East. In her position as executive secretary to the Committee on Federal Employment of the Presidential Commission on the Status of Women and later to the Interdepartmental Committee on the Status of Women (ICSW) and the Citizens' Advisory Council on the Status of Women (CACSW),[6] East fostered crucial contacts among feminists during the early years of the second wave and her position inside the state gave her access to information and resources that were crucial to the movement.

Catherine East's position as executive secretary of the ICSW and CACSW gave her a good sense of the individuals within government who were both responsible for and sympathetic toward feminist concerns. Her job also involved active work with the Commissions on the Status of Women in the individual states (East 1982: 167). As she noted in an oral history in 1982, "I got to meet and talk with women all over the country ... and I found out what was going on all over" (East 1982: 162). Although during most of her years as a government bureaucrat she eschewed membership in women's organizations, she had ties to all of them and often used these ties to connect activists with one another (East 1982: 208). She sums up her role in the women's movement in this way: "I think the role that I kind of played, was that of catalyst, in furnishing information and knowing who knew what, and where you went for information" (East 1982: 170). Her interview goes on to indicate that she felt sure her position would have been compromised if she had been an active member in a feminist organization because of the Women's Bureau's hostility to organizations that opposed protective legislation for women. The exception was under Women's Bureau Director Elizabeth Duncan Koontz who encouraged membership in women's organizations. It was only under Koontz's directorship that East finally felt free to join many of the organizations she had been covertly helping (East 1982). Her connections went beyond traditional women's groups as well; several letters in her papers show connections with local women's liberation movement organizations, including Kathy Amatniek (now Kathy Sarachild) of New York's Radical Women and Redstockings (Amatniek n.d.; East 1969).

Particularly in the early years of the movement, when informal networks were not well-established, these connections provided an

---

[6] East (1982: 90) mentions that one of the reasons that she took the position of executive secretary to the ICSW and CACSW was her anger at the two-committee structure that was created after the Presidential Commission on the Status of Women. In her opinion, the structure was very weak and allowed "all sorts of built-in opportunities for conflict, and for lack of any kind of strength for the council, for the citizen's group, and with the government group essentially in control."

important means of building solidarity, gaining information, and mobilizing individuals. One activist described meeting with a bureaucrat in the Office of Federal Contract Compliance to look into the possibility of using the office to work on equal pay and hiring in academia: "He said 'Do you know Catherine East?' and I said 'No I don't know Catherine East.' And he said 'You have to meet her, let me call her right now.' And 'here she's available.' . . . She immediately provided people I should talk with. I didn't realize how literally that day would change my life. She gave me some names and I called people" (Interview, October 16, 2003). East was often consulted on who should serve in government commissions dealing with "women's issues" particularly in the years after the Presidential Commission on Women (Interview, March 25, 2002). She continued this role as a central node in the women's movement network long after she left her position in the federal bureaucracy, even encouraging young and old feminists to stay at her home when they came to Washington (East 1982: 292; Fuentes 1998: 37).

If feminist activists inside the bureaucracy served to connect feminists with each other and with policy makers, their position in the federal government also gave them access to information and resources that helped the fledgling movement mobilize. East, for example, actively supported the repeal of protective legislation for women in the mid 1960s. Although the Women's Bureau supported protective legislation for women at the time, East's position in the Women's Bureau allowed her to provide necessary information to the lawyers who were attempting to repeal such laws:

I was sending out briefs and things to these lawyers who were trying to get it [protective legislation] superseded in the courts. And that's the way it finally worked. Mary Keyserling [the head of the Women's Bureau] never knew I was doing that. But we were supposed to be a clearing house, so it was completely legal. . . . Mary Eastwood and I used to go down at night and use the Xerox machine to run off copies of briefs that had been done in one jurisdiction on protective labor and send them to another people [sic], and any kind of materials that we got that were anti-protective labor legislation, we sent out to these lawyers who were working on the cases. . . . But as I say, it was completely legal, but she [Mary Keyserling] would have tried to get me reassigned. They wouldn't have fired me, but I would have been reassigned to some other position in the Labor Department. (East 1982: 126–127)

In addition, East made sure that information relevant to the women's movement circulated among activists:

We furnished papers to all the women's movements by the thousands. They called in when they were having conferences or when they were making up packets for the state legislators.... So I guess we spent many a night, Burt and I did there, getting out packages of materials for big conferences, and we furnished an unlimited quantity. And no one ever raised any question about our ordering all this stuff. We kept ordering and reordering on the materials. (East 1982: 215–216)

Other activists also recognized the importance of information at the beginning stages of the movement. As one activist noted:

There were no newspapers that carried women's issues. When there was an article about women, my kids would come running up the stairs to tell me. There were no newsletters, so there was very little information. And Catherine East had the Xerox. Xeroxes were [just] coming out. The only people that had them were large industries, colleges and universities, and government. They were frightfully expensive – about in the mid 70s you began to see them. But in the early 70s, having a Xerox was wonderful.... She was getting phone calls from people, so she had a network of various kinds. It wasn't organized, but she had networks of people. But there was an article on women's credit – these articles are beginning to come up because of NOW and people are looking at this. Catherine East xeroxes the article and sends it out to everybody who was interested in that issue.... And then they, because many of them work in government or big corporate agencies or colleges and universities, re-xerox it and send it to their friends. And these articles would get re-xeroxed and in those days each successive Xerox got faded. (Interview, October 16, 2003)

This example shows the power that such information played in mobilizing the nascent movement, and these informal networks occurred in many places within Washington. Another group that brought together a number of high-level women labeled itself "the Sisterhood":

That was a group of Congressional wives, high official's wives, some women on Capitol Hill, some women interested, some women in organizations. That was a free-floating group. The Sisterhood was the start of it.... The Sisterhood was pretty much – I sometimes say – women who were too old and established to be a conscious-raising group. But that's exactly what we were. We started out talking about abortion. But we had a rule, as you probably read, you introduced yourself, you couldn't use your husband's name. One of the saddest things was at one of our first or second meetings, one woman said, 'This is the first time in 20 years in Washington that anybody's asked who I am.' (Interview, December 18, 2003)

Although East was the best known of feminist activists who facilitated action by providing information, many other insider feminist activists participated in similar networks. In Chapter 6, I show how other inside activists within these other networks played important roles in mobilizing outsider activists about specific policies.[7]

Thus, insider feminists helped to connect feminists both with each other and with people within the federal system who would be helpful with feminist causes. Their positions within the federal bureaucracy brought insider activists into contact not only with policy makers in other bureaucratic units and in local and state governments, but also with a wide array of outside activists. As a result, insider feminist activists were well placed to build the connections the women's movement needed to mobilize and to affect government policy.

Human Rights for Women (HRW)

Human Rights for Women, Inc. was founded by several lawyers who split from the National Organization for Women legal committee (which later created the National Organization for Women Legal Defense Fund) in 1968.[8] Like the later National Organization for Women Legal Defense Fund (NOWLDF), it was set up as a 501c(3) organization for "handling litigation and assisting with litigation for people whose cases indicate some humanitarian case or benefit some exploited group" (Berger 1982: 56). Several issues caused some of the lawyers active on legal issues within NOW to split from the organization as it founded NOWLDF. As Freeman (1975: 82) notes, delays in the establishment of NOWLDF caused several of the women to become

---

[7] For example, several later feminists mentioned their role in providing grant money to feminist groups (Interviews, September 25, 2003 and December 18, 2003). While there are many individuals who could be mentioned, one little-known feminist who appears to have developed strong informal networks is Morag Simchak, who worked in the Department of Labor.

[8] While I focus here on HRW, several insider feminists also played an important role in starting the NOWLDF.

concerned about the organization. Although conceived in 1966, in late 1968 NOWLDF still had not incorporated and several issues about bylaws and board membership were still being debated. A second issue was the question of who would choose the legal counsel in cases that NOWLDF funded. The proposed bylaws required that the defense committee "be in direct control of any litigation endorsed by the fund" (NOW Legal Defense Fund, November 2, 1968: 1). Thus, NOWLDF would designate which lawyers would serve as counsel for the cases they funded. At the time, two important sex discrimination cases were seeking funding from NOW, both originating from a team of three lawyers (all of whom were current or retired federal government employees). Only one of the three had been proposed as a member of the NOWLDF board, which led the other two lawyers to think they might be removed from the cases when the NOWLDF came into existence – a concern magnified by disagreement about how the cases should be litigated.

Finally, ideological differences existed between the lawyers proposed for the NOWLDF board and the lawyers who left to form Human Rights for Women. The lawyers that remained and helped to found NOWLDF – Marguerite Rawalt and Phineas Indritz – had in several cases attempted "to tone it down saying we were asking for too much in one step" (Interview, March 22, 2002). For example, in one brief they added a rider claiming that a finding for their client did not mean that protective legislation for women was contradicted by Title VII. On the other hand, the lawyers in HRW actively supported using these cases to repeal protective legislation.

The creation of Human Rights for Women, Inc., also occurred around the same time as another split in NOW around the issue of organizational structure (Freeman 1975: 81). Radicals like Ti-Grace Atkinson argued that NOW was elitist because it created hierarchical organizations where professionals controlled the national offices. While the initial creation of HRW did not concern issues of organizational structure, HRW soon incorporated these ideas and their advocates into its organization. While fully one half of the initial board of directors of HRW were feminist activists who worked in government, the board also included New York radical feminists Ti-Grace Atkinson and Ann Calderwood, a member of Columbia University Women's Liberation group and first editor of *Feminist Studies*. Mary Eastwood, a founder of HRW and an employee of the Justice Department, was also a founding member of the radical October 17th Movement (October 17th Movement, n.d.).

Human Rights for Women, Inc. followed feminist theories of participatory democracy in assigning offices by lot.

What we do is, we have everybody's name for secretary, everybody's name for treasurer and at each meeting, we draw. Then when you've served your term, it goes into another envelope, and you start all over again. (Eastwood, 1990–1993: 75)

Board members signed an agreement that they would "perform the functions of the offices that I am selected by lot to perform" (Human Rights for Women, n.d.). As Mary Eastwood (1990–1993: 55) noted, her thoughts on participatory democracy:

was kind of an intriguing idea – so intriguing that when we started Human Rights for Women, that's the way we are set up.... You see, it's much more practical when you just have a handful of directors and no members... especially if you don't have a staff – that way you can just theoretically rotate the work.

Thus, although Human Rights for Women brought together both insider and outsider feminist activists to litigate issues of sex discrimination (occasionally even against the federal government), it was largely organized by feminists within the state. Much of the organization reflected the social characteristics of these professional women. The focus on litigation was a result of their background in law; the nonprofit status they sought and maintained reflected their ability to work within and accept the existing law on nonprofits. Yet, their status as federal employees did not mean that they worked only within the state, nor that they recreated the hierarchical organizational structures of the federal bureaucracy. Indeed, these government women saw a need to experiment with the consensus democracy being developed in the more radical wing of the women's liberation movement.

Summary

The organizations discussed here are only a few of the feminist groups that insiders helped to create and run. Insider activists were also involved in rape crisis centers, consciousness-raising groups, and a myriad of other organizations that mobilized both insider and outsider feminists. However, the organizations discussed here are unusual because of the important role that insider feminists played in their founding. In both NOW and Human Rights for Women, insider feminists played significant roles in creating these organizations. Moreover, both of these organizations were founded early in the period of women's mobilization, before the women's movement had achieved much notoriety or success. Thus, insiders' role in the movement preceded the institutionalization of the movement. Finally, although admittedly the adoption of radical feminism organizing principles was not common among insider activists, employment in the state did not *preclude* a belief in and the practice of such principles.

Organizations for Feminist Activists Inside the State

While we normally think of the mobilization and organization of the women's movement occurring outside of the state, from the very first years of the women's movement, feminist activists working within the federal government also organized to effect social change. While many of these organizations focused on the issue of sex discrimination in employment, they also fought for a wide range of other feminist goals. Moreover, the organizations mobilized members within the state to participate in activities both inside and outside of the bureaucracy. The organizations that were created varied in their organizational structure. Some were national federal organizations with officers and professional staff. Others were smaller groups of women who came together around specific problems they faced at the workplace. This section provides three case histories designed to provide a sense of the breadth of organizations formed for activists working within the federal government.

Federally Employed Women (FEW)

Federally Employed Women was founded in 1968 by a small group of women who were taking a training course for executive women run by the Department of Agriculture's Graduate School. Few women at the higher levels of civil service (the equivalent of GS13 or higher) had access to executive training opportunities. At the time the training course taught by Helen Dudley was one of the few opportunities for career development available to women in the mid to upper ranks of the civil service, so many enrolled in it. In 1968 – the third time the course was offered– a number of issues were raised during the three-day seminar about the problems women faced in getting jobs, promotions, and training in spite of the fact that President Johnson had signed Executive Order 11375, prohibiting employment discrimination on the basis of sex within the federal government, the previous year.[9] As a result of this order, the Federal Women's Program was established to encourage and monitor the hiring of women in the federal government. All agencies and departments of the federal government were required to appoint a Federal Women's Program coordinator (Harrison 1988: 202). Only a few women at the training seminar had heard of the changes and in the discussion that followed it became clear that many parts of the federal government were not appointing coordinators nor enforcing the executive order. As Allie B. Latimer tells it:

On the last day at the lunch break, I went around asking those who had expressed the most interest, how many people were interested in getting together again to see how the Federal Women's Program was being implemented, that is, to see which agencies were actually implementing the program and what was being done. I also assumed that maybe we could coordinate with unions and women's organizations, although with the exception of one union most were uninterested in women's issues and NOW was just getting off the ground. Almost everyone was interested, especially those that were hearing about the Federal Women's Program for the first time. Since this was the third class that Helen had had, she also made available the class lists from the previous two classes, and we used those lists to hook up with potentially other interested women. The result was a chair and ad-hoc committee that eventually organized Federally Employed Women. (Private Communication, May 2002)

Several of the founding members of Federally Employed Women were Federal Women's Program coordinators, usually women within the bureaucracy who had simply been given the positions as additional

---

[9] Executive Order 11375 simply added sex to Executive Order 11246, which prohibited discrimination in the federal government based on race, color, religion, or national origin.

duties on top of their existing responsibilities. For example, Tina Hobson, the first head of the Federal Women's Program, was also an early member of FEW and helped with some of the early projects on agency compliance with the executive order.[10] As a result, leaders of FEW and Federal Women's Program officials often coordinated activities and discussed problems together, and FEW became an advocate for strengthening the program. For example, one of the first actions of FEW was a comprehensive study of the activities that departments and agencies were doing within the Federal Women's Program.

In addition, FEW also served to raise feminist consciousness within the bureaucracy. Federally Employed Women began a series of training programs for women employees of the federal government to compensate for the lack of training available through the government. As one activist told me:

One of the most important things to come out of these training programs was the consciousness raising that happened. As women talked about their experiences, they came to realize that the problem was neither idiosyncratic or limited to them but rather was widespread. They were not the only ones to experience a particular type of discrimination. (Interview, May 14, 2002)

However FEW's focus was not limited to the employment issues of women inside government. From its very inception FEW's focus and ideology also centered on larger feminist issues as well. When Betty Friedan issued a call for a "Women's Strike for Equality" to be held on August 26, 1970, Federally Employed Women chose to organize a rally in Washington, DC. It also tried to coordinate with the Federal Women's Program to create a government-wide program celebrating the fiftieth anniversary of women's suffrage and to highlight women's inequality within the federal government. When the Civil Service Commission refused to encourage agencies to participate in such a program it continued to organize its own rally and encouraged widespread participation by federal employees in strike events. Although FEW's focus on wider feminist events has waxed and waned over the years of its existence, it has often promoted general feminist causes

[10] One of the feminist activists interviewed in the project, who had served as Federal Women's Program Coordinator in her department, also noted the overlap between the leadership of FEW and the Federal Women's Program although she was not a member of FEW (Interview, January 8, 2004).

such as the Equal Rights Amendment, abortion rights, and issues of women in poverty. FEW has maintained an independent status from government so it can lobby and participate in other ways outside of the purview of the federal government. For example, FEW's current projects include a voter registration drive, lobbying for the Convention on the Elimination of Discrimination against Women, and for the inclusion of women in more biomedical research (Federally Employed Women n.d.: 10–11).

Thus, although FEW is a national professional organization of women in the federal government, it has also been an active part of the network of feminist organizations that operate outside of the state. In its first few years, FEW served as a consciousness-raising group that mobilized women into action by helping them identify and recognize the problems with discrimination that they faced. Throughout its years, FEW members have also fought for women's rights outside the state and the organization continues to push a wide feminist agenda.

National Institutes of Health Organization for Women/Self Help for Equal Rights

Beginning in 1971, women working at the National Institutes of Health (NIH) started meeting together informally to talk about the problems they faced in the institution. A number of women, particularly scientists at the mid-levels of the organization, found themselves subject to discrimination and were seeking ways of calling attention to this problem. This group of "about 20 women" quickly realized that they needed to organize and began "meeting . . . regularly to develop the program and the guidelines and how we would be organized" (Interview, October 17, 2003). After convincing NIH officials to allow them to use meeting areas, the women founded National Institutes of Health Organization for Women in 1972 (NIHOW) (Goodman 1997: 10).

NIHOW initially focused on three goals. First, the women felt that the NIH needed an employee daycare center to allow female employees to maintain family lives. The initial daycare center idea was very successful, and soon the NIH agreed to help with its operations. As a result, those concerned solely with daycare issues soon left NIHOW. Those concerned with other issues continued to meet, later renaming the organization Self-Help for Equal Rights (SHER). A second concern was how NIH policy – both civil service rules and legislative initiatives – affected women's treatment by NIH. A third goal was to deal specifically with issues of sex discrimination in hiring, promotion, resources, and pay equity. To deal with this NIHOW (and later SHER) focused on collecting statistics to document the problems with sex discrimination within the institution, and supporting individual women as they fought their own sex discrimination suits (Interview, October 17, 2003).

SHER continued to meet until late 2003, although the NIH later also created an official committee focused on women's issues.[11] SHER continued to pursue both general policy goals and serve as a support group for those dealing with their own cases of sexual discrimination or harassment, although over time the emphasis on the latter increased. Formally, SHER's organizational structure mirrored that of the NIH – an elected president and four policy area committees. However, the philosophy and actual meetings of NIHOW and SHER were generally nonhierarchical. The meetings typically took the form of individuals sharing problems, and receiving support and suggestions for solutions from other members. This became increasingly so as SHER focused on individual law suits to address grievances.

Although NIHOW/SHER's primary focus was the status of women employees at NIH, these feminist insiders were also concerned with the relationship between women and science generally. For many members of SHER, there was a clear connection between the treatment of women at NIH and women's health research in the United States. As Billie Mackey, a long-time president of SHER, noted:

People tend to research what they're interested in. If you don't have any women doing research, then research in women's diseases suffers. (Laurence 1994: E-3)

SHER activists pursued independent campaigns around issues of women's role in scientific research and women's health and helped

---

[11] This organization – Women Scientist Advisors (began as Women's Action Committees) – consisted of individuals chosen by various institutes. While in the early years, the Women's Action Committees also dealt with these issues and coordinated with NIHOW/SHER, interviews and other documents show that some members of NIHOW/SHER felt that in its later years Women Scientist Advisors moved away from meaningful action.

to mobilize organizations of outsider feminists on the wider issue of women's health. They met with members of Congress to discuss the problems within NIH as private citizens concerned about women's health (Goodman 1997: 10). They set up hotlines to provide information to interested individuals and the press about existing lawsuits and how they affected the wider public. They also worked with other organizations like NOW, the Association for Women in Science, and Human Rights for Women to raise these larger feminist issues (Interview, October 17, 2003; Interview, January 7, 2004).

In the case of NIHOW/SHER we see feminist activists within NIH creating a self-help organization that was largely informal in its organization. Although the insider activists in the organization were primarily focused on addressing women's grievances within the NIH, they recognized the larger feminist implications of these problems and they were tied into a larger network of feminist organizations concerned with these issues. More importantly, their efforts to spur more research on women's health had far-reaching consequences.

Women's Action Organization

Similar organizations of insider feminists arose throughout the federal government as the women's movement blossomed throughout the United States. Some parts of the U.S. government were slower than others, however, to react to the women's movement. The State Department and the Foreign Service were particularly slow to include women and still had fundamentally discriminatory regulations into the 1970s. Women constituted only 4.8% of the foreign service officers (FSOs) in 1969 (Good 1993: 14) and female FSOs were channeled into the less prestigious consular and administrative work (Leader 2001: 2; McGlen and Sarkees 1995). Moreover, regulations required women in the Foreign Service to remain unmarried. Even when female foreign service officers fulfilled these requirements, they were still barred from many areas of the world for cultural or security reasons (Leader, 2001: 2). For example, women were not allowed to serve as foreign service officers in the USSR or any of the Eastern bloc countries because single people were seen to be a security risk and of course women were required to be single to serve as a foreign service officer.

Beginning in the summer of 1970, women in the Department of State began meeting informally to discuss their dissatisfaction with the situation of women in the Foreign Service areas (Marcy, 1974, p.5; Olmstead 1985, p.31). After trying and failing to get the professional organization in the area (American Foreign Service Association) to look into discrimination against women in the field, approximately thirty women in the United States Information Agency (USIA), the State Department, and Agency for International Development formed an ad hoc task force – the Ad Hoc Committee to Improve the Status of Women in the Foreign Affairs Agencies– to bring their complaints to the Department of State. From that initial action, the women formed the Women's Action Organization (WAO) (Good 1993: 14; Marcy 1991: 93; Marcy 1974: 11).

Initially, the women who formed the task force focused largely on consciousness raising and therefore created no elected offices. Not even a chair was appointed to lead the meeting; rather people took turns discussing their problems. After multiple meetings, the group decided to focus on positive action by bringing complaints to the State Department (Marcy 1974: 11).

Largely, the Women's Action Organization "decided to work within the system" (Jean Joyce quoted by Marcy 1974: 18). The organization testified before a congressional subcommittee sometime after 1980 that women were not being given appointments commensurate with their grade (Dillon 1988: 38). It also encouraged the Department of State to develop a new policy on wives in the Foreign Service that would clearly allow them to pursue their own interests. One way it did this was by instituting a Skills Talent Bank for spouses of Foreign Service Officers, which was later made into a program by the Department of State (Family Liaison Office 2003: 8). However, not everyone within the organization worked the same way. In 1976, Alison Palmer bypassed WAO and initiated a class action sex discrimination suit, which was finally settled in 1996 (Leader 2001: 3). Several USIA members also began to organize a sit-in and picket at USIA in connection with the 1970 "Women's Strike for Equality" (Marcy 1974,: 19), although they were eventually convinced by others to organize a less confrontational program on inequities for women in government.

Of the three examples of feminist organizing within the state, Women's Action Organization represents the example closest to that of a professional organization designed to advance the professional interests of the women involved. Although the actions of WAO remained largely focused on advancing women's status within foreign service agencies, the advancement of women in these agencies is often credited with the new focus on women in development and foreign aid (Tinker 1983: Kardam 1994). Moreover, although WAO did not work with other feminist organizations, many of the feminist activists in the organization had ties to these other organizations. Finally, the WAO provides an example of feminist activism in areas of the state traditionally seen as not related to "women's interests."

Summary

These five examples are illustrative of the many organizations that feminist activists employed by the federal government helped to create. Insider feminist activists also organized themselves to promote women within the federal bureaucracy in such varied agencies as the Civil Aeronautics Board and the Bureau of Alcohol, Tobacco, and Firearms. These organizations of insider feminists existed from the very beginning of the movement, working alongside other feminist organizations to mobilize for a variety of feminist causes and ideals.

When they did organize themselves, feminist insiders utilized a variety of the organizational forms that characterized the second wave of the women's movement. Most feminists within the state were liberal feminists and, like liberal feminists elsewhere, tended to choose more formal and hierarchical organizational forms with elected offices. We would expect this to be true given their occupations, education, and experience. Insider feminists who organized to influence state policy may have chosen these organizational forms to give them greater access to the state; that is, the opportunity to have influence might have been greater for formal hierarchical organizations than for more informal organizations.[12] Yet, a number of the women I talked to advocated organizational forms more typically associated with radical feminism. Thus, insider feminist activists could be found creating organizations based on radical feminist principles of participatory democracy

---

[12] I'm grateful to an anonymous reviewer for pointing this out to me.

and consciousness-raising models, in addition to more traditional forms.

CONCLUSION

Feminist activists within the state, rather than being constrained by their positions in the federal government, were an active part of the U.S. women's movement from its very inception. They participated in the mobilization of feminists located inside and outside the state and were important, sometimes vital, participants in the creation of a wide range of feminist organizations. They participated in the building of a vibrant feminist movement in the same ways as their sisters employed outside of government.

Working inside the government bureaucracy made feminist activists no less active in organizing for feminist causes than those outside the state. Indeed, many of my interviewees insisted that they understood better the need for movement mobilization precisely because of their experiences within the state. Although they often acknowledged and used their positions within the state, these insider feminists were not acting in the state's interest when they mobilized and organized the women's movement. This supports the view that the state is a diverse set of actors and institutions with multiple and sometimes conflicting interests. Their status as insiders did not mean that they only "pursue[d] movement goals through conventional bureaucratic channels," as many scholars of movements inside institutions suggest (Santoro and McGuire 1997: 504; see also Eisenstein 1990; Outshoorn 1997, 1994).

Moreover, their positions inside the federal bureaucracy were consequential for the mobilization and organization of the women's movement. As we look at the beginning of the second wave of the feminist movement, there appears to be an abundance of feminist bureaucrats in the liberal feminist organizations, more than one finds today. Why? One reason is that women who wanted to seek a career in the years before the women's movement often ended up in the federal government because there were more opportunities there, particularly in professions like law. Another reason for their prevalence in the early movement has to do with their being uniquely placed to encourage mobilization in the very early years. Because of their positions in government they saw the need for women to mobilize to take advantage of short windows of opportunity that had been created in the federal government. They also had access to information that could be used to mobilize women into action; many held jobs that required connections both inside and outside of the state, allowing them to reach individuals who could be mobilized. Through their positions in government they also had access to concrete resources (money, meeting spaces, copy machines) that facilitated mobilization. So they were particularly well placed to aid in the initial mobilization of the women's movement.

Ironically, even as they helped to found feminist organizations for both insider and outsider feminists, they also mobilized themselves against the state – building organizations of insider feminists to contest state practices and policies. Organizations of insider feminists did not result from the institutionalization of the movement but were part of its initial mobilization. FEW was organized only two years after the National Organization for Women; NIHOW/SHER and Women's Action Organization were created in the early 1970s. Those writing about feminist organizing within institutions generally see such organization as occurring after the movement has matured, as the pressures for institutionalization begin. However, the case studies here show that feminist organizations within the state began simultaneously with other second-wave organizations. Moreover, these insider organizations were motivated by the same issues as the larger feminist movement; they participated in larger actions of the movement; and they interacted on a daily basis with that movement. To separate these organizations out from the others because they were organized within the state is to create an artificial barrier among feminists, one that hinders social and scientific understanding of social movements and distorts the history of the women's movement.

5

Choosing Tactics Inside and Outside the State

> I think the forms of nonviolent resistance that have been used in the past, society has adapted to and learned to deal with, and I hope that the women who are the militant types can [come] up with some new form of nonviolent resistance that will be effective... Its particularly suitable to women, as a powerless group, to engage in... those tactics.
>
> – Catherine East (1982: 284–285)

This chapter examines the tactics used by feminist activists employed by the federal government. Both social movement and feminist theory have long assumed an association between *location* inside the state, with *insider strategies* and *conventional tactics*. According to this view, feminists who choose to be employed by the state have chosen a set of strategies and tactics that conform to the norms of these institutions. There are two possible processes by which being employed by the state may limit insider feminist activists' ability to represent certain positions, advocate certain issues, take to the streets, and create radical change. First, some view the limitation as external: The state's primary interests, or the interests of the bureaucracy as an institution, are imposed upon these feminist activists. This leaves insider activists with a choice either to conform and work within the system or to exit and take positions as outsiders. A second view focuses on self-selection: Feminists who choose to enter the state already believe in conventional tactics, and are focused more on reforming existing institutions than creating major institutional change. In this view, the state attracts a certain kind of feminist into its ranks.

I have already shown in Chapter 3 that a significant number of the feminist activists that I interviewed believed in the necessity of radical change. Here, I examine how insider activists chose to pursue that change. Following Katzenstein (1998) and Zald and Berger (1987 [1978]), I argue that we should not conflate location and tactics. I examine the tactics of feminist insiders, providing evidence that this group is quite willing to take to the streets when they believe it necessary. By focusing on feminist activists as individuals, rather than concentrating on the agencies or bureaucracies devoted to women, I can distinguish between insider feminist activists and the bureaucratic structures that they occupied. This is important because it is the network of insider feminists that chooses strategies and engages in tactics, not the offices engaged in women's policy. As part of the larger network within the feminist movement, feminist insiders were largely willing to use confrontational, "outsider" tactics when they thought it necessary. One major difference between insider and outsider feminists, however, is that feminist insiders were much more informed about alternative tactics (both inside and outside the state)[1] and about political opportunities that arise within the state. As a result feminist insiders often used conventional tactics because they understood precisely how to employ these to the greatest effect. On the other hand, at several crucial points feminist insiders initiated outside action precisely because they knew that opportunities for change within the government were closed. Thus, the assumption that location inside the state necessarily leads to conventional activity is both false and ignores the strategic considerations of these activists.

In looking at the use of tactics, I also argue that we need to reexamine our definition of unconventional or confrontational tactics. Instead of simply labeling specific tactics as confrontational or conventional, we must examine the dimensions that underlie these endpoints. I identify three different dimensions of strategies and tactics, and argue

---

[1] Although their tactical repertoires were not limitless and it is likely that the resources they had at their disposal (particularly their knowledge of the law) influenced their choices.

that a single tactic may differ on its placement along these dimensions depending on the circumstances of its use. In particular, I argue, as others have, that sometimes institutional tactics can be disruptive and designed to fundamentally alter the system, and in this sense be highly confrontational. In essence, there are *occasions* when the master's tools can be used to dismantle the master's house (to counter Audre Lorde's famous phrase). In making this claim, I focus specifically on the use of lawsuits as a confrontational and radical tactic, even as I argue that there are only certain periods when these legal tactics might have a radical effect.

The discussion centers largely on tactics rather than strategies. Tactics and strategies are different concepts that often blur together in the discussion of social movements. Tactics are the specific means employed by groups within a movement, while strategies are longer term and more comprehensive plans of action focused on achieving a specific goal or set of goals (for similar definitions see Beckwith 2007: 315 and Meyer 2007: 82). Nonetheless, in practice the two concepts are often muddled because strategic concerns often accompany the choice of a single tactic (e.g., does the choice of this tactic preclude other choices later?), and because both time frames and the degree of comprehensiveness – important elements distinguishing tactics from strategies – are continuous in nature. Moreover, it is difficult to claim that all social movements act in strategic ways. Because of the polymorphous nature of many social movements and even many social movement groups, true strategic calculations that associate tactics with a goal are uncommon, and assessments of resources and political opportunities are rarely performed (for an alternative view see Beckwith 2007: 315). When such strategic calculations are made, it is by social movement organizations or networks of activists and/or organizations. As a result, movements usually have several, potentially conflicting, often partial, strategies.[2]

---

[2] I do not explore here the connection between choosing particular types of strategies and particular types of tactics. Although having conventional strategies likely means that one chooses conventional tactics as well, this correlation is by no means perfect. As McAdam, Tarrow, and Tilly (2001:7–8) point out, for example, transgressive contention, such as movement groups engaging in civil disobedience or violence, often includes traditional tactics, such as legal activities for those arrested, as well.

The specific choice of tactics is an important issue for women's movement scholars. In analyses of protest events – that is, confrontational tactics that generate media coverage – women's movements in many countries appear less confrontational than other social movements (Kriesi et al. 1995; Rucht 2003; Tarrow 1994). In the United States, for example, van Dyke, Soule, and Taylor (2004) show that between 1968 and 1975 the women's movement had fewer protest events than the civil rights and peace movements (184 compared to 803 and 923, respectively).[3] Given that this period incorporates the initial period of mobilization and one of its most protest-ridden periods, it is puzzling that so few protest events were recorded. The analyses in this chapter help to explain this puzzle.

I examine the connection between "inside" tactics and the U.S. women's movement in two steps. First, I unpack the underlying dimensions of conventional and confrontational tactics, focusing specifically on the issue of using litigation to bring about social change. Second, I use the qualitative data from my interviews and archival research to examine the tactical decision-making of feminist activists inside the federal bureaucracy.

THE CONVENTIONAL VS. THE CONFRONTATIONAL
AND THE CASE OF CAUSE LAWYERING

Although insider feminist activists often chose to fight their battles within the state, this by no means made their tactics moderate or conventional, as both Katzenstein (1998) and McAdam, Tarrow, and

---

[3] The environmental movement had slightly less with only 171 as did the human rights movement, which had 149 protest events during this period. It is possible that women's protest events are underreported relative to other social movements. Van Dyke et al. (2004) also note that significantly fewer women's movement events focused on the state, which they argue supports the idea that the movement was not always focused on altering the state or state policy. Similarly, other accounts of the women's movement (Ferree and Hess 1985, 2000; Ryan 1992) have noted that women's movement activity also centered on building alternative institutions such as music festivals, bookstores, and communes. While perhaps not "confrontational," such activities reflect a rejection of current societal institutions and an underlying belief in the need to build an alternative society. While these institution-rejecting tactics help to explain the lack of protest events, I argue the use of institutional tactics also helps to account for the small number of protests as well.

Tilly (2001) argue. To understand this distinction it is necessary to examine the different ways that tactics can be confrontational.

Social movement scholars have used the term confrontational or contentious to refer to three different dimensions.[4] One way that tactics (or strategies) are confrontational is if they *raise the public's attention to an issue by polarizing the resulting conflict.* This is precisely what McAdam (1996a: 342) argues occurred in the case of the civil rights movement, which used noninstitutionalized tactics to heighten public attention. The disruptions to the public order that resulted from violent responses to civil rights movement protest raised public attention to the issue and framed the issue in stark terms (see especially his Figure 15.1). Here, even though the goals of the civil rights movement were to reform the political system, the tactics were confrontational in their effect because they dramatically raised issue awareness and polarized the sides of the debate. While McAdam (1996a: 342) clearly connects the use of "noninstitutionalized" tactics to the ability of groups to have these confrontational effects, I argue below that tactics employed within state institutions sometimes have the same effect.

Scholars also describe strategies and tactics as contentious or confrontational if they *disrupt existing institutions.* Piven and Cloward (1978) argue that only disruption allows poor people's movements to win any sort of concessions from the state. In particular, they argue that there are only a few exceptional historical moments when such movements are able to create sufficient disruption of existing institutions. In their view, protestors must disrupt the everyday functioning of the state in order to effect social change. If protestors move to institutionalized tactics, they neutralize the only weapon that they have and this results in, at best, symbolic appeasements. Hence, tactics are confrontational along this dimension only to the degree that they create disorder and interrupt the normal functioning of institutions.

A third criterion scholars have used to determine if tactics and strategies are confrontational is the degree to which the tactics themselves (as opposed the demands made using the tactics) signal

---

[4] Following other scholars, I judge tactics to be confrontational or contentious based on their effects. For example, Piven and Cloward (1979) are most concerned with the ability to disrupt.

underlying *acceptance of the system* (see for example Lorde 1984: 113 and McAdam 1996a: 341). In this view, the specific choice of a tactic also embodies the degree to which the movement accepts the existing political order and confrontational tactics are those that challenge the routine means of influencing politics, either directly or by building alternative political orders.[5] By accepting political institutions, conventional tactics limit the degree to which change can be achieved precisely because so much of what might be changed is accepted as given. In this sense of the term, only tactics and strategies that challenge the underlying system are able to create true system change, and can be characterized as confrontational.

While social movement scholars often make distinctions between conventional and confrontational tactics and strategies, it is not always clear which of these three dimensions – heightening public attention and polarizing the conflict, disrupting the functioning of institutions, or denying the legitimacy of the system – underlie their use of the term. In addition, as Marshall (2006: 167) notes, dividing tactics into dichotomous categories of institutional and extrainstitutional tactics (or disruptive and nondisruptive) relies on a relatively strong assumption that such differences are stark. I suggest that it is better to talk about the degree to which tactics are more or less confrontational.

Regardless of which dimension of confrontation scholars highlight and whether or not they see these as dichotomous categories, they share an assumption that confrontational tactics provide greater possibilities for *changes in the state*. Such changes are usually judged by the amount of innovation from a previous policy, their duration, and by the degree to which they challenge the underlying assumptions of the state itself. Implicit in most social-movement research is the notion that strategies and tactics within institutions cannot create such dramatic innovations (see for example Rosenberg 1993 on the use of the courts). In the rest of this section, I examine one institutional strategy – the use of law – and its related tactics, showing that these can under certain contexts qualify as confrontational along all three dimensions (see also Marshall

---

[5] The most dramatic form of alternative political orders are revolutionary armies that create alternative states, but a lesser form of building alternative communities can be found in separatist feminism's focus on building alternative institutional and social spaces for women only.

2006). In later sections, I will return to these three dimensions as I examine the degree to which feminist activists within the state utilized confrontational tactics.

The Confrontational Nature of Legal Tactics

Use of the legal system as a means to further social movement aims is in many ways the consummate institutional strategy; the law is itself the foundation of the democratic state and the state controls both the means for enforcing the law and the institutions that resolve disputes. Moreover, by their very training, lawyers are elite professionals often very far removed from the movements they serve.[6] Yet, lawsuits and other legal tactics have been an important tactic for a number of social movements, such as the civil rights movement (McCann 1994; Meyer and Boutcher 2007; Sarat and Scheingold 2006, 2005).

The use of litigation as a specific tactic may take on any of the characteristics of confrontational tactics described previously. Lawsuits can polarize a conflict at the same time as they raise public attention. As Luker (1984) demonstrates, *Roe v. Wade* changed the tenor of the abortion debate in the United States; prior to the 1973 Supreme Court ruling, the abortion conflict largely involved reformers from the medical community working outside of the public's view. *Roe v. Wade* polarized the public debate (although public opinion has changed little) and increased the level of conflict between pro- and antiabortion advocates, drawing new pools of activists into both sides of the debate (Luker 1984; Staggenborg 1991 but see Rosenberg 1993, part 2).[7]

Some litigation also has the ability to disrupt the operation of the state in significant ways. For example, *Brown v. Board of Education* while not responsible for creating huge policy changes on its own, did ignite massive disruption: "the Brown decision generated fears in the south that led to the counter campaign of 'massive resistance' . . . angry

---

[6] A literature on cause lawyers has developed which focuses on those lawyers who work first and foremost for "a cause rather than a client" (Woods and Barclay 2008, see also Sarat and Scheingold 2005). Much of this work focuses on their position within the law profession (see, for example, Jones 1999; Sarat and Scheingold 2005, 1998). Here I focus more on the political effects of particular cause lawyers.

[7] In this sense, it also fits McAdam, Tarrow, and Tilly's (2001) definition of a transgressive contention.

crowds at schoolhouse doors, the use of cattle prods, and the unleash-
ing of dogs during desegregation demonstrations, as well as the murder
of civil rights workers" (Sarat and Scheingold 2006: 7, see especially
Rosenberg 1991). In this case, the use of litigation inspired disruption against the state.[8] But the disruptive capacity of legal tactics also
exists in their ability – where the rule of law is well-established –
to directly create disruption within the state. To maintain the rule
of law, states may accept and enforce judicial decisions regardless of
the degree to which they cause havoc with the regular functioning
of the state. Here *Brown v. Board of Education* provides an additional example for it not only inspired external disruption but also
engendered conflict within the state itself as the national government
sought to impose the decision on local governments. For example, in
1963, President Kennedy nationalized the Alabama National Guard to
block the governor of Alabama's attempt to obstruct the integration
of the University of Alabama. In this and several other cases, internal
conflict within the state resulting from litigation led to the use of armed
personnel being employed against another branch of the state (see, for
example, Patterson 2001).

Finally, litigation may be used to challenge the accepted political and
social order of the state and society in fundamental ways. As Chapter 1
notes, the state is not hegemonic and so the law may be used to contest the assumptions underlying specific aspects of the state, even to the
point of questioning the very validity of specific state institutions themselves. For example, lawsuits filed by Israeli feminists disputed the state
power of religious authorities to determine local religious councils in
1988 (Woods 2005; Woods and Barclay 2008), even though the role
of religious authorities was enshrined in the Constitution and accepted as a part of the Israeli state. The ability to use litigation to challenge existing state institutions is limited because legal institutions and
legal categories themselves remain uncontested. However, as I show
later; litigation can also be used to confront society in fundamental
ways; these challenges often involve altering accepted norms through

---

[8] Legal tactics are also used in support of activists who are disrupting and have disrupted
the public order; "grassroots" lawyers can both file injunctions to keep people from
being arrested and quickly get people out of jail so they could continue participating
in disruptive protests (Hilbink 2006; Sarat and Scheingold 2006: 9).

changes in discourse.[9] Hence, while lawsuits leave the existence of the state uncontested, this tactic may be more confrontational than social movement scholars recognize (although see McAdam, Tarrow, and Tilly 2005).

While the use of litigation and other legal tactics may on occasion be characterized as confrontational along the three dimensions I describe, we cannot characterize *all* uses of the litigation as confrontational. Even where we can identify some legal tactics as polarizing the public, being disruptive, or challenging existing institutions, in most cases the same tactic (sometimes even employed by the same social movement during the same time period) may not have these same characteristics. Moreover, some movements may be better placed by their ideology to utilize legal tactics confrontationally. For example, civil rights activists were better able to use legal tactics to disrupt the legal system than antiwar activists because the claims of the civil rights movement fit within the legal opportunity structure (Meyer and Bouchert 2007; for a definition of legal opportunity structure see Andersen 2004) but also because some of the movement's claims were more congruent with legal strategies and tactics. This suggests that we cannot *prima facie* define legal tactics as confrontational or conventional but must look at the position of a particular legal tactic along the three dimensions. More generally, I would argue that the contingent nature of the confrontational–nonconfrontational dimension is true for all types of tactics.[10] Even those that we define as universally confrontational – like demonstrations and boycotts – can in some places or some periods be considered conventional (see, for example, Meyer and Tarrow 1998 on the institutionalization of protest).

The opportunity to engage in confrontational litigation occurs only at certain periods, often in the early stages of social movements. Punctuated equilibria are examples of short periods when policy systems can be fundamentally altered and when regular policy making can be

---

[9] Most social-movement scholars have ignored social movement practices of framing within the law. For exceptions see Ferree et al 2002; Kenney 2004, 1992; Pedriana 2006.

[10] Indeed it is true of most actions. Marriage for example can be seen both as a conventional action (i.e., creating the traditional nuclear family) or as a confrontational act (i.e. the marriage of two individuals of the same sex) depending on contextual factors.

disrupted and new institutions or coalitions put into play (Baumgartner and Jones 1991; Givel 2006; see also Piven and Cloward 1976).
Social movements may contribute to the development of punctuated
equilibria by creating alternative ways of viewing an issue (Rochon
1998; Snow and Benford 1992) and by mobilizing new populations in
support of change. Movements may also inspire new legislation that
provides opportunities to reevaluate existing legal codes and norms.

The Use of the Litigation by Feminist Activists within the State

Because of their place within the federal bureaucracy, insider feminist
activists understood both that they could use lawsuits to challenge the
system and that there were limited periods during which they could do
so effectively.[11] In some cases, their position inside the state allowed
these women to assess the degree to which litigation could challenge
the existing political order and gave them access to unique information
that allowed them to engage in these tactics more effectively. This is
best illustrated by the development of equal opportunity law under
Title VII. As Pedriana (2006) has clearly pointed out, the elimination
of states' protective labor laws for women was by no means assured by
passage of Title VII and the creation of the Equal Employment Opportunity Commission (EEOC), nor was it supported by all women's
organizations of the time. Yet, many *insider* feminists supported the
elimination of state protective legislation, and their early engagement in
equal opportunity litigation focused in part on eliminating those state
institutions. Thus, these lawsuits had some confrontational aspects and
certainly were effective in changing women's status in the economic
and social order.

The Window of Opportunity for Equal Employment
and State Protective Labor Laws

As I suggest in Chapter 4, feminist activists inside the bureaucracy
recognized a need to press for change immediately after the establishment of Title VII of the 1964 Civil Rights Act and the establishment

---

[11] While I focus on those feminists who worked for the federal government, outside
     feminists also recognized the importance of, and engaged in, legal strategies (see for
     example Hartmann 1998, Chapter 3).

of the EEOC. Of particular concern to many of these insider feminists was the issue of state protective labor legislation for women, which enshrined the view that women needed special protection in the form of maximum working hours, weight-lifting restrictions, and prohibitions against night work. The institution of protective legislation for women was well-established within the American state (Skocpol 1992: chapter 7). More than forty-five states had laws restricting women's hours of work, many sought by women's organizations at the beginning of the twentieth century, and protective legislation for women had been upheld by the United States Supreme Court (see *Muller v. Oregon* 1908) even as protective labor legislation for men had not. The acceptance of protective legislation for women was based on the need to protect women as mothers or potential mothers; "healthy mothers are essential to vigorous offspring, the physical wellbeing of woman becomes an object of public interest and care in order to preserve the strength and vigor of the race (*Muller v. Oregon* 1908).[12]

Neither the passage of Title VII nor the work of the President's Commission on the Status of Women (PCSW) reflected a change in this particular gendered political order. Both the Equal Employment Opportunity Commission (EEOC) and PCSW initially supported the state protective legislation for women, as did trade unions and some women's organizations; the positions of these state institutions were changed only because of litigation by feminist activists (Pedriani 2006). However, many (although not all) feminist activists within the state both rejected the maternalist view of workers associated with protective legislation[13] and realized that the window of opportunity to change existing state institutions existed mainly during the initial years of the EEOC. As one insider feminist activist noted:

We didn't have time. EEOC was making policy; courts were going to start deciding and might rule the wrong way. If you don't capture law in early stages it is hard to revise. That's why we had to throw something together. (Interview, March 22, 2002)

---

[12] See also Judith Baer's (1978) *The Chains of Protection: The Judicial Response to Women's Labor Legislation.*

[13] At the beginning of the women's movement, many activists supported protective legislation for women (Rupp and Taylor 1987; Skocpol 1992). As Pedriana (2006: 1747–1750) notes the movement itself was transformed by the litigation against protective legislation.

While this concern inspired insider feminist activists to mobilize women to protest the inaction of the EEOC (see Chapter 4), it also led them to engage in lawsuits specifically designed to make sure that protective legislation for women was abolished and women's equal opportunity was enshrined in law. Feminist activists did this both by pursuing potentially precedent-setting lawsuits and by attempting to radicalize the ideas behind Title VII.

Developing Precedent Setting EEOC Cases

Feminist activists inside the state were vital to the invalidation of state protective legislation laws because they spearheaded several of the landmark cases and utilized their networks to assure that such cases were brought before the courts. The EEOC's ambivalence, combined with its lack of authority to litigate, meant that any change was very dependent on private litigants' pursuit of their own EEOC complaints (Lieberman 2006).

Feminist activists inside the state recognized that challenging the established institutions of protective legislation for women necessitated encouraging private litigants to pursue their complaints in court, and so they developed a network of lawyers to work on these cases.[14] The network began within the Equal Employment Opportunity Commission (EEOC) itself where Sonia Pressman Fuentes would forward potential cases to a network of women lawyers, many of whom worked in other parts of the federal bureaucracy (see also East 1982: 121–122):

I passed on to this network information on women's rights cases that were developing at the EEOC, which the members of this network would then pass on to Marguerite Rawalt. (Fuentes 1999: 134, see also East 1982: 121–122)

Another activist noted that the legal network would be activated when Fuentes would

call and say a terrible thing happened... [Another feminist activist within government] would just pick up the phone and call the women. Before we had

---

[14] While I focus here on their litigation in the area of employment law, the early network of insider feminist activists also worked on a number of other issues including sexual discrimination in prison sentences, contraception for single women, and some early abortion cases (Harrison 1988: 183; Human Rights for Women 1971; NOW Legal Defense Fund 1968).

[other attorneys] to sign their names we wrote legal briefs and of course the judges knew they were ghost-written.[15] (Interview, March 25, 2002)

This group of insider feminists participated in the litigation of the first cases seeking to invalidate state protective legislation for women. These included *Weeks v. Southern Bell Telephone & Telegraph*, *Bowe v. Colgate-Palmolive*, and *Rosenfeld v. Southern Pacific Railroad*. While feminist activists inside the federal bureaucracy also contributed to other lawsuits, they had the largest impact in the area of women's employment law.

Their employment within the federal bureaucracy meant they were unable to take on such high profile cases as the lawyer of record.[16] Caruthers Berger, a member of this network of insider feminist lawyers, even asked for a ruling from the solicitor of labor as to whether she could sign a brief as a charitable donation but she was told that this was not permitted (Berger 1982: 48). Despite their inability to take credit for their work, these inside feminists were actively involved in developing the legal strategies, briefs, and motions that constituted these landmark cases. These lawyers all of whom were or had been government employees – Mary Eastwood, Caruthers Berger, Marguerite Rawalt, and Phineas Indritz – worked behind the scenes on these cases, researching and writing the briefs and preparing the arguments that would be submitted in court. In contrast to most cause lawyers, these activists had to conduct this legal work after hours because of their fulltime jobs within the federal bureaucracy. Marguerite Rawalt's biography notes the amount of time that just one case took for this group:

For months . . . Marguerite, Phineas, Caruthers, and Mary worked on the Mengelkoch brief, trying to prove that the state laws of California denied women opportunities to which they were entitled under the Fourteenth Amendment. . . . The work was slow and tedious and the weight of their inexperience heavy. They were in new territory. No one else had experience either. (Paterson 1986: 175)

[15] See also Caruthers Berger's 1982 interview with Verta Taylor and Leila Rupp, Schlesinger Library, Radcliffe Institute.
[16] One exception was Marguerite Rawalt, who retired from the Internal Revenue Service in 1965, just as many of these cases were beginning to be tried (Paterson 1986: 160). Because she no longer worked for the government she was able to serve as the attorney of record on a number of these cases.

Caruthers Berger noted that even after months of work, the final production of the brief meant very long hours:

The day I produced this [Mengelkoch] brief, I worked around the clock to get it done because I had to do it on a weekend. I think I spent about 28 hours straight and then I turned it over to Marguerite. (Berger 1982: 49)

Thus, although insider feminist activists were not always listed as the lawyers of record, they initiated and were actively involved in the litigation.[17]

Thus, feminist activists within government recognized that litigation could fundamentally restructure state institutions and fundamentally alter the nature of women's rights, setting the courts against state protection laws and eventually changing the EEOC's position as well (Pedriana 2006: 1745). In the 1960s, when protective legislation for women dominated women's employment policy and the notion of women as mothers dominated the state's policies, insider feminist activists' litigation signaled a clear rejection of this gendered political order.[18] Moreover, insider feminists' position within the state was also important to their actions and their success. They understood that timing was essential to challenging the state. Although feminist activists continue to be active in legal challenges, the nature of legal precedent in the United States means that this early mobilization was vital to changing equal employment law throughout the country. The courts are an obvious arena for social movements to create discursive change (Jones 1999; Kenney 2004: 87; McCann 1994; Pedriani 2006). In their lawsuits, these activists fundamentally challenged the accepted social order for women – radically revisioning women not as mothers *and* workers but simply as workers without regard for their parental or marital position. This confrontational litigation helped to bring about large-scale social and cultural change for women (Pedriana 2006: 1753).

INSIDER ACTIVISTS AND INSIDER TACTICS

Feminist activists within the state had a wide array of nonprotest tactics – such as lawsuits – available to them, and these activists often

---

[17] While I focus here on insider feminist activists' litigation, in the next section I discuss ways that they also used government institutions, often in unusual ways, to support their legal battles.

[18] For the importance of discursive politics to social movements, see Rochon (1998).

chose those methods as the means of eliciting social change. Yet, as we shall see, insider feminist activists were neither opposed to protest, nor unwilling to use it themselves. Indeed, in this sense, feminist activists inside the state appear no different from those outside. Feminists inside the federal government did talk more about conventional political activities than about protest when they discussed their activism. While these conventional activities were often used in an innovative manner to gain concessions for the movement, they remain conventional tactics. Yet, many of these same insiders supported the idea that the movement should utilize confrontational tactics and they engaged in these tactics as well.

Attitudes Toward Confrontational Tactics

The insider feminist activists that I interviewed most often expressed their support of confrontational tactics when discussing the contrast between insiders and outsiders within the women's movement. Contrary to the assumption that insiders prefer conventional tactics, almost all of the women interviewed championed the need for confrontational activism. As one insider activist noted:

My theory is that on women's issues – on all kinds of issues, but certainly women's are included – you need agitators and persuaders.... I think the sad part is that you get agitators and persuaders being so critical of each other for not working in the way they work, when I think it's a complementary system. (Interview, June 11, 2004)

Indeed, those insider activists who recognized the constraints of working within the system were often the most supportive of others using confrontational tactics because they openly acknowledged that insider tactics could not bring about change on their own.

You have certain constraints when you work inside any institution, whether it's a union or a church or a government agency, you have to follow certain policies. You can press the envelope a certain amount, but there are constraints. It is very necessary for the more strident voices that are free, and often the strident voices would criticize some of the slower moving voices inside, but you live with some of that... some people have to push the slower moving people, and then the slower moving people sometimes know more facts about how things are working. (Interview, May 13, 2002)

Insider activists often saw their role as providing the information that was necessary to mobilize and coordinate confrontational tactics. While not all insider feminist activists were willing to engage in confrontational tactics themselves (although many were, as I show in the next section), many of those who felt unwilling or unable to participate in such tactics saw their role as inspiring confrontation in the system by providing a necessary element for confrontational tactics: information about issues, people or institutions that needed to be targeted for mobilization. Several were quite proud of their role in developing confrontation even when they did not participate in the confrontational tactics themselves:

What I did was create a dialectic, I call it, where the department was sort of dragging its feet on something I'd call a few of those groups and have them start rebel around here. . . . So I call it my own personal dialectic. I could generate this energy just by planting a seed there and it made a huge differences. (Interview, July 30, 2004)

Didn't you feel so wonderful when you had successfully subverted something? I used to sort of live for that thrill. (Insider Feminist Activist, to others at a dinner party, May 13, 2002)

Above all, even when insider activists were not engaging in confrontation themselves, most remained movement activists who appreciated the importance of confrontational strategies and tactics and the need for movements to challenge the existing order.

The Use of Conventional versus Confrontational Tactics and Strategies

As one would expect, feminist activists within the state overwhelmingly used conventional tactics and strategies. In their capacity as civil servants, insider feminists often provided information and advocated for policies among other branches of government. However, insider activists were also willing to disrupt institutional operations, to polarize conflicts and to challenge existing institutions when they felt that insider tactics would not work. Just as their attitudes toward confrontation suggest that they were accepting of such tactics, so too did the behavior of many insider activists involve confrontational tactics and strategies.

As I've suggested in discussing litigation, even as feminist activists engaged in institutional tactics, these tactics often were designed to raise public awareness and polarize a conflict, or to disrupt existing institutions. For example, because the EEOC had no enforcement powers before 1972, its feminist lawyers utilized other institutional means to encourage compliance. In the case of AT&T, a company that accounted for about 7% of the EEOC's workload in the early years, several initial attempts to use institutional means to change the company's policies were unsuccessful (Shapiro 1973). David Copus, later on the board of directors of NOWLDEF and of NOW, and Susan Deller Ross, a long-time feminist lawyer, were both working within the EEOC in 1970 when AT&T petitioned the Federal Communications Commission (FCC) for a rate hike.[19] Copus than developed the idea of blocking the rate increase by having the EEOC lobby the FCC to reject the rate hike for the utility based on its active discrimination policy (Freeman 1975: 189; Shapiro 1973). In so doing Copus and Deller Ross coordinated actions with NOW and other women's groups who put pressure on the FCC from the outside. In this case, insider feminist activists employed a conventional political activity – lobbying a branch of the government – as a means of disrupting private economic institutions.

Conventional tactics were often successfully employed to direct attention to an issue or obtain regulatory or legislative changes. For example, feminist activists in the National Institute of Health, organized as Self Help for Equal Rights (SHER), used private lobbying to increase public attention to the issue of sex discrimination within the NIH and women's health issues more generally. As the Anita Hill scandal broke in 1991, activists within the NIH contacted congresswomen about sexual discrimination and harassment within the NIH and its effect on women's health more generally.[20] For example, feminist

---

[19] While much of the book has focused on female insider feminist activists, it is important to note that there were a number of men who fit the definition of insider feminist activists. Another example is Phineas Indritz, who worked in the Department of the Interior and later as a staffer for the House of Representatives. He was a founding member of the National Organization for Women and the National Organization for Women Legal Defense and Education Fund.

[20] Although one individual I interviewed (January 7, 2004) suggests that lobbying of women in Congress occurred even before 1986.

activists within NIH gave a presentation to Congresswoman Connie Morella about the issue of sexual discrimination and harassment within the NIH (SHER, 1992); they also testified before Congress about the issue. The publicity surrounding this activism increased the mobilization of feminist and professional women's organizations in support of the Women's Health Equity Act.

The use of conventional tactics did not preclude the use of confrontational tactics as well. In some cases, confrontational and conventional tactics went hand in hand. When an ex-NIH supervisor accused of sexual harassment received an award from a scientific association, SHER organized a picket. As one feminist insider described it, they:

> wanted to call attention . . . so she wanted to set up a blind at noontime, out in front of the place just before – this award was supposed to be given at 1:30 – and she wanted this from 12–1. NOW helped us with the picket line. They provided people. . . . We wanted to get it going at noontime when people are moving in and out and would be aware of it. (Interview, January 7, 2004)

In another well-publicized case, Maureen Polsby – one of the NIH scientists to file a sexual harassment suit – joined a hunger strike with other scientists to call attention to irregularities within the NIH (Hilts 1993: A24).

More importantly, there is evidence that many insider feminist activists engaged in confrontational tactics even though my interview protocol was heavily focused on gathering information about insider tactics. More than 30% (thirteen out of the forty) of the insider activists that I interviewed mentioned participating in protest demonstrations.[21] Most of the activists pursuing more confrontational tactics were among those in the career civil service. For civil servants,

---

[21] This estimate is likely to be lower than the actual participation in confrontational activities by the feminist activists I interviewed. Because the interviews were focused on activities related to the interviewees' positions inside of the federal government, no specific question about respondents' participation in confrontational activities outside of government was asked. Media searches on these insider feminist activists were used to supplement the interviews; this located two additional participants in confrontational activities. Given the absence of a specific question about confrontational activity participation in the interviews and the high threshold for being named in a media or web account of a protest or demonstration, the numbers of individuals who participated in confrontational tactics is likely to be higher.

the degree to which being inside the state exerted constraint on individuals depended partly on the presidential administration as well as immediate supervisors (see Chapter 7), and partly on the degree to which individuals were willing to accept the constraints imposed from above. On one side stood civil servants like Catherine East (1982: 293) who argued that effective action inside required acceding to such constraints: "Inside, . . . in order to be effective, you have to not be openly critical of the people or things." On the other hand, other civil servants found ways of participating that allowed them to avoid the constraints. For example, some civil servants who participated in protest demonstrations hid their activity. Indeed, Mary Eastwood's appearance in the *Washington Post* (December 15, 1967) described in Chapter 1 elicited a warning from her supervisor that she not be caught photographed at another demonstration. After this conversation, Eastwood continued to participate in protests but chose to wear a wig. Another interviewee told me that she used her maiden name when engaging in activism. Others were more willing to accept negative consequences of confrontation: "we put our jobs on the line to get that done" (Interview, January 7, 2004). Thus, feminist activists in the civil service varied in their willingness to succumb to the constraints of being on the inside.

For political appointees, participation in protest demonstrations and other confrontational activity during their tenure within the state was much more circumscribed, and when political appointees participated in protests, they usually did so both as individuals and as spokespeople for the administration. Thus, one feminist activist noted that she "spoke at the July 9 march in Washington [for the ERA]. I spoke at that march and I spoke for the President of the United States" (Interview, March 15, 2004). In these cases, participation was designed to show alliances between a presidential administration and a social movement. Although the insider feminist involved was participating in confrontational activities, doing so in an official capacity was in fact a conventional activity associated with her position. This illustrates the importance of looking at the underlying dimensions of confrontation, because in this case choosing to engage in a confrontational activity – protest – is in fact conventional activity. Moreover, it also shows that insider feminist activists who are political appointees are more likely to be circumspect in their tactical choices, and may be called upon by presidents to serve as indicators of administrative alliances with the movement.

Thus, contrary to the belief that feminists inside the state would be less supportive of confrontational tactics or would be constrained to only work within the system, the in-depth interviews I conducted suggest that feminist activists inside the federal bureaucracy did participate in and support protest and other confrontational tactics. However, as was the case with legal tactics, we also see that the degree to which participation in protest is confrontational can be context specific. When a presidential administration sends a feminist activist political appointee to a demonstration, that individual's participation in a particular demonstration does not represent any of the dimensions of a confrontational tactic.

We also see that each feminist activist inside the state felt a different level of constraints from her position. Political appointees who were supposed to represent the presidential administration were the most constrained in their activity, and were the least likely to be connected to protest demonstrations. Yet, the major external constraint on political appointees was remaining in the state itself. One of the feminist activist political appointees I interviewed was unwilling to change her behavior as a result of this constraint: "I was not constrained, which is why I did not last more than a year and half. You either decide when you get appointed to a job like mine, you're not an activist anymore. You can't be. But I never stopped. So I knew my time was limited" (Interview, March 15, 2004). Most political appointees argued that their position required loyalty to the president who had appointed them, and therefore also employed a high degree of self-constraint as well.[22]

CONCLUSIONS

The moderation of movements by insiders represents a major thesis within social movement theory. The preliminary evidence on insider feminist activists presented here suggests that insider feminist activists did not necessarily embrace conventional tactics or wish to moderate

---

[22] Borelli (1997) in studying the executive branch notes that loyalty to the president is one characteristic affecting how political appointees are chosen.

protest. Therefore, there is little evidence to suggest that state–movement intersections contribute to either growing moderation or a demobilization of the movement. Moreover, the qualitative case studies provide a number of examples of insiders choosing protest activities, particularly when opportunities for inside action are closed.

Nonetheless, it is important to put insider feminist activists' confrontational activities in perspective. Feminist activists inside the state did differ from the larger array of feminist activists in their demographic characteristics. The women I interviewed were older, more highly educated, and already working at high-level careers; they were a part of the women's movement that Freeman (1975) has described as older and more established. In that sense, the range of confrontational tactics that they employed did not include guerilla theater and other "zap actions" conducted by the women's liberation movement of the late 1960s and early 1970s. Yet, these women were not simply working inside the system either. Rather, they chose tactics that were both confrontational and conventional.

In contrast to the assumption that they would limit themselves to internal bureaucratic channels, feminist activists within the state could be found mobilizing outside of the bureaucracy on issues they felt were important. Even inside the state, they behaved like the movement activists they were. This suggests that women's movement scholars, and social movement scholars more generally, need to carefully separate location from tactics. Indeed, the illustrative case studies above suggest that there is much theorizing to be done about the tactical decisions individuals make. We do not yet know under what conditions activists within the state choose outsider tactics and when they are constrained to normal channels.

Finally, I have also argued that we need to explore the different dimensions of tactics rather than categorizing some tactics as confrontational and others as conventional. If the purpose of confrontational tactics is to disrupt the system, or polarize a conflict, or even to challenge the existence of established institutions, then any single tactic may vary in its degree of confrontation depending on the context of its use. As Katzenstein (1988: 121, 123–124) shows, in the Catholic Church, the presence of a woman in certain venues is itself a confrontational act whereas the presence of that same woman in another venue is not. Thus, institutions can be confronted in the courts and on the streets. The normal function of government can be disrupted by violence but also by employing some state institutions against others. What appears to matter most is not just the tactic itself, but the tactic in the context of the surrounding political issues.

6

How Insider Feminists Changed Policy

The women's movement has been relatively successful in changing the policy and culture of U.S. society, especially when viewed from the standpoint of visible actions. Indeed, Tarrow (1994: 184) argues that "the women's movement [is] among the most successful in American social history" even as he acknowledges that other movements produced larger demonstrations and more dramatic publicity than the U.S. women's movement. In this chapter, I argue that part of the success can be attributed to a specific characteristic of the women's movement – the extent to which women's movement activists were part of the state. The presence of women's movement activists in a variety of government agencies helped the movement utilize routine legislation and regulatory actions as political opportunities.

Moreover, the extensive nature of the social changes demanded by the feminist movement allowed it to pursue these political opportunities in a wide array of locations within the state, even as insider feminists were limited to areas where the federal government was involved in policy making. However, because insider feminists were drawn from a particular section of the women's movement, some policies important to other sections of the women's movement were harder to enshrine into government policy. In making this argument, I focus not only on the adoption of new policies – as is common in most studies of social movement outcomes – but also on policy implementation, and its implications for pursuing feminist agendas.

I also contend that the characteristics of particular federal bureaucracies are an additional type of political opportunity that influences the relationship between mobilization and outcomes. The definition and usefulness of the political opportunities concept has been hotly debated (see Jasper and Goodwin 2003) and opportunity issues extend to other social movement concepts (see, for example, Ferree 2003 on discourse opportunity structure and Gamson and Meyer 1996 on the cultural aspects of political opportunity). Yet, even the more narrow definition of political opportunity – the openness of the state to movements, the position of allies within the state and competition among political elites – does not sufficiently cover the range of opportunities that operate through movement-state intersections (Amenta 2005; Kitschelt 1986; Kriesi 1993; McAdam 1982; Tarrow 1989).[1] While sympathetic administrations certainly helped insider feminist activists implement feminist policies and hostile administrations inhibited insider feminist activists (see Chapter 7), two characteristics specific to the federal bureaucracy also influenced whether the women's movement could achieve and maintain policies.[2]

First, those parts of the bureaucracy that had a stronger client orientation were more likely to permit the explicit expression of non-state interests, allowing insider activists to act for the movement more openly. Scholars of the bureaucracy have long understood that some bureaucratic agencies are more oriented towards meeting the demands of their clients than necessarily following state interests (Carpenter 2001; McConnell 1970). Moore (1999: 101–102) argues that institutions like the state are more open to change by social movements

---

[1] The particular definition of political opportunities has varied from author to author (c.f., for example, Kitschelt 1986; Tarrow 1994). In discussing the elements of the traditional concept I utilize the common elements of different definitions recognized by Brockett (1991).

[2] The addition of opportunities specific to the bureaucracy is not unprecedented. Andersen (2004), for example, argues for the need to examine political opportunities within the legal system in understanding the adoption of gay and lesbian rights. It is also important to note that the means by which a movement influences outcomes differs for each of these two types of bureaucratic political opportunities; client oriented bureaucracies require influence from organized outside organizations (even as insider help is still necessary), but bureaucratic change can be subverted by a few well-placed insider activists.

when their claim to legitimacy lies in serving a specific set of clients. In such cases, she argues, organized groups of clients can influence the activities of the institution. Thus, we might expect that insider feminists located in the parts of the U.S. bureaucracy where the clients are expressly women will both employ bureaucratic means in their movement activities more and that this part of the bureaucracy will be more open in their activities.

Second, changes in the bureaucratic structures, including both the creation of *new* agencies and also *routine* changes in policy or implementation processes, provide opportunities for insider activists to create dramatic policy change. Established procedures are difficult to change. But when bureaucratic change is already occurring or when bureaucracies are built from scratch, it is easier for insider activists to introduce additional changes that reflect the interests of the movement. Sometimes insider activists functioning within new bureaucratic structures can implement new rules or regulations "under the radar," in ways that are barely visible to non-state actors or even other parts of the state. Yet, as I shall show in the case of Title IX, these barely visible regulations may have large effects in the way that legislation gets implemented.

I begin this chapter by discussing the issues that insider feminist activists pursued within the federal bureaucracy. As will become clear, the network of insider feminist activists encompassed a wide range of locations within the bureaucracy even as feminist activists tended towards a few key agencies. To examine policy change, I then develop case studies of policy changes in equal employment issues, equity in education, and women in development, focusing specifically on the role that feminist activists within the federal bureaucracy played in the adoption and implementation of each policy. I conclude with the implications of this study for our understanding of the women's movement and for social movements in general.

ISSUE AREAS PURSUED WITHIN THE STATE BY INSIDER FEMINISTS

While my interviewees represented a fairly diverse (albeit nonrandom) set of activists spread across the agencies and departments of the federal government,[3] there was considerable overlap in their areas of activism within government.[4] Here I define activism within government in one of two ways. First, I include feminist activists who worked on an issue as part of their job as engaging in activism within government.[5] For example, feminists opposed to sex discrimination in the workplace who worked within the Equal Employment Opportunity Commission (EEOC) would be considered as engaging in activism within government. Second, activists who addressed feminist issues by mobilizing other government employees are also considered to be engaging in activism within government. For example, feminists who organized women within the National Institutes of Health to fight sex discrimination would also be considered engaging in activism within government.

Table 6.1 presents the range of issues pursued within government by the forty feminist activists I interviewed. The feminist activists in my sample largely focused on one or two issues. Thirteen of the forty feminist activists described their activism within government as focusing on a single issue, twenty one mentioned two issues, and six women pursued three or more different issues within government. As Table 6.1 shows, feminist activists within government used their offices to pursue a wide range of issues including abortion and international issues (such as the status of women in developing countries). However, the greatest emphasis among the population interviewed in this study was on issues of equal employment for women. A sizeable minority of this group also pursued educational equity issues.

---

[3] I have chosen not to report the specific agency or department where feminist activists worked, to maintain the confidentiality of the people I interviewed (some would be easily identified by their location within the bureaucracy). Table 3.4 shows how many worked specifically in areas of the federal bureaucracy focused on policies toward women and I have attempted to give a flavor of the different areas in the text above.

[4] Table 6.1 indicates only the activities pursued within the federal government. Feminist activists inside the federal bureaucracy were also active in a wider array of issue areas, including war and pornography, through feminist actions and organizations outside the state. In some cases, that was because interests shifted over time (and interviews covered periods after government employment), but in other cases, women were working on one issue in their private lives while simultaneously pursuing other issues within government.

[5] By that I mean that either their official duties were related to these issues or they utilized their positions within the state to pursue these issues (albeit not always with the official blessing of their supervisors).

TABLE 6.1. *Issue Focus of Insider Feminists' Activism within the Federal Bureaucracy*

Issue	Number of Activists Involved*	% of All Activists Involved
Equal Employment	25	62.5%
Educational Equity	7	17.0%
Status of Women in Other countries	4	10.0%
Childcare	4	10.0%
Equal Rights Amendment	3	7.5%
Abortion	3	7.5%
Status of Women of Color	3	7.5%
Violence Against Women	2	5.0%
Other issues	6	15.0%

* Activists may be involved in more than one issue area.

One potential reason that such a high percentage of women pursued the issue of equal employment was that feminist activists could tackle this issue within the government bureaucracy even if they worked in a location that did not otherwise address women's issues. Indeed, regardless of the philosophical issues involved, these feminist activists often pursued equal employment issues because they themselves had been subject to discrimination. Thus, I found women in the Department of Commerce, the Treasury Department, and the Foreign Service all actively attempting to change their government agencies or departments to ensure that supervisors or other bureaucrats did not discriminate on the basis of sex and that there were equal hiring and promotion opportunities as well as equal pay and benefits.

Another reason that equal employment dominates the activities of the feminist activists I interviewed may be related to political opportunities. From 1967 on, executive orders mandating equal employment and prohibiting discrimination on the basis of sex within the federal government provided opportunities for insider activists to pursue this issue in all of the parts of the U.S. bureaucracy.[6] Even during the Reagan and Bush administrations – known to be particularly hostile to many feminist issues – equal employment claims could still be

[6] Although those executive orders were also the result of feminist activism itself, see Harrison 1988: 198–202 among others.

pursued. Second, equal employment and antidiscrimination issues correspond easily to principles of liberal government that underlie the U.S. government. Hence, the choice of these issues may fit easily within a political opportunity framework.

In addition, the feminist ideology of the interviewees themselves may account for the focus on equal employment. As I discussed in Chapter 3, most of the feminist activists in the sample could be best characterized as liberal feminists. That is, while they recognized the existence of sexual discrimination, many felt that strong legal sanctions requiring equal treatment would go far in solving women's problems.[7]

With this overview of the sample in mind, I examine how the specific actions of feminist activists within the state influenced policy outcomes in three issue areas: equal employment, educational equity, and foreign development policy. These issues differ in their centrality to feminist activism within the state. While equal employment was the most important issue for the activists I interviewed, foreign aid to women in developing countries was important to only three of these insider activists. The outcomes in these three policy areas also vary somewhat. I first discuss the issue of equal employment and the role that feminist activists played in developing policies and assuring that they were implemented. I then turn to the issue of education equity, where feminist activists played a similarly vital role but where a hostile administration and strong countermovement reduced the gains made by feminists. Finally, I examine the issue of supporting women in development as an area of limited interest to many feminists but one where insider feminist activists nonetheless played an important role.

EQUAL EMPLOYMENT AND FEMINISTS WITHIN THE STATE

One of the major successes of the U.S. women's movement has been the changes that have occurred in the workplace. Legally, women's equal opportunity in the workplace was advanced by the Equal Pay Act of

---

[7] Again my method of finding interviewees may also have played a role in determining the issue areas that feminist activists pursued. Because the sample was chosen in part to maximize variation in location (agency and department), the emphasis on equal opportunity may simply be a result of a sample biased toward maximizing variation in location. Unfortunately, we simply cannot determine the degree to which the focus of activism is biased because we have no way of knowing the distribution of insider feminist activists across different locations within the federal bureaucracy.

1963 and Title VII of the Civil Rights Act of 1964. The Equal Pay Act of 1963 requires that employees doing the same work must receive equal pay regardless of sex. Title VII also prohibited discrimination in hiring, firing, and compensation on the basis of sex. These two pieces of legislation were followed by over four decades of legal battles that helped to define the specific parameters of these laws and helped to assure enforcement. Although women still do not occupy top positions in most occupations and are underrepresented in others, the equal employment legislation of the 1960s had a revolutionary impact on women's employment. There has also been a concurrent change in the cultural understandings of women and work. While women were largely portrayed as limited to particular occupations, and often as not part of the work force at all, American culture now expects to find women in a wider array of occupations and girls largely grow up expecting to be part of the workplace throughout their life (Conway, Ahern, and Steurnagel 1999: 68).

The passage of the Civil Rights Act of 1964 and the creation of the Equal Employment Opportunity Commission (EEOC) provided an opportunity for entrée into the state by feminist activists. The EEOC created one hundred initial openings for staff whose job it was to deal with complaints of sexual and racial discrimination (EEOC 2000: 5). While most of these positions were filled by personnel from other parts of the federal bureaucracy, others were filled by employees entering the government for the first time. Although the foundation of the EEOC predates the resurgence of the women's movement, in its early years feminists and women with an interest in discrimination sought positions there because it appeared to be an exciting place to work (Interviews, May 11 2002 and October 11, 2002).[8]

Feminists within the state played several important roles in the elimination of employment discrimination against women. First, insider feminists were vital in assuring that the legislation was enforced. The

---

[8] Other legislation or presidential initiatives have created opportunities for entrée into the state as well. The Violence against Women Act resulted in the creation of the Violence against Women Office in 1995. Presidential initiatives in hiring women at top administrative levels, such as Lyndon Johnson's 1964 decision to appoint fifty women or Richard Nixon's Task Force on Women's Rights and Responsibilities (and the subsequent nomination of Barbara Hackman Franklin as his staff assistant responsible for recruiting women to high level positions in the federal government) have also created opportunities for personnel changes specific to particular administrations.

Equal Employment Opportunity Commission (EEOC), which came into being in July 1965, was charged with the task of enforcing the Title VII of the Civil Rights Act of 1964. Although fully one-third of the complaints registered with the EEOC during the first year alleged sex discrimination (EEOC 2000; Hernandez 1975: 9), leading commissioners downplayed the sex provision emphasizing instead the importance of the race and religion clauses of the bill. For example, EEOC executive director Herman Edelsberg commented in the *Washington Post* that "no man should be required to have a male secretary" (Shelton 1965: B1), and in April 1966 the EEOC Commission voted three to two to allow employers to place sex-segregated job advertisements in newspapers (Harrison 1988: 188).

As Chapter 4 details, insider feminist activists facilitated the founding of the National Organization for Women (NOW) when existing women's organizations showed little interest in protesting the EEOC's lack of support for the "sex" clause[9] and, not surprisingly, many of NOW's initial actions focused on employment issues; these included filing a suit of mandamus against the EEOC to require them to enforce the sex clause as well as protests (such as the one mentioned in Chapter 1) and petitions against the EEOC's ruling in support of sex-segregated job advertisements. In August 1968, the EEOC finally reversed this ruling (Carabillo et al. 1993: 52).

As I show in the Chapter 5, feminist activists within government also played a large role in the early legal cases that assured that Title VII became a powerful piece of legislation. The cases pursued by these feminist activists within government were among the most important precedents in equal employment law (Hernandez 1975). These included the two cases against state protective legislation (*Mengelkoch v. Industrial Welfare Commission* and *Rosenfeld v. South Pacific*), as well as against prominent companies' and trade unions' discriminatory practices (*Bowe v. Colgate Palmolive* and *Weeks v. Southern Bell*). Several of these early cases – especially *Weeks v. Southern Bell Telephone & Telegraph* and *Bowe vs. Colgate-Palmolive Co.* – are cited in overviews of equal opportunity case law (see, for example Sedmak and Vidas 1994). *Weeks v. Southern Bell Telephone and Telegraph*

---

[9] Although Pedriana (2004: 191) notes that Esther Peterson wrote a letter complaining about the jokes at the expense of women workers.

was particularly significant because it was the first case to invalidate existing state protective legislation for women (The Association of the Bar of the City of New York 2007)[10] and the first case in which the court held that Title VII applied to women (Tully 1973). This case developed from an EEOC complaint by Lorena Weeks who had applied for the job of switchman only to be told that the position was not open to women because of state and company regulations against women lifting more than thirty pounds. Her case was one of those passed on to feminist lawyers within government by Sonia Pressman Fuentes.

Insider feminist activists also helped to develop the concept of *systemic discrimination* as a violation of equal opportunity under Title VII (McCann 1994). In this case a group of feminist lawyers within the EEOC working on the landmark pattern and practice case against American Telegraph & Telephone (AT&T) influenced the way the case was pursued, specifically focusing on the use of statistics to show systemic discrimination in its investigation within the EEOC (Interviews, May 10, 2002 and October 11, 2002; Stockard 2004: 50–52). Attorneys at the EEOC also moved beyond proof of individual discrimination to argue that sexual discrimination within the Bell system inculcated sexual stereotypes into the larger society. As one insider told the story, the EEOC's argument was molded to present a "really revolutionary view of sex discrimination.... We wanted to present the whole sociology and psychology of sexual stereotypes as it was inculcated into the Bell System structure" (Shapiro 1973). In the end, AT&T decided to settle with the EEOC in what became the largest award in a discrimination lawsuit to date. The settlement resulted in 13,000 women receiving back pay awards and over twice as many who were given immediate raises (Shanahan 1973).

More importantly, the AT&T case led the EEOC to focus on systematic discrimination by the country's largest employers. In 1973, EEOC established task forces to investigate General Electric, General Motors, Ford, and Sears Roebuck and filed "commissioner charges" against

---

[10] However, it was not the first suit brought by this group in an attempt to invalidate state protection laws. The same group of feminists had also aided in the suit *Mengelkoch v. North American Aviation Co.*, but this suit was dismissed on appeal. *Rosenfeld v. Southern Pacific Company*, which also invalidated restrictive state laws, came later. Many of the same feminist activists worked on this case as well.

these employers (EEOC History: 35th Anniversary: 1965–2000). A later feminist insider noted that this activism around AT&T led to the:

> whole idea of systemic investigation. So he [David Copus] had done the first systemic investigation... of AT&T. So after that was successful they set up a division at EEOC and he became the head of it and then recruited five of us to take on five organizations. (Interview, May 10, 2002)

As McCann (1994: 50) notes, the EEOC's power to charge systemic rather than individual discrimination was important because it allowed the EEOC to pursue claims without relying on individual complainants to stay the course, and it opened up opportunities later for the comparative worth movement which moved beyond a focus on discrimination to the issue of pay scale differences between occupations in a largely sex-segregated job market.

Feminist activists within the state also pursued their own equal employment claims within government in ways that strengthened equal employment practice more generally, often bolstered by feminist activists and organizations outside of government. Early on, "insider" feminist activists sought to eliminate discrimination on the basis of sex for federal contractors and subcontractors. In response to President Johnson's Executive Order 11246 of 1965, which barred discrimination among federal contractors on the basis of "race, creed, color, or national origin" but not sex, feminist activists within and outside the federal government organized to have sex added to the executive order. As Freeman (1975: 193) notes, Catherine East helped to coordinate the battle to amend E.O. 11246 by lobbying Secretary of Labor Willard Wirtz and by encouraging women's organizations outside the federal government to pressure for such a change. Continued intransigence in adopting equal employment policies within various departments led feminists within the federal government to organize both within their specific agencies and departments (e.g., National Institutes of Health, Foreign Service, Department of Justice) and also across the federal bureaucracy through Federally Employed Women (see Chapter 4).

Feminist activists within the state also helped to ensure continued vigilance on the issue of equal employment even under the administrations of Ronald Reagan and George H.W. Bush. For example, insider feminist activists within the state have continually tried to ensure that laws were not stripped of their enforcement power. While insider feminists are not always able to advocate for specific policies, they can pass on information about minute changes in regulations that might otherwise get buried in the Federal Register. This was particularly useful under those administrations that were less supportive of Title VII. One activist I interviewed noted that the Bush administration had tried to use regulations to handicap enforcement of equal opportunity. In her job reviewing regulations, she discovered "the most outrageous things just tucked away in a little paragraph like the repeal of Title VII" (Interview, June 25, 2002). This activist then passed information about the changes on to others outside of government, allowing outside feminists to mobilize in defense of existing policies.

Thus, in the case of employment equity, feminist activists played a role in both the adoption and implementation of legislation. Although Title VII was not specifically the work of feminist activists within the state,[11] they helped to spread equal employment to other venues through their work and through their battles to extend these rights to the federal government through an Executive Order. More importantly, feminist activists within the state played a large role in assuring that the sex clause of Title VII was implemented. They did so using an array of tactics that included creating or mobilizing outsider organizations, filing lawsuits (including some suing the government itself), and informing outside feminists of the problems regarding implementation.

EDUCATIONAL EQUITY AND FEMINISTS WITHIN THE STATE

A second important outcome for the women's movement has been the cumulated changes in the educational system that occurred since the 1960s. As East (1982: 220) notes, the President's Commission on the Status of Women and the later Citizen's Advisory Council on the Status of Women were focused largely on employment opportunities, the Equal Rights Amendment, and maternity leave and largely ignored issues of educational equity. Thus, the focus on education and the creation of Title IX developed after the initial mobilization of the

---

[11] Nonetheless, some of these feminists lobbied for Title VII and several congresswomen were influential in its passage.

women's movement, and insider feminist activists played an important role in Title IX.

Second-wave feminists' actions on the issue of educational equity developed at first out of equal employment policies. In 1969, Bernice Sandler, who had received an Ed.D. in education and was teaching part-time at the University of Maryland, sought a position in the same department (at the time they had seven openings). When she inquired why she was not considered for one of the openings, she was told "You come on too strong for a woman" (Sandler 1997: 1). Seeking to file a sex discrimination charge, she discovered that Title VII of the Civil Rights Act exempted educational institutions, meaning that academics could not file charges of discrimination. Encouraged by Vincent Macaluso in the Office of Federal Compliance and with the help of the Women's Equity Action League,[12] Sandler filed a complaint against the university and a class action suit against all colleges and universities using Executive Order 11246, which prohibited federal contractors from discrimination. While issues of equal employment in education initially dominated the fight for educational equity, other issues soon came to the fore, including the existing barriers to training in nontraditional occupations (such as informal quotas in graduate and professional schools and separate vocational training for boys and girls in high school), as well as sex stereotyping in educational materials.

Two important pieces of legislation were eventually adopted that attempted to rectify these problems: Title IX of the Educational Amendments of 1972 and the Women's Educational Equity Act of 1974. Feminist activists within the state played a role in the passage of Title IX as well as in monitoring its implementation, but in contrast to the issue of equal employment, the opposition to educational equity policy was much fiercer. As a result, feminist activists inside the state were limited in what they could achieve and, particularly during Ronald Reagan's administration, found themselves battling anti-feminists inside the state. Feminist activists found themselves subject to campaigns to terminate their employment or to limit their freedom to act. Even under these circumstances, however, feminists inside the state still managed to advance programs of educational equity.

---

[12] Sandler was made chair of WEAL's Federal Contract Compliance Committee.

The Passage of Title IX

The first consideration of educational equity issues centered around the legislation that became Title IX of the 1972 Higher Education Amendments. Title IX empowered federal agencies providing any form of education aid to revoke federal funds to institutions that engaged in gender discrimination and at the same time allowed the Department of Justice to file suit against institutions that refused to comply (Conway, Ahern, and Steurnagel 1999: 25–26).

Title IX was the work of Representatives Edith Green (D-OR) along with Patsy Mink (D-HI), both of whom had long been aware of issues of sexual discrimination in education. As chair of a subcommittee of the House Education and Labor Committee Edith Green was uniquely situated to deal with this issue, and feminists within the state had encouraged her to do so. One key connection was congressional staffer Phineas Indritz. As a board member of National Organization for Women and close associate of Catherine East, Mary Eastwood, Sonia Pressman Fuentes, and other feminists inside the bureaucracy working on employment equity, he had been urging Green to hold hearings on educational equity. In 1970 she convened the hearings on a new piece of legislation that she had drafted (Sandler 1997: 4).

In addition to the women's groups and educators who largely testified in favor of the bill, the Nixon administration sent a representative from the Department of Health, Education, and Welfare (HEW) to testify *in opposition to* the bill. Yet, the text of the administration's statement helped to develop support *for* the passage of the bill. How this happened illustrates the influence that political activists within the state can have. The testimony had been written by a feminist activist in HEW who had been trying to convince the administration to support Green's bill. As she recalls it:

> I wrote a fairly strong draft, detailing all of the instances of sex discrimination in education that I could find, with all the statistics I could find, and concluded with a statement that the administration supported the bill. It was very strong testimony.... The last part of this process was a meeting at the White House with representatives of ... other departments that were considered to be stakeholders.... I argued that the administration should support the bill but the decision of the meeting was that the administration would oppose it.... All I did was change the last couple of paragraphs. And that's all I was required to

do. So I left all the statistics and what a general problem this was, and how unequal this was.... I was required to cut out the last paragraph and two, and instead of saying 'and therefore we support the bill,' say 'however, we do not believe this legislation is necessary at this time.' (Interview, May 25, 2004)

Activists in the education area noted that the result of the testimony was to encourage support for the legislation and to give Representative Green's argument about the need for such legislation stronger credence (Interview, October 16, 2003; Millsap 1988: 21–22). As Millsap (1988: 22) notes, the reaction to the HEW testimony was immediate:

In questioning the officials, Representative Green pointed out the discrepancy between the 'effective and eloquent testimony'... and HEW opposition to the bill, and expressed doubt whether existing law or executive orders were sufficient.

While the legislation did not pass that year, the testimony from the hearings was widely distributed and even two decades later was considered "an excellent source of information about the status of women's education" (McBride Stetson 1991: 108). The legislation was incorporated into an education bill two years later; it was adopted largely under the radar of educational specialists.[13]

Implementing Title IX

If the passage of Title IX attracted little attention, a large battle developed over the initial regulations implementing the bill. Because controversy around the initial regulations was so intense, it took from July 1972 to July 1975 (spanning the Nixon and Ford administrations) to publish initial regulations (McBride Stetson 1991: 109; Nash et al. 2007: 65–67). Several different debates were occurring within the bureaucracy at this point with feminist activists within government pushing for the strongest regulations possible. Feminist activists within

---

[13] McBride Stetson (1991: 109) noted that the major controversy in congressional debate around the bill involved the issue of court-ordered busing for racial integration. Moreover, several interviewees noted that Representative Green urged feminists not to lobby or call attention to Title IX and was content that debate focused on other aspects of the bill. The bill also closed loopholes in the Equal Pay act – a feat accomplished by another feminist activist in government – Morag Simchak – who attached a technical rider to Title IX.

government, including B. Ann Kleindienst, also worked to assure that the women's movement's voice was included in the public comment process (Millsap 1988: 32–33; Interview, May 25, 2004).[14] The result was that 10,000 comments were provided on the draft regulation, where most regulations elicited less than one thousand (Millsap 1988: 35). Many of the suggestions from women's groups were included in the final implementation including a "self assessment, a grievance procedure and the Title IX coordinator" (Nash et al. 2007: 66).

Feminist insiders also influenced the final regulations about the complaint process under Title IX. After the public comment period, the HEW transmitted final recommendations to the president that included newly added wording that placed stronger limitations on when individuals could register complaints under Title IX:

They put in a clause at the last minute that would have said that before you could file a complaint you would have to go through an internal grievance process in . . . your . . . college. . . . So again, this was the inside stuff we found out. I was best buddies with . . . [name withheld] – by this time she was inside, I was outside – so we found out about this . . . this horrible clause in the draft regulation. We thought it would absolutely be a disaster because then there would be no enforcement; people who wanted redress would cool their heels for years with some internal grievance process. . . . So we finally got a meeting with an aide to the President where we jumped up and down and said how horrible this requirement of exhausting the internal remedy before filing a complaint was, and it had to come out. In the end they did take it out. . . . If we hadn't had people who had been inside . . . we wouldn't have known about it until it went on the Hill and then it would have been too late. (Interview, May 25, 2004)

In the end the final regulations did not include the requirement that individuals complete internal grievance procedures; instead they allowed complaints to go through the Office for Civil Rights in the Department of Education, which could then threaten to cut federal

---

[14] Equally important for this issue was the existence of feminist activists within many of the traditional educational organizations like Dr. Bernice Sandler at the Association of American Colleges and Universities (Nash et al. 2007: 66). These women were often able to utilize these larger organizations to lobby for changes although, in all likelihood, the membership of the organizations would not have been strongly supportive of the positions these women took. For a look at women in several such organizations see Hartmann (1998).

financial aid, and allowed individuals to sue as well (Millsap 1988; McBride Stetson 1991).

These recommendations that feminists organized to fight were not public, and as Millsap (1988: 37–38) notes feminists had no direct access to the White House or Cabinet officials who could have provided information on the new regulation or supported feminist positions. The political opportunities, as conventionally understood, were thus largely closed to the women's movement. However, feminist activists within the state changed that by providing information about what was about to happen and by encouraging women's organizations to mobilize. Although other factors were also important in getting these regulations changed (especially the existence of Republican women who arranged the White House meeting), feminist activists within the state helped to change the political opportunities affecting the women's movement.

Of course, feminists inside the bureaucracy, like their counterparts outside of the state, were unable to get all of the policies they wanted into Title IX regulations. As one activist noted, they also attempted to get the issue of sexist teaching materials included in the regulations:

We tried, me and [another activist], to get coverage for sex bias in textbooks . . . There had been some very dramatic studies out on sex bias in textbooks. So I tried to get . . . the group drafting the regulation at HEW to accept some language covering sex bias in textbooks. We may have gotten that in at some point but it got knocked out at the upper level. (Interview, May 25, 2004)

In the end, the elimination of sexist teaching materials was not part of Title IX regulations.

Thus, feminist activists within the government bureaucracy played a large role in assuring that Title IX passed and that it was implemented in such a way as to provide some enforcement protection. While there are many ways in which Title IX has been weakened (e.g., in excluding many types of extracurricular organizations and some types of sports), feminist activists inside the state influenced in positive ways both the adoption and the implementation of Title IX.

The results of this activity have been mixed. On the one hand the number of women in professional schools has risen dramatically and the informal quotas that limited women's attendance in many schools have disappeared. There have been large increases in the percentage of women graduating in the fields of law, medicine, and mathematics (Brown n.d.: 8). In several fields, including law, the sea change has reached to the upper levels of the higher education system as women have entered administrative ranks as well. For example, Barbara Babcock (2001: 722) notes: "In 1972, I came to Stanford Law School as its first woman on the tenure track. For five years I was the only one.... Today I teach on a Stanford faculty, almost a third women, all stars, led by a famous woman dean." However, educational advances have not been uniform. Some fields, such as mechanical engineering, computer and information sciences, and physics continue to be dominated by men. Moreover, studies into the 1990s continue to find that curriculum materials shortchange women and girls (Klein et al. 2007; Wellesley College Center for Research on Women 1995). An analysis of government programs for creating gender equity in education found that Title IX enforcement is limited and that many government programs encouraging gender equity had disappeared, particularly under the Reagan and George H. W. Bush administrations (Nash et al. 2007: 72). Hence, although feminists can point to many changes it is clear that educational equity has not been achieved.

The Women's Educational Equity Act

The issue of sex-role stereotyping and bias in educational materials failed to be incorporated into Title IX, but soon became the focus of another piece of legislation – the Women's Educational Equity Act (WEEA) of 1974. As Nash et al. (2007: 70–76) point out, while much of Title IX enforcement involved a "stick" approach, WEEA was designed as a "carrot" to promote educational equity through assistance for compliance and for training in appropriate practices. Feminists in Congress and outside of government fought hard to create the program, finally getting it incorporated into a Special Projects Act that included a number of small programs.[15] As was the case with Title IX, Patsy Mink – WEEA's sponsor – discouraged active feminist lobbying because she hoped the act would be adopted with little public notice (Millsap 1988: 29–30). The initial bill authorized

---

[15] Fraser (1983), Millsap (1988) and others note the importance of feminist staffers on Capital Hill in providing the initial impetus for this bill.

$30 million for encouraging educational equity and established the National Advisory Council for Women's Educational Programs in the Office of Education.[16]

Feminist activists quickly became involved in WEEA implementation. One activist noted, for example, how she was able to turn the programs toward some of the pressing issues within the women's movement when she entered government in the late 1970s:

> When I came in, the statute had been reauthorized, there were some changes, and it was time to write new regulations. We made substantial change in the focus; we added priority for funding – strict ones that hadn't really existed – one of the priorities was for programs to promote educational equity for disabled women and girls. That had never happened before or since I regret to say. Another was promoting equity for women and girls of color that has not happened before or since sorry to say. (Interview, September 25, 2003)

However, the WEEA program quickly became a particular target of conservative politicians and the Heritage Foundation, which published specific attacks on the program (see Faludi 1991: 259–263; Nash et al. 2007: 71). Consequently, feminist activists within the state and connected to the program were specifically targeted by the Reagan administration. The Reagan administration requested zero funds for WEEA in 1982 and Leslie Wolfe, WEEA's director, was the target of a lengthy campaign to discredit and remove her. At first, the department political appointees "detailed" her to be the senior officer on a task force examining waste and fraud in the department. She was told to move immediately to her new position even though Wolfe was in the middle of organizing the reviews of grant proposals for the WEEA program. Before she went she "did communicate with some grantees and some field readers and some colleagues and some advocacy groups – women's groups – and they launched a campaign to save the program, which worked" (Interview with Leslie R. Wolfe, Fall 2003). Although at the end of ninety days, she returned to her position as WEEA director, her position was downgraded soon thereafter.

The Reagan administration did other things to reduce the power of feminist activists within government. Millsap (1988: 141) notes that

---

[16] The 1976 amendment of the Vocational Education Act of 1963 also focused on the reduction of gender bias and stereotyping in vocational education.

one effective strategy was to eliminate the ability of feminist activists to pass on information. The Office of Civil Rights, for example, required all information requests to be cleared by the Office of the Assistant Secretary. Another mid-level bureaucrat in the area of sex equity in education reported being monitored by members of Congress and denied promotions (Interview, March 8, 2004). Nonetheless, outside activists were often able to receive information about upcoming regulations. This information allowed them to stop the administration from eliminating funding for sex equity coordinators for vocational education for a while (Millsap 1988: 146; Klein et al. 2007).

While the program and its funding rallied somewhat during the Clinton presidency, when George H. W. Bush assumed the presidency, conservative activists both inside and outside the state renewed their attack on WEEA (Gahr 2001; Kafer 2001, 2007). The appropriations for WEEA, which previously constituted only .02% of the Department of Education's budget, were whittled down to less than $3 million and the federal contract to fund a center to distribute equity materials was closed (Nash et al. 2007: 71). Although George H.W. Bush continued to slate WEEA for extinction, women in Congress have managed to provide the program with a small budget through 2008, allowing it to continue on in a very limited form.

Thus, the story of educational equity is at best mixed. Feminist activists within the state did contribute both to the passage of Title IX legislation and to stronger implementation of educational equity programs. But focused opposition, particularly throughout the 1980s and during the George H.W. Bush presidency, limited opportunities for policy successes. Indeed, the George H.W. Bush presidency was characterized by the wholesale movement of prominent antifeminists into the state (Morin and Dean 2001). Yet, even with such intense and focused opposition, feminist activists within the state have still been able to influence policy, largely by being in places that allow them to pass on information and mobilize support for educational equity programs.

WOMEN AND DEVELOPMENT

In the early 1970s parts of the U.S. women's movement began to focus on women in developing countries, arguing that because foreign development aid was driven by economic statistics and much of women's work did not appear on these statistics, aid tended to ignore women's needs. Indeed, feminists criticized economic aid from advanced industrialized countries for hurting women in developing countries by undercutting existing economic activities of women (Tinker 2004: 69). However, there was little initial response to these critiques from the male dominated foreign service and foreign policy communities. With the exception of population and health policy, women were almost totally ignored in economic aid up to the early 1970s. As Chaney (2004: 203) notes: "women were viewed only as 'targets' in the agency's population and mother-child health programs and the word 'women' rarely appeared in documents unless prefaced by the phrase 'pregnant or lactating.' Nonmothers, girls, and older women were invisible."

The Percy Amendment of 1973

Beginning in the 1970s, there was a major change in the focus of development aid – known as the New Directions or Basic Human Needs mandate. This new focus affected many programs ranging from infrastructure grants to humanitarian aid (Sartorius and Ruttan 1989). Feminists within government took advantage of the opportunity presented by the rise of new models of foreign aid to introduce a focus on women into the Foreign Assistance Bill of 1973. Mildred Marcy, one of these insider feminists, was a foreign service officer married to Carl Marcy who was chief of staff for the Senate Foreign Relations committee. At discussions with women's groups around the International Year of the Woman, several women asked her if women could not benefit from the current bill before the Senate. Mildred Marcy read the bill and wrote an amendment saying that the New Directions mandate should focus specifically on women and, through connections on Capitol Hill, managed to get Senator Percy to introduce it (Tinker 1983). The amendment was not in the House version and so when the bill hit the conference committee, House members dropped the amendment thinking that no one really supported it. "Mildred Marcy was informed; she in turn called several women who had been at the State Department and congressional hearings; and the lobbying began" (Tinker 1983: 231). Marcy herself reports having called Virginia Allan at the State Department, along with activists in the League of Women Voters and the National Council of Jewish Women (Marcy 1991: 57). The representatives on the conference committee found their mailboxes inundated with letters in support of the Percy Amendment from women around the country. As a result, they reinserted the Percy Amendment into the bill, which was adopted by both houses and signed by President Nixon.

Increasing the Focus on Women in Development

As a consequence of the Percy Amendment, the Office of Women in Development (WID) was created within the United States Agency for International Development in 1974. However, in the first years after the adoption of the Percy Amendment, the office remained small – the total budget was only $300,000 – and largely marginal to the work of AID. In 1977, Arvonne Fraser, former president of the Women's Equity Action League, was appointed to be coordinator of the office. Under her purview, the office engaged in several activities that strengthened policies toward Women in Development.

First, under Fraser's tenure, the budget was significantly increased so that by 1980 the budget had risen to $10 million (Jaquette 2004: 194). While the budget remained fairly static in following administrations and was miniscule compared to those of other offices, the budget increases enabled the office to continue to press for a focus on women in development through several administrations. One reason the Office of Women in Development was particularly effective was that it utilized its funds to influence existing projects in other units. Rather than funding women's components of aid projects, Fraser argued "that the Percy Amendment required integrating women; that the various bureaus were supposed to use their own budgets to make women beneficiaries" (Fraser 2004: 169). While Fraser experienced resistance toward WID from much of the agency, there was increasing realization among other USAID bureaucrats that they must address women's needs in proposals, even if only in a pro forma language (Jaquette 2004: 194). These changes represented a strengthening of the focus on women in development within an agency previously indifferent to the issue.

Second, Fraser also developed an outside support network by funding many women's organizations. As she notes: "I soon learned that contracts under $10,000 could be let with little bureaucratic paperwork. I also knew from my own experience with women's organizations that $10,000 could be a great boon to women's groups, including U.S. women's groups doing women in development research, and therefore began to write numerous contracts" (Fraser 2004: 169). The funding from the WID office had two effects: It contributed to the rise in women as a political force among those interested in development issues, and it increased the networks among those groups, creating closer ties within the existing transnational movement on women and development. By strengthening outside organizations that could mobilize around issues of women in development, it created an important external force (Tinker 1983: 236).

Third, the WID office encouraged the collection of data and research about women, often through its small grants to women's organizations. WID feminists then used this information to lobby within the institution for a greater focus on women in the spending of development aid. For example, Jane Jaquette and Elsa Chaney – both academic feminists active in women's and development issues, and recruited into WID by Fraser – worked with the International Division of the Department of the Census to develop a set of standard indicators of women's status in countries receiving aid. These indicators, particularly those on women's education and literacy, later became the basis for continuing foreign aid policies.

Thus, feminist activists within the state played a major role in creating legislation that included women in development aid and in implementing the legislation in ways that guaranteed a permanent focus on women within USAID. The adoption of the Percy Amendment in 1973 and the development of the Women in Development office contributed to wider acceptance and implementation of policies toward women in development aid. One example of the mainstreaming of these policies is the degree to which the George W. Bush administration touted its policies toward providing economic aid to *women* in developing countries and toward abolishing the international trafficking of women. Many of the programs developed by feminists – particularly those focused on education, microcredit, and antitrafficking – continued to thrive under the George W. Bush administration, although the resources devoted to these programs continues to be a small part of all foreign aid (Sharma 2001: 1). In both the adoption of the Percy Amendment and in its implementation through the Office of Women in Development, feminists took advantage of political opportunities but they also created opportunities themselves by actively seeking allies both within and outside of government, and by molding the resources available to the bureaucracy.

CONCLUSIONS

Looking at women in government during the New Deal, Susan Ware notes that: "Obviously no single group can claim exclusive credit for a piece of legislation or a new program, but in many cases the network of women in the New Deal played a crucial role in developing and implementing the New Deal's social welfare policies" (Ware 1981: 87). In each of the three previously discussed case studies, a complex web of causes influenced both the introduction and implementation of the policy. Yet, as was the case in the New Deal, there is evidence that feminist activists inside the state played important roles in the introduction and implementation of equal employment law, Title IX, and policies toward women in development. Their contributions often occurred under the radar – in ways almost imperceptible to the usual studies of policy implementation. While I have provided here the accounts of insider feminist activists themselves (and they have incentives to overstate their role), outsider feminist activists have also acknowledged the contributions insider feminists have made in these cases (see e.g., Freeman 1975: 230; Tobias 1997: 82–85).

The three case studies show feminist activists within the state playing several roles in the adoption and implementation of feminist policy. Feminist activists within the state helped to write legislation, provided the rationale that convinced outsiders to support feminist legislation, provided information and resources to outsider women's movement organizations that helped them organize and mobilize in support of policy, and conducted lawsuits (in many cases against the government) to assure that existing policies were followed. In doing so, they were certainly influenced by the political opportunities and constraints that existed around these specific issues (as well as by the character of the presidential administration as discussed in Chapter 7). Mildred Marcy's writing of the Percy Amendment was aided by the New Directions mandate that had already suggested a need to change aid policy. In the case of education policy, strong countermovements and hostile administrations limited what feminist activists within the state could achieve. Yet, by writing legislation and regulations, by mobilizing allies when they were needed, and by creating legal precedent through litigation, feminist activists within the state also created political opportunities. While feminist activists within the state were not decisive on all issues, we should not ignore the activities of these insider feminists, nor should we lump them together with the federal bureaucracy or specific presidential administrations. For in doing so, we would miss many of the ways that the feminist movement in the United States influenced its own future.

Moreover, feminist activism within the state was not limited to a few women's policy agencies. Some of the feminist activists important to the case studies in this chapter were part of agencies that were expressly there to serve women, but many were located in other parts of the federal bureaucracy. Even on an issue as specific as gender equity in education, Nash et al. (2007: 79–82) note that important programs were located not just in the Department of Education but throughout the federal bureaucracy, including the Department of Labor, the National Science Foundation, the Agency for International Development, the Department of Health and Human Services, and the Millenium Challenge Corporation. Hence, research concentrating on a few parts of the government will inevitably miss much feminist activism within the state. Because a wide variety of policies affect women, feminist activists can have profound effects even when located outside of women's policy agencies.

Finally, these case studies illustrate how policy outcomes themselves influence whether movements have activists in the state. Any time the state adopts or modifies policies (even informal ones) that affect a movement or its goals, it may alter the movement–state intersection. Title VII and the creation of the Equal Employment Opportunity Commission, for example, not only legislated equal employment policy for women, it also affected the intersection of the women's movement with the state by increasing the opportunities for movement activists to become insiders. The creation, combination, or elimination of specific departments or agencies also opens or closes opportunities for movement activists to enter the state. New bureaucratic structures create the greatest opportunities for movement activists to enter the state because of the lack of incumbent personnel and the attraction of movement activists to being able to build the organization from the ground up. But any organizational change may alter the intersection between social movements and the state.

However, even when organizational charts remain unchanged, policies and the operating rules and norms of government organizations can make working within the state more attractive or make particular locations more (or less) open to the activities of insider activists. In the case of the EEOC, the hostility toward enforcing the sex provision of Title VII was so explicit in the first years of the EEOC that it provoked the resignation of Aileen Hernandez, the five-member commission's only woman (Harrison 1988: 196). On the other hand, as I shall show in the next chapter, the rules and norms of particular state institutions and their leaders play a large role in creating space for insider feminists to act even when Presidents and their political parties are hostile to feminism.

7

Changing with the Times – How Presidential Administrations Affect Feminist Activists Inside the State

> Every administration comes in suspicious of the career employees who are beneath them because they think they were in . . . with the previous administration.
>
> (Interview, September 25, 2003)

> I think the Clinton administration was a wonderful moment for women inside government. It was partly because you had Cabinet officers who were not just people with ovaries.
>
> (Interview, September 23, 2003)

Having explored the existence, activities, and influence of feminist activists inside the federal bureaucracy in previous chapters, I turn now to examining their activities within those administrations considered to be inimical to the women's movement. Bashevkin (1998) chronicles the serious challenges faced by feminist activists outside the state during the Reagan and Bush presidencies. She argues that during these years U.S. feminists faced a strongly organized anti-feminist movement, which often (although not always) found sympathy and support from the presidential administrations (198). This chapter seeks to answer three sets of interrelated questions about insider feminist activists under these presidential administrations.

First, to what degree is the presence of feminist activists within the bureaucracy dependent on the sympathy of each presidential administration? Do feminist activists only enter government during sympathetic administrations and do administrations hostile to feminist goals also cause insider activists to exit the bureaucracy? Feminist activists enter the federal government at all levels: as political appointees or as civil servants interested in a particular job or career (sometimes even unrelated to their activism). When administrations hostile to feminism are elected, feminist activists do not usually receive political appointments (although there are exceptions). But civil servants, whose jobs are protected, may already be in the bureaucracy and theoretically could even enter during hostile administrations. But in practice, what happens to civil servants who see themselves as part of the feminist movement? Do they chose to leave, or do they remain under unpleasant administrations? And do we see fewer feminist activists entering the civil service during hostile administrations?

Social movement scholarship assumes that social movement activists will only enter government after the initial mobilization of the movement and usually in response to some initial movement success (Burnstein, Einwohner and Hollander 1995; Gamson 1975; Santoro 1999). Piven and Cloward (1978), for example, argue that the state may incorporate some movement elites into the political system to moderate their demands and demobilize protest. Others such as Gamson (1975) and Santoro (1999) see the movement of activists into government institutions as a sign of the movement's ability to achieve desirable outcomes – such as increasing its representation in electoral institutions. Similarly, Stetson and Mazur (1995: Chapter 1) argue that political leaders and political parties created new state offices focused specifically on women – "women's policy machinery" – in response to women's movement demands, fashioning opportunities for feminist activists to enter the state. If this literature is correct, and antifeminist administrations close such opportunities for feminist activists, we should find feminists entering government positions during Democratic administrations and exiting government during Republican administrations, especially those after 1980.

Second, I ask to what extent insider feminist activists are responsive to the agendas of administrations, particularly those opposed to feminist goals. What tactics, if any, do they use to push a feminist agenda under hostile regimes? If feminist activists remain in the bureaucracy during presidential administrations that oppose many of their goals, what are they able to achieve as activists within the bureaucracy? Social movement scholars in the United States have tended to view whole administrations as indicators of the opportunity structure. Democratic administrations have generally been viewed as increasing political opportunities for the environmental, civil rights, and women's movements, while alternatively Republican control of the presidency and Congress has been assumed to restrict political opportunities (Amenta, Dunleavy, and Bernstein 1994; Johnson 2004; McAdam 1982; Meyer and Minkoff 2004).[1] For example, Costain (1992) finds direct connections between individual Presidential administrations and the number of acts initiated by the federal bureaucracy. Such a view of political opportunities assumes that bureaucrats carry out the wishes of the presidential administration like loyal footsoldiers, and do so consistently in every agency. In this case, insider feminist activists should be constrained to act in ways that represent administrative interests no matter what their personal beliefs. However, research on bureaucracies has demonstrated that they are not very responsive to presidential policy initiatives (e.g., Aberbach and Rockman 2000).

Instead, the literature on the bureaucracy has focused on two other models of bureaucratic actions. On the one hand, a number of authors have looked at policy networks or interest groups to examine the degree to which bureaucracies are "captured" by the interests they represent (e.g., Heinz, Laumann, Nelson, and Salisbury 1993; McConnell 1966). In this case, bureaucrats in each agency work closely with a group outside of government; over time, bureaucrats adopt the group's interests as their own, either because the network develops a common set of norms and goals, or because promoting the group's interests aids the office's own survival.

Alternatively, scholars have argued that bureaucrats have their own interests in advancing their part of the bureaucracy (Carpenter 2001; Golden 2000). These interests are neither those of the presidential administration nor those of a client. Carpenter suggests that bureaucratic autonomy is strongest at the middle levels of the bureaucracy – "bureau or division chiefs, program planners, and monitors"

---

[1] Similarly, extensive literature inside the United States and elsewhere finds greater representation of women and feminist issues in Left parties (Beckwith 2003; Clark 1998).

(2001: 19). Yet how do bureaucrats pursue their own interests when they conflict with those of the presidential administration? Here Carpenter (2001) provides some suggestions. He argues that the way to "change the agendas and preferences of politicians and the organized public" (2001: 15) is through coalition building, rhetoric, and innovation. According to Carpenter (2001: 15) bureaucrats can be autonomous even when opposed by a presidential administration but in such cases they do not use "strategies of consistent fiat or defiance."

These two theories of bureaucratic interests lead to very different conclusions about how insider feminist activists will act. If bureaucracies are largely captured by outside interests, we should see civil servants carrying out the will of the clientele they serve. In such a case, we expect the actions of feminist activists within particular agencies (those most likely to be "captured" by the women's movement) to reflect movement goals but this behavior should be limited to specific agencies. Theories of bureaucratic autonomy suggest that insider feminist activists will take actions to support the movement, but these actions are not likely to openly oppose the positions of presidential administrations.

These theories also help us examine a third set of questions about how location within the bureaucracy influences how insider feminist activists respond to presidential administrations. Is the bureaucracy's responsiveness to presidential administrations uniform or are there locations within the federal bureaucracy where insider feminists may still act as movement activists under hostile administrations? The tendency of social movement scholars to treat the executive branch as a single unit means that they rarely seek to distinguish among different locations within the government. Nonetheless theories of bureaucratic autonomy suggest that social movement scholars' classification of administrations as positive or negative political opportunities is too general. Rather within the state at any time, one is likely to find both political opportunities and political constraints, with some locations serving as better places for movement activists to achieve policy ends.

One important distinction within the bureaucracy is, therefore, between locations of government recognized as related to the women's movement and those that are not. According to theories of interest group capture, bureaucratic agencies even partially captured by the movement should be more accessible to movement actors than other bureaucratic agencies. However, bureaucratic agencies with multiple constituencies will find their loyalty and attention divided. For example, Bonastia (2000) has argued that affirmative action policies failed in the Bureau of Housing and Urban Development (HUD) while it fared better in the Equal Employment Opportunity Commission in large part because HUD had multiple purposes and served multiple constituencies. This suggests that feminist activists will fare best in government offices focused solely on women but will still do better in offices whose multiple constituencies or purposes include women rather than in those where women are not an express constituency.

In addition, presidential control of the bureaucracy is uneven. Wilson (1989: 261) notes that historically presidents focus on a few key political appointees, which can leave other agencies with leaders who have little commitment to the president's ideology or policy. However, this may be changing; Wilson (1989) finds that Carter and Reagan initiated an increasing use of ideology as a criterion for appointments. In attempting to explain the autonomy of bureaucracies, Carpenter (2001) also argues that managers and other civil servants in the layer of management under political appointees have access to information that rarely gets filtered to the top. As a result, political appointees must concentrate on only a few reforms if they are to have any effect. This suggests that insider activists will be freer to act within the bureaucracy under appointees chosen for nonideological reasons, or in areas that are not the main focus of an ideological appointee.

Thus, we have several different expectations about how location influences actions under hostile administrations. First, we expect departments or agencies with a significant clientele of feminists to be less responsive to hostile administrations than those with a mandate unrelated to feminist goals. Second, we expect insider activists to be more able to act in agencies with a single goal or constituency than in those with multiple goals and constituencies. Third, we expect that the type of political appointee, and whether an office or agency is targeted by the administration, will influence the ability of feminist activists within the bureaucracy to act.

To examine these expectations, I begin by briefly describing the different administrations that existed during the time period that I am studying. I then discuss whether the entrance into and exit from the bureaucracy by feminist activists is related to the presidential administration. The third section explores the tactics feminist activists within the bureaucracy took under hostile administrations, and the fourth section examines feminist activists in different agencies across the bureaucracy to see if certain locations were better under both sympathetic and hostile administrations. Finally, the last section summarizes the findings and discusses the implications for our understanding of the feminist movement, social movements more generally, and our conceptions of how American democracy functions.

ADMINISTRATIONS DURING THE U.S. WOMEN'S MOVEMENT (1961–2000)

Despite the tendency among social movement scholars to talk about Democratic and Republican administrations, the party of the president is not sufficient to differentiate hostile from sympathetic administrations. This is because the parties in the United States underwent a dramatic shift in their identification with the women's movement starting in 1980 (Costain 1992; Freeman 1987; Wolbrecht 2000; but see Sanbonmatsu 2002). Republican Presidents Nixon and Ford could be counted as at least indifferent to, if not supportive of, some women's movement goals. Yet, after 1980, Republican administrations became more antithetical to women's movement interests.

Women's movement activity did not begin to emerge until the Johnson presidency of November 1963–1968. Yet, the Kennedy administration is commonly viewed as the starting point. Because Kennedy created the President's Commission on the Status of Women, which investigated legal and economic discrimination against women, he is also heralded as a staunch ally of the women's movement. The equal pay bill was adopted during his administration as well.

Johnson maintained this support for equal opportunities for women. Under his administration the commission begun by Kennedy continued and he signed the Equal Pay Act, Title VII of the Civil Rights Act in 1964 and an executive order prohibiting discrimination against women in federal government employment practices. Finally, Johnson engaged in a very public campaign to increase the appointment of women into the top levels of government.

The Carter (1977–1980) and Clinton administrations (1993–2000) represented perhaps the pinnacle of support for the women's movement among Democratic administrations prior to 2000. As Costain (1992: 93–95) argues, the Carter administration gave the women's movement extensive access to the White House. The Carter White House also lobbied extensively for the Equal Rights Amendment,[2] and appointed a large number of women to government positions. However, Carter did not support the feminist position on abortion. Carter proclaimed to be personally prolife and in 1977 he signed into law the Hyde amendment, which prohibited federal funding for abortion.

The Clinton administration also had a reputation for being supportive of the women's movement. [Clinton nominated more women to his administration than ever before and put them into key positions in the Departments of State and Justice](Borelli 2000). He signed into law both the Family Medical Leave Act and the Violence against Women Act, and was vocally in favor of a woman's right to choose. Yet, like Carter, there were some policy areas where he differed from many feminists including his support of the Personal Responsibility and Work Opportunity Reconciliation Act and the Defense of Marriage Act. Despite variation among Democratic presidents, however, the combined records of Kennedy, Johnson, Carter, and Clinton share support for women's rights and generally good relations with the women's movement.

In contrast, there is much greater variability among Republican administrations. The Nixon and Ford administrations are comparable to the early Democratic presidents in supporting some women's rights issues while opposing others. Nixon supported the ratification of the Equal Rights Amendment and lobbied on occasion for its passage. He created a second Presidential Commission whose report endorsed the Equal Rights Amendment and a host of other policies (Costain and Costain 1987: 203). He also hired Barbara Hackman Franklin to be a staff assistant in charge of recruiting women to leadership positions. Yet, Nixon vetoed the Comprehensive Child Care Act and opposed most abortion reforms (Wolbrecht 2000: 38). His administration also fought attempts by Republican feminists to change the party's rules to include positive action toward increasing women's representation

---

[2] Although Wolbrecht (2001: 174) notes that the National Organization for Women criticized Carter for not allocating sufficient resources to the ERA campaign.

(Wolbrecht 2000: 38–39), and he personally was hostile to women's rights (see, for example, Dean 2001: 104; Deckard 1983: 128).

Ford was a stronger personal supporter of women's rights than Nixon. During his tenure as president, he signed into law the Equal Credit Opportunity Act and the Women's Education Equity Act. His White House was often on the forefront of the ratification campaign for the Equal Rights Amendment; he hosted meetings with women's organizations to discuss the best strategy for assuring ratification of the ERA, and White House staff often spoke in support of the ERA at rallies and campaign events (Interviews, January 9, 2004 and October 16, 2003).

Ronald Reagan and George H.W. Bush, on the other hand, opposed many of the goals of the women's movement. Reagan was the first president, for example, to appoint fewer women than his predecessors. He opposed the Equal Rights Amendment and abortion rights, and his administration targeted some women's equity policies, specifically in education, for elimination. While George H.W. Bush was perhaps less fervent in his attacks on women's rights, he vetoed the Family Medical Leave Act and was strongly prolife. Thus, Reagan and Bush differentiated themselves from previous Republican administrations by being more clearly opposed to issues on the agenda of the women's movement (see Bashevkin 1998: 115–117).

As I show, there was also variation within each administration that can be attributed to the political appointees chosen by the president. The specific head of a department or agency often made an important difference. For example, several interviewees spoke glowingly about the directors of the Women's Bureau under Reagan and Bush. Lenora Cole Alexander, director of the Women's Bureau under Reagan, for example was seen as "a very independent thinker among Republicans.... They didn't know what to expect from her. I found out afterwards, that she was more independent in her thinking and had some ideas about women that maybe other people might take an issue with.... I would say that our strongest connections with women's groups were under Carter and [Alexander], even though it was a Republican administration" (Interview, October 10, 2002). On the other hand, other respondents noted specific appointees under Democratic administrations who weakened its otherwise strong record on women's rights. One was Clinton's education secretary, Richard Riley. Several respondents remembered that Riley's "support for gender equity issues was not particularly strong" (Interviews, March 8, 2004 and January 7, 2004). As we shall see, political appointees also make a significant difference in whether feminist activists stay in government during hostile regimes and what they do if they stay.

FEMINIST ACTIVISTS: EMBEDDING SYMPATHIZERS AND PURGING THE STATE

How were feminist activists in the federal government affected by changes in presidential administration? To explore this question, I look in this section at the civil servants among the people I interviewed. While political appointees are clearly tied to a specific presidential administration – leaving with the administration that appoints them – the entry and exit of civil servants from the federal government is formally separate from the presidential administration. Yet, there are a number of reasons we might expect the presence of feminist activists to be tied to the politics of the president. First, feminist activists are motivated in part by the ideological concerns they have, and so we might expect them to enter during sympathetic administrations and leave during hostile ones. Second, presidents and their administrators also recognize the importance of having sympathizers among the civil service as well as among political appointees. Ingraham (1995: 97), for example, notes that Nixon encouraged political appointees to help screen bureaucratic appointments as well. This leads to two sorts of activities by presidential administrations: the process of routing out civil servants that they find opposed to their agenda, and embedding individuals sympathetic with their own political agenda in civil servant positions. Finally, sympathetic presidential administrations might create new women's policy agencies, thereby inspiring feminist activists to enter the state and creating locations that demand their expertise.

Entering the Bureaucracy

Examining entering and exiting among civil servants is difficult. The career paths of civil servants at the middle and upper levels of the federal bureaucracy often include stints in the private sector (Heinz et al. 1993; Salisbury and Johnson 1989).³ Consistent with that, about 19% (six) of the thirty-two civil servants I interviewed "entered" the federal government multiple times.⁴ In addition, several individuals served both as civil servants and political appointees.

Many of the feminist activists I interviewed entered the bureaucracy in the early administrations (see Table 7.1). Six entered before the second wave of the women's movement began, and another eleven entered during the Kennedy–Johnson years. Eleven women entered the civil service during the Nixon administration and an additional four entered during the two-year Ford administration. Only two civil servants entered the bureaucracy during the Carter administration, while two entered during the Reagan administration. None of the feminist activists I interviewed took civil service positions during George H.W. Bush's administration, and only one took such a position during the Clinton administration.

There are a number of possible explanations for the decline in insider feminist activists during the later years. One possibility is that the timing of entering the bureaucracy corresponds with the most active, public phases of the women's movement.⁵ Perhaps women entered public service in the earlier years of the movement, and entrée into the bureaucracy tapered off as the initial publicity died down. Alternatively, the reduction in the number of women entering in these later years may reflect the nature of my snowball sample, which began with feminist activists from the early years and relies on others to identify them.⁶ Feminist activists in these later years may not have achieved the notoriety that leads them to be identified by others, or generational

---

³ Some women may also enter the bureaucracy first and become feminist activists after they are already civil servants. Because it is difficult to pinpoint when women became feminist activists, in the analysis below I look only at when the women I interviewed entered and exited from the bureaucracy.

⁴ For example, one individual that I interviewed began her career in the civil service, went into public service, and later became a political appointee. To focus on civil servants in Table 7.1, I include only entrances that were made as civil servants. Thus, for this individual and others, dates of entry and reentry into the civil service are noted, but not any political appointments.

⁵ I am grateful to an anonymous reviewer for pointing out this alternative to me.

⁶ It is also important to note that some of the women who entered the bureaucracy in these early years didn't become feminist activists until later.

TABLE 7.1. *Number of Feminist Activists Entering and Leaving Civil Service Positions by Presidential Administration*

Presidential Admin.	Entered pre-1960	Kennedy (1961–1963)	Johnson (1964–1968)	Nixon (1969–7/1974)	Ford (8/1974–1976)	Carter (1977–1980)	Reagan (1981–1988)	Bush 1 (1989–1992)	Clinton (1993–2000)	Bush 2 (2001–interview date)
Avg. Number Working	n.a.	6.3	10.6	20	22	23	19.25	12.5	7.375	3
Total Number Entering	6	1	10	11	4	2	3	0	1	n.a.
Total Number Leaving	1	1	1	6	1	1	11	2	8	n.a.
Avg. Hazard Rate of Leaving		0.048	0.025	0.049	0.024	0.011	0.071	0.036	0.139	n.a.

differences may have simply kept the networks of older women apart from newer civil servants. A third possibility is that the phenomenon results from increasing prospects for women's employment in the private sector, such as described among women lawyers in Chapter 2, which gave feminists other opportunities for satisfying careers.

Overall, the individuals that I interviewed were as likely to enter the civil service during Republican as Democratic administrations, although that finding is largely due to the large number who entered during the Nixon administration. However, these numbers do not include political appointments, which brought many feminist activists into the federal government during both the Carter and Clinton administrations.

Most of the activists who entered the civil service did so without viewing their entrance as a means of extending their activism. This was true of course for those respondents who joined before the women's movement had become a visible presence. However, many feminist activists also took jobs in government initially for career reasons rather than reasons of activism. These women did not view their jobs as part of their activism, regardless of how involved they were in the movement. For example, one of the respondents who entered government during the Nixon administration said: "I moved from New York to Washington with a one year job. I had no intent to go into government whatsoever. And my brother was here, and he suggested I fill out a 171 in case I should see a job I wanted, I would have my credentials, and I guess I never thought of that. I didn't want to work for the government; I mean we were always telling the government how wrong they were" (Interview, June 25, 2002).

On the other hand, other activists interviewed were clearly attracted by the chance to work within state institutions that dealt with issues important to the movement. For example, one activist just out of law school talked about her decision to enter the Equal Employment Opportunity Commission (EEOC):

As far as I could tell, it was the only place in the country where you could go and do women's rights work. So I applied. I got the job. I went. I was thrilled. I was already exposed to these issues. I had applied for a law firm. I got my offer with ... And I remember going and talking with the professor who ran the ... civil liberties program. And he really wasn't much help in terms of making up my mind. But somehow in the middle of that I decided to go with what attracted me the most. (Interview, October 17, 2003).

In some cases, activist networks provided connections to particular agencies and avenues for recruitment among activists. The result was that in some agencies there was a steady stream of activists recruited by the existing activists in the agency: "We got more to come. . . . Word of mouth, the same way with my successors working for [elected representative's name removed]. Some of them followed the same career. They worked . . . as women's rights assistants. Then they went to EEOC. It was all just word of mouth" (Interview, October 17, 2003).

Thus, feminist activists were more likely to enter the civil service during sympathetic presidential administrations, although not all sympathetic administrations were led by Democratic presidents. Many feminist activists entered during the Nixon and Ford presidencies as well. Moreover, not all feminist activists entered the civil service for reasons related to their activism although many did, often facilitated by networks of insider feminists.

Exiting the Bureaucracy

Were the feminist activists who entered government positions within the civil service more likely to leave under presidential administrations that were hostile to feminism? Table 7.1 also describes the number of activists who left the federal government under each administration, and reports the average hazard rate at which the feminist activists I interviewed left government. The hazard rate represents the relative risk of an insider feminist activist leaving during a particular year; it is calculated from my interviews by taking the ratio of people who left during a year and dividing by the number of feminist activist civil servants who were working in the bureaucracy in that year. Again the numbers describe only those who held nonappointed positions within government because political appointees are assumed to exit when an administration leaves office. As the fourth row of Table 7.1 suggests, feminist activists left the government during every administration and were no more likely to leave in Republican administrations. The highest rates of leaving were found in the Reagan and Clinton eras, and the lowest were during the administrations of President Johnson, Carter, and Ford.[7]

[7] I did not interview individuals about the George W. Bush presidency. However, at least one of the people I interviewed left during this administration, and several others mentioned that the climate was hostile to feminists who remained in the bureaucracy.

How can we account for the large number of activists leaving during the Reagan and Clinton administrations? In the case of the Clinton administration, the results are heavily affected by the demographics of the snowball sample itself. Because I began by interviewing women in the civil service during the rise of the women's movements in the 1960s, there were a large number of retirements during the Clinton era (six out of the eight people who left). Of the two other individuals who left, one left to pursue an advanced degree, and the other left for a private sector job. As a result, by the end of the Clinton administration there were very few activists from my sample who still worked in government (only four by 2000).

In the Reagan era there were fewer retirements and more individuals who attributed their departure directly to the administration. Of the eleven who left during this time, five appear to have left for normal career reasons. In these cases, the individuals did not mention hostility for leaving but rather explained their resignation from government jobs as a normal part of their careers. One person retired and the others moved on to other jobs. For example one activist noted that: "this really good friend who saw a job on sex discrimination called me and said 'There's an ad in the paper. I think you might like this job'" (Interview, October 17, 2003). While it is unclear what role the hostile administration played in making the private sector jobs look more attractive, in hindsight, these activists identified their exit from government as a career move.

Nonetheless, there were also three cases of civil servants who felt forced from their positions because of administrative policy. Two of the three people interviewed were working in the area of women's equality in education – an area particularly targeted by the Reagan administration. As I noted in Chapter 6, the program associated with the Women's Education Equity Act (WEEA) was specifically targeted by the Heritage Foundation and other conservative organizations, and Leslie Wolfe, WEEA's director was subject to a lengthy campaign to discredit and remove her (see also Faludi 1991: 259–263). "[T]hey abolished the job of director – and they offered me a job (it would have been at the same GS15 salary) as a GS3. That's what you do in the civil service. You can't just fire somebody.... And I said they could just take that job and give it to someone who needed it" (Interview with Leslie Wolfe, Fall 2003). A second person interviewed, who was working on women's equity in education in a different part of government, similarly reported being forced from her position.

Yet, even the Reagan government was unable to eliminate all of the feminist activists in government. Rather, much seemed to depend on whether the White House or the particular political appointee in a department or agency focused on eliminating particular types of civil servants. There were other places within government where civil servants were targeted: "Reagan appointed a bright young man... and he came in to clean house. He got rid of all the senior attorneys, but not me because I was protected by civil service.... So he decided that he would transfer me to the San Francisco office. I didn't want that and was eligible for retirement and so I retired" (Interview, March 25, 2002). In contrast, several others reported that the political appointees in their departments protected them. "I was not a political appointee. I was a fed. They came after me. There was a whole thing that happened where they alleged that I was using my office to do political work – which I was not.... We had one good woman who came from Minnesota. She was a Republican, but she actually protected me the couple years that she was there" (Interview, March 11, 2004). Other activists interviewed noted no pressure to leave their jobs, but suggested that other changes in the civil service (e.g., budget cuts) affected their decisions to leave.

In short, my interview data suggest that administrations have only a little impact on civil servants' decisions to leave the bureaucracy. Even during the Reagan administration, when there were clearly attempts to eliminate feminist activists from some positions, the interview evidence suggests that feminist activists had a range of experiences. Much depended on where activists were located. Administrations tend to focus on a few priorities, and in those particular areas – like education under the Reagan government – feminist activists found themselves clearly targeted by the administration. However, in other parts of the bureaucracy feminist activists could remain in a hostile administration because they were under the radar of political appointees who were focused on other issues, or because an administration's political appointees even supported their activities. The fact that such diversity of experiences exists clearly shows that the party in power, or even the presidential administration, does not determine the opportunities afforded feminist activists within the bureaucracy.

EXAMPLES OF FEMINIST ACTIVISM IN HOSTILE
ADMINISTRATIONS

Movement activists within the government are likely to be better informed than outsiders about many political opportunities. This high level of information is important because several theorists have argued that social movements must recognize the existence of political opportunities in order for these to affect social movement activities (Banaszak 1996; Sawyers and Meyer 1999). If movement activists within the state are most likely to be aware of the array of political opportunities within the bureaucracy, what activities do they engage in when administrations hostile to feminist ideals are at the helm?

Feminist activists who remained in government during administrations that were not sympathetic to feminist goals used a number of tactics to continue to advocate for women's rights. First and foremost, many used their offices' responsibility to provide information to the general public to inform outside activists about government actions that might threaten feminist interests. Second, when the administration clearly opposed some feminist policies, these activists attempted to further other feminist policies that might be deemed acceptable to the administration. Finally, some simply tried to work under the radar in ways that were helpful to the movement.

The Use of Information

Most departments and agencies have a mandate to provide information to the general public. Government offices charged with regulating, for example, are expected to provide information about the rules and regulations they propose and enforce. Other offices have, as their raison d'être, the production of knowledge that can inform decision making. All government offices are expected to freely provide information about changes or proposed changes in their operations to other parts of the government and to interested parties outside the state. Information, then, is a basic element in the functioning of a democratic government's bureaucracy, and the modern state produces huge amounts of information. For example, the 2007 *Federal Register* – one source of information about rules and regulations of the U.S. bureaucracy – contained over 74,400 pages.

Insider activists used this function of information dispersal to aid feminist causes during hostile administrations. Several of the individuals I interviewed mentioned using the power to inform in order to slow reversals in policy. For example, one activist noted that even though the administration would hide changes to existing legislation in among new proposed regulations, the following also occurred:

it was a long process with regulations and the proposed regulations in the *Federal Register* with weeks or months to comment on them. So you can talk to people, you can say . . . 'such and such a regulation will appear in the *Federal Register* next week.' We were allowed to say that and then they would read what was in the public record. (Interview, June 25, 2002)

Moreover, feminist activists in government offices whose principle purpose was to disseminate information often felt able to influence decisions by providing the right kind of evidence. For example, several feminists in the Women's Bureau argued that the research conducted by the Bureau had the power to alter debates regardless of the administration. One respondent argued that although George H.W. Bush opposed the Family and Medical Leave Act, the Women's Bureau's literature on the family leave already provided on the state level helped bolster arguments for the adoption of the act on the federal level and in additional individual states.

Yet even then, activists noted how important it was for the information to be carefully neutral. In the case of the research on state family leave policies, the activist noted that the Bureau was protected from charges of bias because the research became fodder for groups both for and against the Family and Medical Leave Act. While there were multiple examples of how dissemination of research helped the feminist cause, some attempts to provide information did result in serious consequences. One activist noted:

I developed an e-list of about 80 people within the Department of Education who said they were interested and wanted to get information on gender equity . . . I got in trouble once because I happened to forward something that was written by someone at the American Psychological Association saying that WEEA was in jeopardy and here were the reasons. If you want to do something about this, here is who to contact in the House and in the Senate. I sent it out to this list and put on the top of it – This Might Be of Interest. I didn't tell them to go do it. I was just sending information as I normally did. . . . Someone – I think I know who it was – sent it to a Congressman from Oregon . . . who was a conservative. He immediately wrote a letter to the Secretary that this was inappropriate behavior for a mid level bureaucrat to be doing and to fire me. I became a scapegoat. They took away a lot of my responsibilities and they never promoted me after that. (Interview, March 8, 2004)

Thus, providing information is one tactic feminist activists used. Although occasionally activists would be reprimanded for inappropriate behavior, information provision was considered a normal function of the bureaucracy and therefore could be used as a tactic regardless of the administration.

Conforming Their Goals to the Administration

A second tactic that feminist activists used under hostile administrations was to try to adapt their desire for action to the goals of the administration. In most cases, this was not difficult. As one activist told me:

I never felt that much [was] impacted by who was in the White House. . . . In the jobs I had, the stuff I was doing was pretty much mandated by federal regulation, if you could make a reasonable case. That's why it was important to figure out the kind of manager you had. If you had a 'Do Good' manager, you made one kind of a case, and if you had a 'Bottom Line' manager then you made another kind of a case. (Interview, May 10, 2002)

Another activist who worked as a legislative analyst argued that even under hostile administrations there was still a chance of shaping legislation: "you were trying to shape the language, sometimes just a phrase added to a sentence somewhere made the law more active" (Interview, June 25, 2002). For example, even in the Reagan administration, she argued that progress toward sexual equality was made because they were able to convince the administration to review and revise laws that mentioned sex differences.

Finally, when feminist activists were asked to conform, they often did as little as possible to meet the requirements of the administration. The example of the government's testimony on Title IX legislation, presented in Chapter 6, showed how minimally conforming to requests could have a positive effect on policy. In that case, a feminist activist, told to alter agency testimony from supporting Title IX to opposing it, changed only a few sentences and left much of the analysis of discrimination against women in education. The form this testimony took weakened the administration's ability to stop new legislation, because, as others in the education area noted, it encouraged support for the legislation and gave credence to those arguing such legislation was needed.

Several activists working in other policy areas also noted the importance of being able to develop the rhetoric that supported the administration's position. Even when they could not be as obvious as the case above, they argued that by making administrative positions more measured or by being able to portray opposite arguments in a better light, activists played an important role in providing fodder to the opposition.

Under the Radar

Finally, the federal government is a large bureaucracy, making it difficult for administrations to make sure that everything done by all of the agencies represents their positions. As one activist pointed out, this allows feminist activists under even the worst conditions to succeed "under the radar – slightly underground. . . . I think some people, people who know how to work their bureaucracy, know how to touch things in terms that are acceptable perhaps, can get some programs moving . . . where programs that are flexible in some ways, where certain things can be funded" (Interview, September 25, 2003).

A number of the feminist activists I interviewed discussed the idea of affecting change under the radar in the bureaucracy. One activist spoke with admiration about the ability of another feminist activist in government to get legislation through the administration and Congress. "What she did was that she drafted it so that if you look at it, it looks like what they call a technical amendment. Sometimes an 'and' is left out or a period is left out or a comma, so that the bill was meant to do something else but technically was wrong, so they had to fix it. What she did with this [piece of legislation] was make it look like a technical amendment. . . . And the Labor Department dropped the ball. They had no idea that their jurisdiction had changed substantially until after the bill was passed." (Interview, October 16, 2003). While no other activist mentioned such a major change that occurred under the radar, others spoke often of being able to influence the distribution of grants, the wording of minor regulations, and the scope of some programs because these things were not the focus of attention.

Individuals who had a supervisory layer above them were often protected from scrutiny or permitted some flexibility in their duties. This provided them with additional independence. For example, one activist mentioned that she: "had some male bosses who sort of weren't all that pleased with the Reagan Administration either. They sort of let me do a few equity things that were related to other things.... So I was able to pay some attention to equity issues, even though my key assignment was not gender equity" (Interview, March 8, 2004). From the standpoint of the feminist civil servants who served many years in office, supervisory staff who protected other forms of action were important to surviving hostile administrations.

Thus, there were many ways that feminist activists within the federal government continued to try to influence policy under hostile administrations. Although these activists were limited in terms of what they could reasonably do while maintaining their positions,[8] their hands were by no means tied. No matter what their beliefs or desire to implement policy, presidential administrations are unable to focus on all parts of the bureaucracy at once, leaving openings for actions by civil servants. Moreover, many government actions are governed by ongoing regulations or functions defined by a specific office's purpose or by larger democratic principles. All of these permit activists to take actions to help the movement within the bureaucracy even under adverse political conditions.

BUREAUCRATIC LOCATION AND ACTIVISM
IN DIFFERING ADMINISTRATIONS

The previous sections suggest that the tendency to view administrations as uniformly hostile is too broad a generalization. In addition

---

[8] Although civil servants rarely lost their jobs for such activities there were many ways to get rid of civil servants who attracted the attention of hostile administrations. Catherine East (1982: 178) describes such means when she discussed her own position: "People think I risked my job. I wouldn't have. I'd been in government too long and I had too good a record, but they would have reassigned me to something I didn't want to do, or wouldn't want to do as much."

to the variations across different feminist goals discussed above, two factors are important to the ability of feminist activists to act during seemingly hostile administrations. First, even when an administration is very hostile toward a social movement, it is unable to implement its ideology evenly across the whole of the federal government, leaving opportunities in some agencies for activists to operate. Second, political appointments enact presidential goals unevenly, creating variation among the overseers of different government offices.

In each administration, some agencies received greater scrutiny than others. It was clear that Reagan, especially in his first term, focused many efforts on removing feminist influences from the Department of Education. All of the feminist activists inside the federal government working in the area of educational equity for women noted that they faced greater scrutiny and pressure to leave during this period. As one feminist activist noted:

I always considered myself to be a member of the underground. In my case, it was difficult because I wasn't able to stay underground...I was under surveillance, the program was under surveillance, there was no way to sneak around and get things done in the appropriate bureaucratic way. (Interview, September 25, 2003)

Agencies that are targeted for change are more likely to receive the added scrutiny, constraining activists even more. The opposite is true under a friendly administration, being within government offices targeted for change provides additional opportunities for action (Banaszak 2005). In the end, this means that extra scrutiny often provides added opportunities under friendly administrations, but increases constraints under hostile ones.

While I have focused specifically on the scrutiny of the presidential administration, that scrutiny can also come from other elected officials, especially under conditions of divided government. In two cases, interviewees mentioned that intense scrutiny by a member of Congress constrained their activity. In one case an activist within the State Department during the Clinton administration noted that during a one-year period: "Everything – memos, mail, graphs, talking points, anything internal – had to go to [North Carolina Senator Jesse] Helms" (Interview, March 8, 2004). According to the individual, the added scrutiny caused every person in the Department to act cautiously, limiting what they would do or say. The result was that civil servants in the State Department during this period of Clinton's administration worked in a politically hostile environment even though they were part of a supportive presidential administration.

Finally, under any presidential administration there is variation in the degree to which individual political appointees convey the tenets of an administration. This occurs because political appointments are made for various reasons. For central departments the ideology of the appointee is likely to be important, but political appointees may also be chosen for their expertise in a particular field, their contribution to the president's campaign or to the political party, or to represent a specific community (Borelli 2000). As a result, throughout my interviews, activists uniformly argued that "the personality of the director and the background of the individual director" were more important than the presidential administration (Interview, January 28, 2004). For example, Catherine East (1982) who worked under both Republican and Democratic administrations noted that her supervisor influenced her ability to join feminist organizations. Even though the Kennedy and Johnson administrations had reputations for being open to feminists, East (1982: 208) noted that it was not until the Nixon administration that she was able to openly join feminist organizations: "I became a member of a number of them during Libby [Koontz]'s administration. Libby was very happy that I had ties with these organizations and used them all of the time." Thus, the constraints on feminist activists within the state were most strongly related to the values and priorities of political appointees. Particular appointees might be very approachable and might protect activists under their supervision from potential retaliation. Yet, even when political appointees were vigilant on an issue, it is also true that layers of bureaucracy can protect activity further down the chain of command.

CONCLUSIONS

This analysis of feminist activists working inside government under hostile administrations suggests we need to reexamine our tendency to judge whole presidential administrations as hostile or sympathetic.

One of the things this chapter shows is that feminist activists are located within the state, even under administrations that are especially hostile to feminism – like the presidencies of Ronald Reagan and George W. Bush. It is true that under the conscious efforts of the Reagan administration, many feminist activists were forced out or pushed out through the creation of a chilly climate. Nonetheless, more activists remained in the state through the Reagan years than left because of it.

Moreover, although insider feminists' abilities to act were constrained during hostile administrations, their feminism continued to influence their activities. These insider activists served as an important resource to the movement during hostile administrations, providing vital information to feminists on the outside and continuing to encourage feminist policies in small ways.[9] While we tend to think of insider feminists existing only under sympathetic administrations, this research suggests that there is still value to being an insider even under the most hostile administration.

Finally, the major argument of this chapter is that the tendency of social movement scholars to focus on the party in power or on presidential administrations is problematic. In the social movement literature, it is common to view turnovers in administration as new opportunities (see, for example, Burstein 1999: 17–18). My research suggests that a more nuanced view is needed. The arrival of a hostile administration does not signal a complete loss of opportunities just as the arrival of a sympathetic one does not provide unlimited opportunities. In looking at the political opportunities afforded by an administration, we need to take into account the uneven nature of administrative scrutiny, the autonomy of civil servants in many of their daily activities, and the diversity of people appointed by presidents to represent their administrations. Taken together, these three factors mean that, at any moment in time, when we look at the openness of the state to social movements, *a range of political opportunities* exist. Even during apparently closed political administrations there will be some opportunities for positive action. Rather than assume

---

[9] Oral histories from outside feminist activists during this time show that they also echo some of the same themes, particularly the necessity of reducing the erosion of existing policies and the importance of small victories (see Bashevkin 1998: Chapter 4).

bureaucratic responsiveness to administrative desires as many of those who measure political opportunities do, it would be better to locate the specific areas of the bureaucracy responsible for influencing movement goals and determine the degree to which that bureaucracy is under administrative scrutiny, is led by hostile or friendly political appointees, and can count insider activists among its civil servants.

8

What Insider Feminists Tell Us about Women's Movements, Social Movements, and the State

In 1975, Jo Freeman, looking at a vibrant and active women's movement, concluded:

There is clearly a symbiotic relationship between feminists within our governmental institutions, feminists operating in the private sphere, and even feminists who are openly opposed to and/or alienated from the American political system. (230)

The preceding chapters confirm this observation and describe in detail the sector of the second wave women's movement that operated inside the federal government. I have shown how insider feminist activists – embodying the intersection between the women's movement and the state – played a significant role in the remobilization of the women's movement and in the development of many of the policies we have today. This group of insider feminist activists has been largely overlooked by scholars who have written about the women's movement. The inattention to insider feminist activists is partly because of scholars' and activists' preconceived notions that movements and states are antithetical and partly because many of these insiders worked under the radar and were known only to a small number of activists and government employees. Although hidden from public view, these insider feminist activists were nonetheless an important part of the women's movement.

One goal of this book is to describe this sector of the movement and the women who comprised it. This will, I hope, allow these activists' stories to be included with those of other important feminist activists, adding to our knowledge of the diversity of this key part of U.S. social history. By examining feminist activists inside the U.S. government, I hope also to contribute to the comparative study of insider feminist activity, providing both a different perspective on the concept of state feminism, and supplementing current knowledge of how insider feminists contribute to the development of feminist policies around the globe. My third purpose is to show that our understanding of social movements generally is enhanced if we discard a rigid demarcation between social movements and the state. Instead, I maintain that we can better understand *all* social movements if we view the movement–state intersection as a central theoretical concept with identifiable dimensions, and examine the degree to which movement–state intersections vary from movement to movement, and over time within the same movement. These three purposes are complementary and spur a number of substantive conclusions.

THE ROLE OF INSIDERS WITHIN THE U.S. WOMEN'S MOVEMENT

Although the second wave of the U.S. women's movement has been the subject of many scholarly works, the role of insider activists is not widely appreciated. Feminist activism after 1920, I have shown, laid the groundwork for a small but well-placed network of insider feminist activists by 1960. Women's organizations during the 1920s, 1930s, 1940s, and 1950s recognized the importance of women in the federal bureaucracy and fought for women's place within the state. This push for women's inclusion, along with opportunities created because the needs of the American state required women's employment, produced a network of (overwhelmingly white) feminists within the federal government even before the second wave arose. This network included women who were active in organizations that pursued feminist policies well before the movement coalesced in the 1960s, as well as civil servants who were not originally feminists when they entered the state but were converted to feminism as events unfolded.

These insider feminists played an important role in the mobilization of the second wave of the women's movement. Feminist activists inside the state had the information and resources that helped to mobilize women as the second wave began in the 1960s. They were certainly central to the creation of the National Organization for Women but they also spawned other feminist organizations as well.

In contrast to what some might have predicted, the groups that insider feminists helped to organize did not reflect a preference for hierarchical modes of organization, incremental change, or exclusively conventional tactics. Like their cohorts outside of the state, insider feminists created different types of organizations – particularly in the initial years of the movement. In addition to building general feminist organizations pursuing social change, insider feminist activists organized themselves within government to help to create a state whose practices and policies better reflected feminist principles. While many of these organizations focused on the things that affected insider feminist activists the most – the employment and promotion practices within the federal bureaucracy – their influence often reverberated outside the state as well, as the example of feminist activists within the National Institutes of Health shows.

Feminist activists inside the state were more diverse than scholars have assumed, although they represented a less diverse spectrum than the women's movement as a whole. Contrary to expectations, feminist activists within the state were not always supportive of established institutions or reformist in their goals; much of the ideological diversity found in the larger feminist movement could be found in the ideology of insider feminist activists. While liberal feminism was more prevalent among insider feminist activists, many were strong critics of the very institutions for which they worked. In that sense, they represented the diverse set of interests of the women's movement, though in other ways – particularly their race, class, and education – they constituted a very limited slice of the women's movement as a whole.

The evidence also contradicts the notion that feminist activists inside the state were married to conventional political tactics. Insider feminist activists were willing to engage in confrontation. Even consummate insiders like Catherine East strongly supported the use of confrontational tactics by the women's movement. What did differentiate insider feminist activists from their outsider counterparts was their keen sense of both the political opportunities available through the American state, and when and how outside forces could successfully assert their influence on government actors. With this information, insider feminist activists encouraged the use of conventional tactics when they were convinced that they had greater probabilities of success. As other scholars have suggested, they also occasionally were able to direct resources from the state to the movement.

However, their insider status also provided these feminist activists with privileged information about where access through normal political channels was blocked. In these cases, we see insider feminist activists choosing two other courses of action. First, like outside feminist activists, they took to the streets. Where insider activists saw the possibilities for change limited by institutions or by state personnel, they did not hesitate to mobilize the feminist movement (including themselves) to protest. Second, insider feminist activists also found ways of employing one part of the state to counteract political constraints elsewhere within the state, as when insider feminist activists used the Federal Communications Commission to fight the battles of a hamstrung Equal Employment Opportunity Commission.

Nonetheless, there were limits to the policies that insiders sought. Most insider feminist activists pursued policies that affected themselves directly. As is to be expected given their occupations, they were more educated and economically better off than the average woman in the United States. As such, they largely focused on those aspects of the feminist agenda that reflected the needs of middle-class white women: equal opportunity issues, rather than issues of poverty for example. And while many mentioned their activity in the early civil rights movement, few beyond the insider activists of color mentioned sustained activity on issues related to race. Thus, the agenda of insider feminist activists was often limited, influencing policy change in some issue areas, but leaving others virtually untouched.

Although there was considerable diversity in their efforts, one common theme was that feminist activists inside the state were able to take advantage of a very different set of political opportunities than their outsider counterparts. The routine operation of the state provided chances for effecting policy change that generally go unnoticed outside the state. In addition, because feminists sought fundamental change in the treatment of women in all institutions and policy areas, insider feminist activists could utilize opportunities in any part of the state, meaning that reforms in any policy arena (like the changes in foreign policy focus during the 1970s mentioned in Chapter 6) might serve as openings to create feminist policies. The widespread nature of women's interests also protected insider feminist activists under hostile administrations and allowed small agencies, commissions, and offices representing feminist interests to be spread throughout the state. Additional political opportunities were available to insider feminist activists because of the nature of the state, which provided prospects for action in the routine operations and transformations that occur within the bureaucracy. While many of the policy changes insider feminist activists achieved appear to be small and incremental (especially vis-à-vis the large regulatory American state), some of them had significant substantive effects on women's social, economic, or political status.

Nonetheless, these findings should not be interpreted as providing support for the argument that the women's movement should focus only on entering the state, nor as suggesting that other parts of the feminist movement were somehow less important than insider feminists. As Van Dyke and her colleagues (2004) rightly have noted, feminism does not concentrate only on the state, nor should it. Scholars who study state feminism note that state-directed change is unlikely to be completely consistent with feminist ideals. Because their facility in negotiating political opportunities within the state leads insider feminist activists to concentrate on policy change, the women's movement also requires an outside independent movement. The insider feminists that I studied understood that. Indeed, they knew that even changing internal state policy required an independent women's movement outside the state. Thus, suggesting insider feminists were important to the U.S. women's movement is not the same as advocating only for insider activists. However, a strong, independent women's movement can and did benefit from insiders within the state. I see this argument as an important corrective to those activists and scholars who have on occasion eschewed insiders. The feminist activists inside the state whom I studied were not simply bureaucratic sympathizers; they identified with the movement and acted like the movement activists they were. Although their actions were not always attractive to outside activists and are difficult to study because they are hidden, insider feminists need to be counted among the diverse groups that make up the modern women's movement.

Taken as a whole, the archival, documentary, and interview evidence that I compiled shows that a thorough understanding of the second-wave women's movement requires that we look at feminist activists inside the state. This initial examination both validates some of the assumptions held about insiders and suggests some revisions in how we view them in relation to the U.S. women's movement. It also suggests a different perspective for understanding state feminism in a comparative context.

IMPLICATIONS FOR THE COMPARATIVE STUDY OF STATE FEMINISM AND "FEMOCRATS"

While this study draws from the wisdom of work on women's policy agencies and "femocrats" in other countries, it examines the same questions from a slightly different perspective. In many comparative studies of state feminism, the focus is often on state institutions and the policies they implement. When the role of women's movements is examined, it is often from the viewpoint of whether they establish strong and enduring agencies that implement feminist policies. Thus, the concern is one of building state institutions, rather than in the existence of individual feminist activists inside the government bur-eaucracy. Even when insider feminist activists are examined, they are often discussed as part and parcel of the offices they inhabit. Here, I focus on the insider activists who are part of the larger women's movement, rather than the bureaucratic institutions creating women's policy. While this choice is dictated by my interest in social move-ments, I would argue that both the bureaucratic structures and the individual activists are important to understanding the success of the women's movement in creating public policy, but that they tell very different stories. Agencies and offices whose mandate is to engage in feminist policies create opportunities for the outside movement to be included in the state. Yet, without some support from inside the state, these women's policy agencies can be marginalized or find it difficult to create substantive policy change. Insider feminist activists can func-tion within a bureaucracy without feminist structures and they can effect meaningful change in agencies not traditionally linked to issues of gender, family, or civil rights (as the American example shows). My research also shows that the creation of bureaucratic structures that focus on feminist issues provides opportunities for insider feminists to act.

However, focusing on a specific part of the state rather than on individual feminist activists provides a very different view of how feminists can influence the state. In the United States, the policy agencies that are designated as devoted to women's issues are not particularly influential when they are compared to other countries. For example, although the Women's Bureau is one of the oldest "women's policy agencies," it is relatively weak and has a very limited portfolio (Stetson 1995; see also Laughlin 2000). Other offices covering "women's issues" are also relatively small and are focused on specific issues like education or foreign aid. Thus, comparative studies of women's policy agencies generally find that the United States is not particularly strong in the creation of such institutions. On the other hand, the few *comparative* studies of individual feminist activists inside government bureaucracies find that U.S. insider feminists were more numerous and more able to engage in creating feminist policies (see, for example, von Wahl 1999). Together, these findings suggest that a better understanding of feminism within the state requires examining both the individuals who occupy positions within the state and the bureaucratic structures that are created to implement feminist policy.

Studies of individuals in government bureaucracies have been conducted in other countries, but their foci have differed considerably from this study. Many other studies examine women bureaucrats, either in women's policy agencies or throughout the government bureaucracy as a whole. This research speaks to important issues of gender and sex differences among political actors. But because such women cannot be assumed to be feminists even when they occupy important positions in women's policy agencies, it cannot tell us much about feminist activism inside the state. The few studies of insider feminists have tended to look at a select group – usually top level political appointees or those that enter women's policy agencies. But as Angelika von Wahl (1999: 33) notes, women's movement issues are dealt with throughout the state. Thus, reducing our focus to the praxis and policies of those locations that are specifically designated as focusing on women ignores the policies that are made in other locations within the state. In addition, much feminist activity within the state will be invisible in studies that focus only top level insider feminists – such as political appointees. As I have suggested in this book, insider feminists who are political appointees are *least* able to act as movement activists while inside the state because their positions are much more precarious and their initial appointments are often based on their loyalty to the governing party (or parties). Such appointees also receive much more scrutiny than civil servants and for that reason it is more difficult for them to act – as many of the insider feminist activists studied here – under the radar. Thus, methodologically, the work here suggests that those researchers studying "femocrats" within government bureaucracies need to cast a wide net to truly understand the ways that individual feminist activists employed within the state influence state policy.

Finally, as feminist scholars, it is also important that we take care in how we label and treat insider feminist activists. Just as women have themselves been excluded by labels and language, so to feminist activists within the government should not be marginalized from the women's movement as a whole. The insider feminist activists I researched saw themselves as movement activists even as they were employed as bureaucrats. As a result, they consistently acted as part of the larger movement, often against the interests of the bureaucracies where they worked. Separating these women from the movement not only reduces our understanding of how the women's movement has shaped our destiny and contributes to the tendency to conflate the presence of feminist activists inside the bureaucracy with insider strategies, but it also unnecessarily erects barriers that divide the movement. Defining insider feminist activists as part of the movement increases our understanding of the agency that the women's movement has, and creates a more complete picture of the women's movement and its effects.

IMPLICATIONS FOR THE STUDY OF CONTENTIOUS POLITICS IN DEMOCRATIC STATES

This examination of feminist activists inside the U.S. federal bureaucracy also can do much to inform the study of social movements and our understanding of democratic politics more generally. Movements are typically defined by their wide mobilization – they exist beyond the confines of individual organizations or even coalitions of organizations – and by their exclusion from normal political channels that leads them to engage in confrontational political actions. Yet, such definitions do not preclude the intersection of movements with the state. I have focused on the fuzzy boundary between social movements and the state in order to better understand the nature of social movements and their implications for democratic politics.

Although this book explores just a single case study, the evidence suggests that studying movement emergence, activities, and outcomes will be enhanced by attention to movement–state intersections. The character of this overlap can influence important aspects of movement mobilization, such as the development of national organizations. Similarly, I have argued that some movement outcomes resulted from the activities of insider feminist activists. All of this implies that a focus on movement–state intersections should be a part of all analyses of social movements. However, two areas of inquiry may find the movement–state intersection especially illuminating: studies of social movement institutionalization and studies of political opportunity structures.

Movement Institutionalization

The evidence suggests that we may need to revise and improve our understanding of movement institutionalization. While scholars vary in how they define the process by which movements become institutionalized, one common definition sees the process as involving increasing alliance with and entry into the state (Walker n.d.). My research suggests that entry into the state cannot define movement institutionalization because movements can intersect with the state even at initial stages before "institutionalization" can take place. Nonetheless, movements do change over time, and many movements – often those who enjoy some initial successes – undergo similar processes that involve a reduced emphasis on protest, a bureaucratization of movement organizations, and the modulation of radical ideology.

If increasing entrée into the state cannot account for movement institutionalization, as my research suggests, what, then, can explain this process that occurs in many movements over time? One possibility of course is that institutionalization does not occur because of the movement–state intersection but depends on other factors. For example, as Walker (n.d.: 29) suggests, organizational demands such as concerns about organizational survival may come to dominate social movement activity over time, leading to other forms of institutionalization such as routinized interactions with the state. Alternatively, institutionalization of movements may require a particular type of movement–state intersection, one that was absent at the beginning of the U.S. women's movement. For example, it may be that activists must be located within specific institutions focused on movement goals in order for the movement–state intersection to contribute to movement institutionalization. In this case institutionalization may be accelerated by government institutions directly linked to the movement, such as the development of a Department of Labor or an Office of Faith Based Initiatives. The creation of a movement–state intersection through organizations or state bureaucratic institutions would explain the move toward institutionalization.

The analyses presented earlier suggest that another potential explanation for movement institutionalization may be the nature of movement successes. The need to defend previously won gains has transformed feminist politics – in part – from a movement demanding change to one defending the status quo. It is not just that there are more insider feminist activists than there were at the beginning of the movement (although there are). Rather feminist activists both inside and outside the state seek to defend state policies from attacks by countermovements, interest groups, and presidential administrations seeking to change those policies. As a result, feminists increasingly find themselves fighting battles for state policy using conventional tactics and seeking to minimize radical change (at least those that would dismantle feminist policies).

The analyses here suggest that movement institutionalization does not just consist of increased movement-state intersections, but it does not solve the puzzle of the processes by which institutionalization occurs. However, my research suggests that detailed and, ideally, comparative analyses of movements that include an examination of movement–state intersections will help us ascertain which characteristics might be responsible for the process of institutionalization.

Revisiting Political Opportunities

Political opportunities that are exogenous to social movements have been a staple of social movement research since the seminal works of Eisinger (1973) and McAdam (1982). Even as social movement scholars have expanded the concept of opportunities (see, for example,

Andersen 2004; Gamson and Meyer 1996; McCammon et al. 2001),
social movement scholars have typically placed the many components
of the state in the category of political opportunities – the environment within which social movements operate. This conceptualization
is born of the view that movements and states are mutually exclusive
entities, and the state is part of the movement's environment. Examining the intersection of the women's movement and the state has led
me to suggest three revisions to our understanding of political opportunities.

First and foremost I have argued here that we cannot merely label
the state as political opportunity because movement–state intersections
mean that some state-based political opportunities are in fact parts of
the movement itself. Increasingly, social movement scholars such as
Gamson and Meyer (1996: 275) have warned against creating overly
broad definitions of political opportunities. I argue that the tendency
to label movement–state intersections as political opportunities contributes to this problem. Keeping the movement and the state distinct
while recognizing the possibility of their *intersection* allows us to avoid
over expanding the concept of political opportunities, and simultaneously recognizes the agency of movement members, as Goodwin and
Jasper (2003) suggest.

But it is not only the mislabeling of insider movement activists that
minimizes the agency of the movement. Social movement scholars have
long recognized that movements actively create their own opportunities. In this case study, the focus on the movement–state intersection
shows that *many* important political opportunities were endogenous –
created by the actions of activists. Outsider feminists fought to increase
access to the civil service, creating the conditions that allowed the
movement–state intersection to exist. But the more interesting cases
are where insider activists create a new bureaucratic institution or
regulation that has clear impacts on the outside sector of the movement. For example, insider feminist activists were instrumental in the
creation of the Office of Women in Development which, in turn, supported feminist research and organizations outside the state. In these
cases, earlier movement outcomes become the political opportunities
for later movement action and mobilization. Many of the political
opportunities created by the movement can be attributed at least partially to the actions of insider activists, which suggests that a great

many political opportunities will be properly recognized as endogenous once scholars look closely at the intersection between movements and states.

Finally, my research shows that insider feminists faced a somewhat different array of political opportunities than outsider feminists; their political opportunities were both more context specific and were tied to the functioning of the state. Presidential administrations still played a role as other social movement scholars have claimed: Some administrations greatly constrained feminist activism while others did much to encourage it. Although there was some connection to the political party of the administration, parties also changed considerably over this period. It was harder, for example, for Republican women to identify as feminists in the Reagan years than during the Nixon administration. Thus, party alone was not a reliable indicator of constraint.

But this generalization hides considerable variation *even within the same movement at a specific time*. In any presidential administration, the political opportunities available to insider movement activists were not uniform across the U.S. bureaucracy. During administrations openly hostile to feminism, there were islands of opportunity for action. Some of these opportunities resulted from sympathetic supervisors who allowed feminist activists to continue their work under the radar. Other opportunities occurred because hostile administrations could only focus on a few major issues at one time; with feminist activists throughout the state, it was difficult in antifeminist administrations to root out all feminist activity. Thus, in hostile administrations, insider activists were occasionally able to take advantage of opportunities, and in sympathetic administrations they might find themselves heavily constrained.

Moreover, many political opportunities for movement–state intersections are found in the everyday operation of the state bureaucracy. For example, insider feminist activists took advantage of reauthorizations of foreign aid legislation to insert gender concerns into U.S. foreign policy. During hostile administrations they utilized bureaucratic regulations to protect gains that were already written into policy. These political opportunities were available only to those within the federal bureaucracy who had both knowledge of these opportunities and were well placed to take advantage of them. Scholars already have acknowledged that political opportunities are specific to the movement and to the dependent variable being explained (e.g., mobilization or outcomes), but my findings suggest that, in fact, political opportunities differ even within the movement itself, as Meyer (2004: 141) also suggests. In delineating how a particular sector of one specific social movement – in this case the part that intersects with the state – has access to different sets of political opportunities than other sectors of the movement, my research suggests the necessity of an intramovement examination of political opportunities that includes a focus on movement–state intersections.

Conceptualizing Movement-State Intersections and Their Effects

While I examine only a single case, my work suggests that a number of dimensions of the intersection between a social movement and the state might be important in explaining movement development or movement influence on policy. One clearly relevant dimension is simply the *relative size* of this intersection in relation to the movement – that is how many movement actors or organizations are inside the state. Included under this dimension is, of course, the case where no intersection between movement and state occurs at all.

Second, in thinking about such intersections it is necessary to consider *location* within the state. Are insider activists sequestered in "policy ghettos"? Are activists occupying a range of jobs reflecting substantial authority and access to policy making? In the case of the women's movement, I have argued that relevant policy is made throughout the state and not just in agencies that deal specifically with women's issues. Insider feminist activists were advantaged because they were diffused throughout the federal bureaucracy, and hence, had access to a multitude of offices where they could seek social change. However, this suggests that examining the location of the movement–state intersection can only be done within the context of the specific demands of the movement. Locating activists throughout the bureaucracy will not be useful for all social movements. For example, in the course of my archival research I ran across an organization in the National Institutes of Health called the Vietnam Moratorium Committee (Walsh 1972). The discussions of their activities suggested that this peace movement organization acted no differently from organizations outside the state; it used a mixture of protest and petition to try to influence the end of the war. Although the organization was composed of movement insiders, their location – in a part of the state uninvolved in making policies about the war – did not allow them to effect change in the way that feminist insiders at the NIH could. Thus, the importance of location is related to the goals of the movement, and the feminist movement has benefited from being able to use many locations within the state in order to advance its goals.

It is important to emphasize that I have also chosen to focus only on the bureaucracy as a location within the state. Studies of the democratic state have often begun with the bureaucracy because it is that part of the state most insulated from societal effects. Yet, if we are to truly understand the effects of movement-state intersections, we need also to focus on the overlap in other areas. Movement–state intersections can occur in the form of elected officials, judges, and nongovernmental organizations pulled into the state. In nations characterized by federalism, location in subnational governments may also be important. Each of these is likely to provide different opportunities to the movement and have different influences on policy and the state. My work suggests that there are linkages across these different venues in the state. In the specific cases examined in this book, insider feminists in the bureaucracy often worked with those in Congress – both staff and elected officials. The interaction across different venues in the state may be consequential for the movement and for insider feminists, but we cannot know unless we focus on insiders in these other areas as well.

Second, *timing* also plays an important role in understanding movement–state intersections. I have argued here that a network of feminist activists existed within the state even at the initial stages of the second wave of the women's movement, but movements will likely differ as to when intersections with the state develop. The research here suggests that the U.S. women's movement was greatly advantaged by the early development of its intersection with the state. The existence of a movement–state intersection in the early 1960s actually helped the women's movement to mobilize. But the timing, as it is relative to changes in the state, may also be important. In this view, the deciding factor may not be that the movement–state intersection was in place from the beginning of the movement but rather that it was in place as new bureaucratic structures – like the Equal Employment

Opportunity Commission – were created. Larger change in the bureau-cratic organization of the state is irregular, but such change represents a great opportunity for insider activists. More careful examinations of the timing of movement–state intersections vis-à-vis the mobilization of other movements or the creation of new agencies are necessary to understand how movement–state intersections influence the political fortunes of a movement.

Third, this study suggests that the *representativeness of movement–state intersections* relative to the movement as a whole has important consequences. In examining insider feminist activists I focused on their social characteristics, ideology, and tactical repertoires, arguing that these characteristics account for successes in the area of equal employ-ment but may also explain the lack of feminist policy change in other areas such as welfare policies. However, given the nature of recruit-ment into government bureaucracies, it is likely that all movement–state intersections are likely to contain an upper-middle-class bias. This suggests that movements representing poor people are least likely to benefit from movement–state intersections. In this sense, movement–state intersections are no different from the bias we see in formal advocacy organizations (Strolovich 2007).

Finally, the *formalization* of the movement–state intersection is undoubtedly important. I focused here on individual feminist activists who were either networked through common memberships in other groups or who forged their own networks once they began working in government. But as I note in Chapter 1, the intersection of social movements and states may also occur in the form of social movement organizations that take on state functions. For example, Smith and Lipsky (1993) note that social movement organizations – like those that advocate against domestic violence – can become part of the state when they are contracted to provide state services. Social movement organizations that intersect with the state may act differently from the informal networks that I study here, and they are likely to experi-ence different constraints and opportunities. Hence, additional studies are necessary to examine how the formalization of such intersections affects their activities and policy effects.

All of this suggests, however, that the movement–state intersection merits considerably more study as a significant *variable* (or set of variables) in social movement research than it has been given to date. While my study finds that insider feminist activists played an important role in the U.S. women's movement, we need to know if and how these findings can be generalized to all social movements.

IMPLICATIONS FOR UNDERSTANDING THE AMERICAN STATE

The results of this study also have implications for our understanding of the American state. Older debates about the state focus on whether the state is an autonomous actor or whether states are fundamentally tools of societal interests. These debates occurr in different literatures, sometimes examining whether social classes determine the actions of the state (see, for example, Miliband 1969) and sometimes looking at whether interested parties can "capture" specific parts of the state for their own purposes (e.g., Stigler 1975). I demonstrate that, at least in the United States, the state is influenced by specific interests even as it also acts autonomously in relation to society.

Recent scholarship on the state focuses on understanding the way that state interests develop, specifically how state interests become imbued with particular racial or gendered orders (King and Smith 2005; Ritter 2006). Here movement-state intersections may play important roles in altering the state, particularly in changing the descriptive and substantive representation of groups among state actors, which likely affects how democratic states see their interests. Chapter 2 describes several aspects of descriptive representation, but one effect of the women's movement has been also to increase women's substantive representation in a number of areas where their voices were silent, as when insider activists helped to change the focus of foreign development aid. Similarly, insider feminists contributed to the multiplication of women's policy agencies in the U.S. bureaucracy. For example, the Office of Women in Development and the Women's Educational Equity Act Program both resulted in large part from the actions of insider feminists. Feminist scholars are rightly cautious in interpreting the existence of these offices as evidence of real change because their actual connection to women's movement goals can vary greatly as can their ability to influence actual policy (Mazur 1995; Stetson and Mazur 1995). Nevertheless, these offices have become relatively permanent parts of the state. A closer look at movement–state intersections can therefore contribute to our understanding of the development of the gender and racial orders of the state.

However, the story of the intersection between the U.S. women's movement and the state also illustrates that larger societal forces play a role in the development of the gender and racial orders of the state. My research shows that state actors were not immune to the changes in gender roles that occurred outside the state. The intersection between the movement and state arose not only because feminist activists infiltrated the state but also because the mobilization of the women's movement influenced state actors as well, converting some of them into insider activists. Thus, while the state is an autonomous actor, and never simply mirrors society, it is affected by the social forces occurring outside the state. The question that remains is when and how the state is altered by these forces and how their influence plays out on state actions and capacity.

In examining the intersection between the U.S. women's movement and the state I found that many of the demands on the state from movement activists also helped to build state capacity and bring new powers to the state. The adoption of at least some of the women's movements demands has increased the American state's power, particularly over the private sphere. But I have focused here only on the U.S. women's movement and the American state is subject to a number of different intersecting interests that have come to be represented within the American state. These intersecting interests give rise, I believe, to many of the contradictions that occur within the American state. Thus, as insider feminist activists injected feminist ideology into state actions, they also created conflict within the state on issues of gender.

Thus, movement–state intersections help to explain the long-term development of the gendered and racial character of the American state as well as the contradictions that arise within the state itself. However, to truly understand both the contradictions and the state's long-term development, scholars need to turn increasingly to studies of the intersection of race, class, and gender within the American state. Here, the concept of movement–state intersections may help parse out the varying influences within the state and contribute to a better understanding of the long-term development of state interests.

WHERE DO WE GO FROM HERE?

There is still much work to be done to understand the causes and consequences of movement-state intersections. Yet, in the course of my archival research, it became clear that movement–state intersections are ubiquitious across a wide range of movements. As I poured through archival material, I ran across numerous examples of activists from other movements employed by the federal bureaucracy and who mobilized both inside and outside of the state. From the Vietnam Moratorium Committee of NIH mentioned previously to Federal Employees for a Democratic Society, many movements have intersected with the American state. In addition, existing literature on social movement organizations shows that these increasingly contracted with the state to take on state functions (Banaszak, Beckwith, and Rucht 2003; Smith and Lipsky 1993), creating other sources of movement–state intersections. These examples are evidence that the intersection between movements and the state is not simply a feminist phenomenon.

Indeed, many of the political controversies that appeared during the presidency of George W. Bush suggest that conservative movements are increasingly recognizing the usefulness of movement–state intersections. From the tempest surrounding the hiring and firing of United States attorneys in the Department of Justice to the resignation of Dr. Susan Wood from the Office of Women's Health in the National Institutes of Health because of political interference in the office's deliberations, there is evidence that conservative movements are also increasingly intersecting with the state and operating under the radar.

In addition, changes in the state bureaucracy appear to provide religious and the new right movements with increased opportunities for movement–state intersections. For example, the development of the Office of Faith-Based and Community Initiatives and the Department of Homeland Security created new government bureaucracies that may enlarge the intersection between conservative movements and the state. These events have occurred even as feminist activists continue to inhabit positions within the federal bureaucracy. The result has been increasingly publicized contentious politics occurring inside the state, with insiders mobilizing outside activists when needed. What remains to be seen is the degree to which insider conservative activists are now working under the radar, and whether, if they remain in these offices, they will operate in ways that are similar to insider feminists. Focusing on the movement–state intersection in this case may give us a better understanding of the development, particularly the institutionalization, of conservative movements, which have made significant inroads into the state in the last eight years. This means we need to compare the state–movement intersection across movements in order to truly understand the role that activists within the state play.

Because recruitment into the bureaucracy and the rules that govern the behavior of individuals once inside differ by country, we also need to examine movement–state intersections in different countries. For example, the number of political appointees is higher in the United States than in the United Kingdom, which in turn is higher than in Germany (King 1995: 9). This suggests that networks of movement activists among the civil service in these countries might play an even greater role than they do in the United States. Similarly, rules like the Hatch Act that govern the political behavior of civil servants also determine what movement–state intersections will look like and how they will act. Some other countries put much greater restraints on the political activities of their civil service. For example, the German Radikalenerlass of 1972 forbids civil servants from engaging in political activity considered antithetical to the German state even on their own time. This rule was used to limit the entry of certain types of activists into the state (Braunthal 1990; Kvistad 1988). In order to generalize about the role of movement–state intersections in contentious politics we need to examine their development and their effects under very different political systems.

This book provides an initial step toward a theoretical perspective that incorporates an understanding of both movements and states as diverse entities with multiple points of intersection. Future comparisons across movements and comparisons of parallel movements in different countries, will better illuminate the ways that movements and states intersect, and the policy consequences of that intersection. As this book shows, ignoring movement–state intersections impoverishes our understanding of movements and their power, of the complex nature of the American state, and of how feminists have altered American society.

Appendix: Supplemental Information about the Research Design

To understand movement–state intersections and their effect on social movement development and policy outcomes, I have chosen to focus on a single case – the United States women's movement. The choice of a case study design of one movement in a single country was one of both practicality and research design. Given the fact that many of the major discussions of insiders within the social movement literature involve the institutionalization of the movement – a process that occurs over time – I realized early on that the theoretical framework required analyses that could be done over time. I began by trying to identify data sets of civil servants that might include information about insider activists, their activities and organizational membership outside the bureaucracy, and which spanned multiple time points. I searched for such data and evidence both crossnationally and within the United States. After considerable effort, I came to the realization that finding a sample of insider activists through a larger sample of civil servants was not possible. Of course, random samples of movement activists are also not readily available, particularly at multiple points in time. Once I narrowed my case to the U.S. women's movement, it was still not possible to develop random samples of insider feminist activists. The few samples of women in the civil service that existed did not ask about organizational membership and activism outside the bureaucracy. Although there were a few surveys of women in government that did (e.g., CAWP 1978), these occurred at a single time point.

Samples of feminist activists from which I could have drawn (e.g., Rossi's 1982 study of women at the National Women's Conference) were also unavailable. Hence, I made the decision to study a single case in-depth using multiple methods.

I chose to focus on the U.S. women's movement because there was already some evidence of a movement–state intersection: a movement where the secondary literature clearly mentioned (albeit usually in passing) the existence of activists working inside of government (see Duerst-Lahti 1989; Freeman1975; Friedan 1998; Ware 1981 among others). Because the literature on many movements makes no mention of movement–state intersections, I thought by examining a case in which a movement–state intersection existed, I might be able to theorize about how the presence or absence of movement–state intersections would affect social movements generally.

In the course of this case study, I have now come across examples of movement–state intersections in the environmental, peace, and civil rights movement. This suggests that movement–state intersections may be more common than I originally thought, although there are still aspects of the women's movement that make that case unusual. In particular, the low levels of protest in the women's movement relative to other movements and the extensive policy change that has occurred in some areas suggest a priori that the U.S. women's movement is a critical case of movement institutionalization (for more information on critical cases see Yin 2008: 47–48).

Having chosen the case I wished to study, the next step was to determine the sorts of evidence I would gather. This project uses both archival research and semistructured interviews with feminist activists inside the state. Both methods provide different windows into this particular group of people. By analyzing the documents of major women's movement organizations and the personal papers of feminist activists inside the state I am able to get a snapshot of the relationship between these two groups, as well as the activities of feminist activists inside of government. These documents provide some evidence of how outsider activists and organizations and insider feminists saw their relationship with each other and the federal government. The advantage of these documents is that they are recorded at the time of the movement, so the evidence they provide is unbiased by hindsight.

Unfortunately, much of the interaction between insiders and outsiders and between insider feminists and the State, did not occur in the form of written communication or activity that was recorded for archives. As a result, the picture provided by documentary analysis is often incomplete.

The semistructured interviews with feminist activists who worked for the federal government provide an alternative perspective on the issue of feminist activists inside the state. I was able to find a wider array of insider feminists to interview compared to the limited archival material that was available. Moreover, with the exception of existing oral histories, archived materials were largely limited in scope, rarely saying much about the activities and attitudes of the individuals involved. As Blee and Taylor (2002: 94) have noted, talking to individuals allows "respondents to generate, challenge, clarify, elaborate, or recontextualize understandings of social movements. . . . This is particularly helpful for understanding little studied aspects of social movement dynamics."

Below I describe the semistructured interviews in more depth, particularly the methods used to locate and interview insider feminist activists. I also document the historical and archival materials used in this research.

THE IN-DEPTH INTERVIEWS

As part of the research on feminist activists within the state, I conducted interviews with forty women's movement activists who held positions in the U.S. bureaucracy. My identification of activists who held positions in the U.S. bureaucracy was done retrospectively using two criteria to identify "insider" activists. First, those included in my sample had to have engaged in clear and sustained activism within feminist organizations. This activism was either documented in the historical record or by information volunteered by at least two other activists. Engagement was not limited to activism in the larger organizations such as National Organization for Women; several activists were long-time participants in other organizations such as local rape crisis centers, Women in Black, or the Women's Rights Law Project. To be considered an insider feminist activist, an individual's activism must have occurred prior to, or during, their employment in the federal government, in order to exclude women who became feminist activists after they left the civil service. This particular sampling strategy did capture both insider feminist activists who entered the federal government as activists and insider feminist activists who converted to feminism while they were employed by the federal government. It is possible that I may have missed insider activists who converted to feminism once inside the federal government but who felt so constrained by their position that they only engaged in activism in organizations once they left government. However, I believe this group is likely to be small, and the nature of insider feminist networks is such that their names would have been mentioned by other insider feminist activists. Hence, I am confident that my measure of insider feminist activists captures the underlying concept well.

The second criterion I used to select interview participants was that they must also have been employed by the federal government. I excluded interviewees who worked for state or local governments, largely because this raised additional questions about how differences between localities influenced the effect of insiders. I also did not include feminist activists serving in the judiciary, elected to Congress, or working as staffers in the legislative branch, although it is clear that all of these locations hosted networks of insider feminist activists. I did include feminist activists employed in the White House, despite the fact that White House staff is not normally considered part of the federal bureaucracy, and despite the fact that these positions are more political in nature than those in the federal bureaucracy. White House staffers were included because they often had ties to the federal bureaucratic machinery and, in part, because I was interested in the differences between political appointees and the bureaucracy.

I also focused specifically on individuals who were in the position to potentially influence policy (which I generally defined as being either in the Senior Executive Service or at the level of GS14 or above). This no doubt excludes a number of feminist activists employed at lower levels of the bureaucracy, and also resulted in a much more narrow socioeconomic background for the activists I interviewed. I did, however, try to vary the type of appointment process – interviewing some political appointees and some career civil servants – because I wished to examine

TABLE A.I. *Characteristics of Interviewees*

Type of Appointment[a]		Year First Entered Federal Government	
White House staff or Political Appointee	10 25%	pre-1961	8 20%
Civil Servants	31 78%	1961–1980	28 70%
		1981 and after	4 10%

[a] Column totals to more than 100% because one woman served both as a civil servant and as a political appointee.
Source: Calculated from interviews with forty insider feminist activists.

whether the stereotypes of insider feminists hold for both types of individuals (see Table A.1).

The Modified Snowball Sampling

To locate the activists I interviewed, I used a modified snowball design. In the course of my interviews, I asked people to identify other feminist activists who were in the federal government. Jo Freeman provided an initial short list of feminist activists in government who had been helpful in her research on the women's liberation movement. I supplemented this list with people I discovered in the course of my research in archives and secondary literature. I interviewed only those people who were identified by at least two sources – either two separate interviewees, one interviewee and one historical source, or two independent historical sources. To get a sense of how location influences their activities, I interviewed insider activists across a range of locations within the federal bureaucracy rather than selecting individuals who were clearly located in agencies related to feminist issues (see Table 3.4).

In order to get a sense of how things have changed over time, I interviewed women who were employed in government over a range of different time periods (see Table A.1 and Table 7.1).[1] The women

[1] The differences between Table A.1 and Table 7.1, which includes the number of activists in each administration and the number entering during each presidential administration, are a result of individuals who entered the federal government multiple times.

interviewed were active in different phases of the women's movement (from 1961–2000). Although, as Table A.1 shows, there are significantly fewer activists who entered government for the first time after 1980.

Two concerns could be raised about the use of a snowball sampling design, because it is a purposive sample based on networks connection. First, we want to know whether it is possible that all networks of feminist activists within government were uncovered, or whether the snowball sample missed the individuals that connected one network of feminist activists to another. The result would be incomplete information about the existing networks of feminist activists in the federal government. However, the snowball sample brought me to very different parts of the government – from the Department of Treasury to the National Institutes of Health – suggesting that at least in terms of bureaucratic location and also locus of activism, I had reached varied parts of the larger network. By relying on historical sources as a second means of locating insider feminist activists, I also mitigated to some extent the possibility that I missed an isolated network of feminist activists, or one with few ties to the networks I interviewed. Hence, I am fairly confident that the methodology I used was one that captured the variety of networks within the federal government.

Second, one can ask whether the snowball sample is biased in such a way that it changed the results I report. Here of particular concern are the characteristics of insider feminist activists described in Chapter 3. Some characteristics are unlikely to be affected by a biased sample. For example, the class and educational levels of insider feminist activists are constrained greatly by their positions within the federal government, and so, sample biases are not likely to alter my conclusions about these characteristics. However, my conclusions about the ideology of insider feminist activists and their choice of tactics might be subject to sample bias. In particular, as Table A.1 suggests, I do have a definite generational bias in my sample. Few of the people I interviewed entered the federal government for the first time after 1980. Thus, I need to consider whether having an "older" sample has biased my conclusions about the ideology of insider feminist activists and the tactics they chose to use.

In terms of ideology, there are two possible directions that bias could take: "younger" insider feminist activists might be more conservative than their counterparts who entered before 1980, or "younger" insider feminist activists might be more radical than "older" insider feminist activists. Both of these possibilities receive some support in the secondary literature. On the one hand, discussions of cohorts of third-wave feminists suggest that they are in some ways more radical than the older generation (see, for example, Whittier 1995). However, such a bias would only strengthen my conclusion that insider feminists are more radical than we expect, and that institutionalization of the movement within government has not occurred.

However, there is also literature that suggests younger women are increasingly unwilling to identify as feminists and are also more conservative about issues (e.g., Bushman and Lenart 1996; but see Huddy et al. 2000). This might suggest the ideology of my sample of insider feminist activists is more radical than would be the case had I interviewed more women who entered the government after 1980. However, the literature on younger women largely suggests that they are unwilling to accept the label of feminists and see no need to engage in feminist activism, rather than saying that feminist activists are more conservative than they used to be. If this is true, it would actually reduce the number of insider feminists in the larger population, not just in my sample. That is, fewer women would meet the criterion of being a feminist activist. Indeed, this literature may in part explain why I found fewer insider feminist activists in the 1980s, rather than suggesting that the insider feminist activists that I did interview should be more conservative. Thus, I believe that any bias that occurred from the use of snowball sampling is unlikely to bias the results in favor of my conclusions.

The Interview Process

Finally, a word on the content of the interviews and their use in the text is in order. I utilized a historical oral history approach to the interview, preferring semistructured interviews because the experiences of insider feminist activists – both in their work inside the bureaucracy and in their feminist activity – was quite varied. The semistructured interview process was particularly useful for discussing at length events critical to the intersection of the women's movement and the state. This structure allowed me to follow up on specific events that might tell me more about how movement–state intersections operated.

All individuals were asked a common series of questions designed to elicit information about both their activism and their work within the bureaucracy. These questions covered how they became involved in the women's movement and their subsequent activities within the movement; all were asked general questions about their career path and how they came to work in the federal government. In each interview I asked about whether they participated in any feminist related activities while working for the bureaucracy, and asked them to describe these in detail. I asked specifically about issues of implementation as well as the development of new policies. If they were present in the federal bureaucracy over several administrations, I asked them how the change in administrations affected both their activism and their jobs. I also asked them to talk about their relationships to feminists outside the state. I ended the interview by asking them who else they thought I should talk to given my interest in feminist activists who worked in the federal government.

To ensure a candid response, the feminist activists interviewed for this project were promised confidentiality. After the initial draft of the book manuscript was completed, I offered every individual who I interviewed the opportunity to see how I had utilized specific quotations within the text. Many of the individuals who were contacted used the opportunity to provide me with additional comments on the events that were described within the book. With one exception (where I expressly asked permission to identify an individual I interviewed), I have maintained the confidentiality that was promised in the interviews. Whenever specific individuals are named in this book, the information comes from publicly available archival or secondary historical sources. When quotations are taken from the interviews, the person being interviewed is identified only by the date on which the interview occurred. Many of the people I interviewed expressly offered to allow me to use their names upon reading a final draft of this manuscript. However, because naming these individuals might make it easier to identify those who were not named and wished to remain anonymous, I maintained the convention of citing people only by the date of the interview in all cases. It is ironic that to maintain social science ethical standards, many of these women must once again work "under the radar."

ARCHIVAL WORK

In addition to the in-depth interviews that I conducted, I utilized three types of archival materials in my research. First, I benefited greatly from the work of other scholars and feminists who had already collected a wide array of oral histories with feminist activists. While most of these oral histories served other purposes – to document women in the federal government or women's movement (Schlesinger oral histories), the history of the foreign service (Georgetown oral histories), or women in the Nixon administration (The Pennsylvania State University oral histories) – they nonetheless contained a wealth of information about the activities, thoughts, and characteristics of insider feminist activists. These were particularly useful in the case of insider feminists who had died before this research began.

Second, I utilized the archives of feminist organizations located at the Schlesinger Library to both examine the degree to which insider feminists were active in these organizations and to obtain the outsider feminist perspective on insider activities. Because the insider feminists were active in these organizations, I could often track their interconnections with outsider feminists and see the degree to which there was documented evidence of insider feminists using their status to help the organization. Where the organizations permitted it, I also used descriptions of members in these organizations to verify that people I would interview met my criteria for being an activist, or to locate new activists to interview.

Third, some insider feminists have also archived their personal papers, and a few of the activists I interviewed allowed me to explore some of their private papers, which provided a perspective of these individuals captured during the moment – in letters and memos they had written and received, articles they had published, and documents they had collected from other insider feminists or from organizations. Others gave me large packets of published information they thought would be helpful for my research. These documents proved invaluable in gaining a deeper view of insider feminists than could be gleaned from organizational records, often allowing me to gather personal opinions of controversies at the time they occurred, uncolored by the passage of time. Because all the interviewees were promised confidentiality, I do not list the personal archives I visited or the individuals who provided published documents, although they played a large role in this final project, nor do I provide any indication of the source of published documents cited in the book outside of the usual citation. Below however, I list the libraries visited and the sources consulted at each library.

List of Archives Visited and Collections Used

Schlesinger Library

1. Oral Histories:
   a. Catherine East
   b. Mary Eastwood
   c. Caruthers Berger
   d. Daisy Fields
   e. Mary Keyserling
   f. Esther Lawton
2. Organizational Papers:
   a. Human Rights for Women
   b. National Organization for Women (including the papers of NOW Officers)
   c. National Organization for Women Legal Defense and Education Fund
   d. Women's Equity Action League
   e. National Women's Political Caucus
3. Personal Papers:
   a. Catherine East
   b. Marguerite Rawalt
   c. Mary Eastwood

Georgetown Library

1. Oral Histories:
   a. Mary Olmstead
   b. Mildred Marcy
   c. Barbara J. Good

The Pennsylvania State University: A Few
Good Women Special Collection

1. Oral Histories:
   a. Virginia Allan
   b. Evelyn Cunningham
   c. Barbara Hackman Franklin
   d. Esther Lawton
   e. Maj. Gen. Jeanne M. Holm
2. Personal Papers:
   a. Barbara Hackman Franklin
   b. Esther Lawton

Bibliography

Aberbach, Joel and Bert Rockman. 2000. *In the Web of Politics: Three Decades of the U.S. Federal Executive*. Washington DC: Brookings Institute.

Amatniek, Kathy. n.d. Letter to Catherine East. From the Papers of Catherine East (MC477), Box 15, Folder 39. Schlesinger Library, Radcliffe Institute for Advanced Study, Harvard University.

Amenta, Edwin. 2005. "Political Contexts, Challenger Strategies, and Mobilization: Explaining the Impact of the Townsend Plan." In Meyer, David, Valerie Jenness, and Helen Ingram (eds.). *Routing the Opposition: Social Movements, Public Policy, and Democracy*. Minneapolis: University of Minnesota Press. Pp. 29–64.

Amenta, Edwin and Yvonne Zylan. 1991. "Political Opportunity, the New Institutionalism and the Townsend Movement." *American Sociological Review* 56(2): 250–265.

Andersen, Ellen Ann. 2004. *Out of the Closets and Into the Courts: Legal Opportunity Structure and Gay Rights Legislation*. Ann Arbor: University of Michigan Press.

Andersen, Kristi. 1996. *After Suffrage: Women in Partisan and Electoral Politics before the New Deal*. Chicago: University of Chicago Press.

Aron, Cindy Sondik. 1987. *Ladies and Gentlemen of the Civil Service: Middle-Class Workers in the Gilded Age*. Oxford: Oxford University Press.

The Association of the Bar of the City of New York. 2007. "Women Lawyers: Women Changing the Law for Women." http://www.abcny.org/Diversity/WomenChangingtheLawforWomen.htm. Accessed March 31, 2008.

Babcock, Barbara Allen. 2001. "Introduction: A Real Revolution." *University of Kansas Law Review* 49(4): 719–731.

Bachrach, Peter and Morton Baratz. 1962. "The Two Faces of Power." *American Political Science Review* 56: 942–952.

Baer, Judith. 1978. *Chains of Protection: The Judicial Response to Women's Labor Legislation*. New York: Greenwood Press.

Banaszak, Lee Ann. 1996. *Why Movements Succeed or Fail: Opportunity, Culture and the Struggle for Woman Suffrage*. Princeton, NJ: Princeton University Press.

———. 1996a. "When Waves Collide: Cycles of Protest and the Swiss and American Women's Movements." *Political Research Quarterly* 49(December): 837–860.

———. 2005. "Inside and Outside the State: Movement Insider Status, Tactics and Public Policy Achievements" In Meyer, David, Valerie Jenness, and Helen Ingram (eds.). *Routing the Opposition: Social Movements, Public Policy, and Democracy*. Minneapolis: University of Minnesota Press. Pp. 149–176.

Banaszak, Lee Ann, Karen Beckwith, and Dieter Rucht, editors. 2003. "When Power Relocates: Interactive Changes in Women's Movements and States." In Banaszak, Lee Ann, Karen Beckwith, and Dieter Rucht (eds.). *Women's Movements Facing a Reconfigured State*. Cambridge: Cambridge University Press. Pp. 1–29.

———. 2003a. *Women's Movements Facing a Reconfigured State*. Cambridge: Cambridge University Press.

Barakso, Maryann. 2005. "Diminished Democracy? Comparing Opportunities for Participation in Women's Voluntary Associations." Paper presented at the annual meeting of the American Political Science Association, Marriott Wardman Park, Omni Shoreham, Washington Hilton, Washington, DC, September 1, 2005.

Bashevkin, Sylvia. 1998. *Women on the Defensive: Living through Conservative Times*. Chicago: University of Chicago Press.

Baumgartner, Frank and Bryan Jones. 1993. *Agendas and Instability in American Politics*. Chicago: University of Chicago Press.

Berger, Caruthers. 1982. Oral History with Leila Rupp and Verta Taylor conducted May 15, 1982. In the Rupp-Taylor Collection of Interviews. Schlesinger Library, Radcliffe Institute for Advanced Study, Harvard University.

Bernstein, Anya. 2001. *The Moderation Dilemma: Legislative Coalitions and the Politics of Family and Medical Leave*. Pittsburgh, PA: University of Pittsburgh Press.

Binder, Amy. 2002. *Contentious Curricula: Afrocentrism and Creationism in American Public Schools*. Princeton, NJ: Princeton University Press.

Birnbaum, Pierre. 1988. *States and Collective Action: The European Experience*. Cambridge: Cambridge University Press.

Blee, Kathleen M. and Verta Taylor. 2002. "Semi-Structured Interviewing in Social Movement Research." In Bert Klandermans and Suzanne Staggenborg, (eds.). *Methods in Social Movement Research*. Minneapolis: University of Minnesota Press. Pp. 92–117.

Bonastia, Chris. 2000. "Why did Affirmative Action in Housing Fail during the Nixon Era? Exploring the 'Institutional Homes' of Social Policies." *Social Problems* 47(4): 523–542.

Borrelli, MaryAnne. 1997. *The Other Elites: Women, Politics, and Power in the Executive Branch.* Boulder, CO: Lynne Reinner Publishers.

———. 2000. "Gender, Politics, and Change in the United States Cabinet." In Tolleson-Rinehart, Sue, and Jyl Josephson (eds.). *Gender and American Politics: Women, Men, and the Political Process.* Armonk, NY: M. E. Sharpe. Pp. 185–204.

Bowman, Geline MacDonald and Earlene White. 1944. *A History of the National Federation of Business and Professional Women's Clubs, Inc. 1919–1944.* New York: National Federation of Business and Professional Women's Clubs.

Braunthal, Gerard. 1990. *Political Loyalty and Public Service in West Germany: The 1972 Decree Against Radicals and Its Consequences.* Amherst: University of Massachusetts Press.

Brockett, Charles D. 1991. "The Structure of Political Opportunities and Peasant Mobilization in Central America." *Comparative Politics* 23: 253–274.

Brown, Cynthia. n.d. *The Thickest Ceiling of All: The Struggle for Female Leadership in Education.* Occasional Paper on Leadership Issues 3. Washington, DC; Institute for Educational Leadership, Inc.

Burstein, Paul. 1985. *Discrimination, Jobs, and Politics: The Struggle for Equal Employment Opportunity in the United States since the New Deal.* Chicago: University of Chicago Press.

———. 1999. "Social Movements and Public Policy." In Guigni, Marco, Doug McAdam, and Charles Tilly (eds.). *How Social Movements Matter.* Minneapolis: University of Minnesota Press. Pp. 3–21.

Burstein, Paul, Rachel Einwohner, and Jocelyn Hollander. 1995. "The Success of Political Movements: A Bargaining Perspective." In Jenkins, J. Craig and Bert Klandermans (eds.). *The Politics of Social Protest: Comparative Perspectives on States and Social Movements.* Minneapolis: University of Minnesota Press. Pp. 275–295.

Buschman, Joan K. and Silvo Lenart. 1996. "'I Am Not a Feminist, but . . .': College Women, Feminism, and Negative Experiences." *Political Psychology* 17(1): 59–75.

Carabillo, Toni, Judith Meuli, and June Bundy Csida. 1993. *The Feminist Chronicles: 1953–1993.* Los Angeles: Women's Graphics.

Carpenter, Daniel. 2001. *The Forging of Bureaucratic Autonomy: Reputations, Networks, and Policy Innovation in Executive Agencies, 1862–1928.* Princeton, NJ: Princeton University Press.

———. 2002. "Groups, the Media, Agency Waiting Costs, and FDA Drug Approval." *American Journal of Political Science* 46(3): 490–505.

Center for the American Woman and Politics. 1978. *Women in Public Office: A Biographical Directory and Statistical Analysis.* Second edition. Metuchen, NJ: The Scarecrow Press.

————. 1991. *The Impact of Women in Public Office: An Overview*. New Brunswick, NJ: Center for the American Woman and Politics.

Chafe, William. 1977. *Women and Equality: Changing Patterns in American Culture*. Oxford: Oxford University Press.

Chaney, Elsa. 2004. "Full Circle: From Academia to Government and Back." In *Developing Power: How Women Transformed International Development*, Arvonne Fraser and Irene Tinker (eds.). New York: Feminist Press at the City University of New York. Pp. 200–210.

Chappell, Louise. 2002. *Gendering Government: Feminist Engagement With the State in Australia and Canada*. Vancouver: UBC Press.

Chester, Ronald. 1985. *Unequal Access: Women Lawyers in a Changing America*. South Hadley, MA: Bergin and Garvey.

Claussen, Cathryn L. 1996. "Gendered Merit: Women and the Merit Concept in Federal Employment, 1864–1944." *American Journal of Legal History* 40(3): 229–252.

Connell, R.W. 1990. "The State, Gender, and Sexual Politics: Theory and Appraisal." *Theory and Society* 19: 507–544.

Conway, M. Margaret, David Ahern, and Gertrude Steuernagel. 1999. *Women and Public Policy: A Revolution in Progress*. Washington, DC: CQ Press.

Costain, Anne. 1992. *Inviting Women's Rebellion: A Political Process Interpretation of the Women's Movement*. Baltimore, MD: Johns Hopkins University Press.

————. 1998. "Women Lobby Congress." In *Social Movements and American Political Institutions*. Costain, Anne and Andrew McFarland (eds.). Pp. 171–184.

Costain, W. Douglas and James P. Lester. 1998. "The Environmental Movement and Congress." In *Social Movements and American Political Institutions*. Costain, Anne and Andrew McFarland, (eds.). Pp.185–198.

Dahl, Robert. 1971. *Polyarchy*. New Haven, CT: Yale University Press.

Davis, John A. and Cornelius L. Golightly. 1945. "Negro Employment in the Federal Government." *Phylon* 6(4): 337–346.

Dean, John. 2001. *The Rehnquist Choice: The Untold Story of the Nixon Appointment That Redefined the Supreme Court*. New York: Free Press.

Della Porta, Donatella and Dieter Rucht. 1995. "Left-Libertarian Movements in Context." In Jenkins, J. Craig and Bert Klandermans, (eds.). *The Politics of Social Protest: Comparative Perspectives on States and Social Movements*. Minneapolis: University of Minnesota Press. Pp. 229–272.

Desali, Manali. 2003. "From Movement to Party to Government: Why Social Policies in Kerala and West Bengal are so Different?." In Goldstone, Jack (ed.). *States, Parties and Social Movements*. Cambridge: Cambridge University Press. Pp. 170–196.

Diani, Mario. 1992. "The Concept of Social Movement." *The Sociological Review* 40(1): 1–25.

Dillon, Dorothy. 1988. Oral History Interview, Foreign Affairs Oral History Collection. Georgetown University Library. May 10, 1988.

Drachmann, Virginia. 1998. *Sisters-In-Law: Women Lawyers in Modern American History*. Cambridge: Harvard University Press.

Duerst-Lahti, Georgia. 1989. "The Government's Role in Building the Women's Movement." *Political Science Quarterly* 104(2): 249–268.

East, Catherine. 1969. Letter to Kathy Amatniek dated February 27, 1969. From the Papers of Catherine East (MC477), Box 15, Folder 39. Schlesinger Library, Radcliffe Institute for Advanced Study, Harvard University.

————. 1982. Oral History in Women in the Federal Government Oral History Project Interviews. Schlesinger Library, Radcliffe Institute for Advanced Study, Harvard University.

Eastwood, Mary. 1990–1993. Oral History in Tully-Crenshaw Feminist Oral History Project. Schlesinger Library, Radcliffe Institute for Advanced Study, Harvard University.

Eisenstein, Hester. 1990. "Femocrats, Official Feminism, and the Uses of Power." In Watson, Sophie (ed). *Playing the State: Australian Feminist Interventions*. Boston: Allen and Unwin. Pp. 87–103.

————. 1996. *Inside Agitators: Australian Femocrats and the State*. Philadelphia, PA: Temple University Press.

Eisinger, Peter. 1973. "The Conditions of Protest Behavior in American Cities." *American Political Science Review* 67: 11–28.

Epstein, Cynthia Fuchs. 1993. *Women in Law*. Second edition. Urbana: University of Illinois Press.

Equal Employment Opportunity Commission. 2000. *The Story of the United States Equal Employment Opportunity Commission: Ensuring the Promise of Opportunity for 35 Years*. Washington, DC: Equal Employment Opportunity Commission.

Evans, Peter, Dietrich Rueschemeyer, and Theda Skocpol. 1985 (eds.). *Bringing the State Back In*. Cambridge: Cambridge University Press.

Family Liaison Office. United States Department of State. 2003. "The Family Liaison Office's Early Years." *FLO Focus* 10(1): 7–9.

Federal Woman's Award Study Group on Careers for Women. 1967. "Progress Report to the President March 3, 1967."

Federally Employed Women. n.d. "The FEW Legislative Agenda." http://www.few.org/108thCongressAgenda.pdf. Accessed August 9, 2004.

Ferguson, Kathy. 1984. *The Feminist Case against Bureaucracy*. Philadelphia, PA: Temple University Press.

Ferree, Myra Marx. 1991–1992. "Institutionalizing Gender Equality: Feminist Politics and Equality Offices." *German Politics and Society* 24 & 25 (Winter): 53–64.

————. 1996. "Institutionalization, Identity, and the Political Participation of Women in the New Bundesländer." *Research on Russia and Eastern Europe* 2: 19–34.

————. 2003. "Resonance and Radicalism: Feminist Framing in the Abortion Debates of the United States and Germany." *American Journal of Sociology.* 109(2): 304–344.

————. 2005. "Soft Repression: Ridicule, Stigma, and Silencing in Gender-Based Movements" In Myers, Daniel and Daniel Cress, (eds.). *Research in Social Movements, Conflicts and Change,* Volume 25. Pp. 85–101.

Ferree, Myra Marx and Beth Hess. 1985. *Controversy and Coalition: The New Feminist Movement.* Boston: Twayne Publishers.

————. 2000. *Controversy and Coalition: The New Feminist Movement Across Three Decades of Change.* Third edition. New York: Routledge Publishers.

Flam, Helena, (ed.) 1994. *States and Anti-Nuclear Movements.* Edinburgh: Edinburgh University Press.

Ford, Lynne E. 2002. *Women and Politics: The Pursuit of Equality.* Boston: Houghton Mifflin Company.

Fraser, Arvonne. 1983. "Insiders and Outsiders: Women in the Political Arena." In Tinker, Irene (ed.). *Women in Washington.* Beverly Hills, CA: Sage Publications. Pp. 120–139.

————. 2004. "Seizing Opportunities: USAID, WID, and CEDAW." In Fraser, Arvonne and Irene Tinker (eds.). *Developing Power: How Women Transformed International Development.* New York: Feminist Press at the City University of New York. Pp. 164–175.

Freeman, Jo. 1975. *The Politics of Women's Liberation.* New York: Longman.

————. 1987. "Whom You Know versus Whom You Represent: Feminist Influence in the Democratic and Republican Parties."In Katzenstein, Mary Fainsod and Carol McClurg Mueller (eds). *The Women's Movements of the United States and Western Europe.* Philadelphia: Temple University Press. Pp. 215–244.

Friedan, Betty. 1963. *The Feminine Mystique.* New York: Norton.

————. 1998. *It Changed My Life: Writings on the Women's Movement.* Second edition. Cambridge, MA: Harvard University Press.

Fuentes, Sonia Pressman. 1998. "Three United States Feminists–A Personal Tribute," *Jewish Affairs* 53(1): 37.

————. 1999. *Eat First – You Don't Know What They'll Give You.* Philidelphia, PA: Xlibris Corporation.

Gahr, Evan. 2001. "Oink! Oink! Isn't it High Time the Federal Government Stopped Playing Lady Bountiful to these Gals?" *The Women's Quarterly* 27: 55.

Gamson, William. 1990. *The Strategy of Social Protest.* Second edition. Belmont, CA: Wadsworth Publishing Company.

Gamson, William and David S. Meyer. 1996. "Framing Political Opportunity" In McAdam, Doug, John D. McCarthy and Mayer N. Zald (eds.). *Comparative Perspectives on Social Movements.* Cambridge: Cambridge University Press. Pp. 275–290.

Gaventa, John. 1980. *Power and Powerlessness: Quiescience and Rebellion in an Appalachian Valley*. Urbana: University of Illinois Press.

Gelb, Joyce and Marian Lief Palley. 1982. *Women and Public Policies*. Revised edition. Princeton, NJ: Princeton University Press.

Giugni, Marco. 1999. *How Social Movements Matter*. Minnesota: University of Minnesota Press.

Givel, Michael. 2006. "Punctuated Equilibrium in Limbo: The Tobacco Lobby and U.S. State Policymaking from 1990 to 2003." *Policy Studies Journal* 34(3): 405–418.

Glenn John. 2003. "Parties out of Movements: Party Emergence in Post-communist Eastern Europe." In Jack Goldstone (ed.). *States, Parties and Social Movements*. Cambridge: Cambridge University Press. Pp. 147–169.

Goldstone, Jack. 2003. "Introduction: Bridging Institutionalized and Non-Institutionalized Politics." In Goldstone, Jack (ed.). *States, Parties and Social Movements*. Cambridge: Cambridge University Press. Pp. 1–27.

Good, Barbara J. 1993. Oral History Interview, Foreign Affairs Oral History Collection. Georgetown University Library. May 25, 1993.

Goodman, Billy. 1997. "Controversial Group Marks Quarter-Century of Fighting for NIH Women Scientists' Rights." *The Scientist* 11(1): 1, 10.

Harrison, Cynthia. 1988. *On Account of Sex: The Politics of Women's Issues, 1945–1968*. Berkeley: University of California Press.

Hartmann, Susan. 1998. *The Other Feminists: Activists in the Liberal Establishment*. New Haven, CT: Yale University Press.

Harvey, Anna. 1998. *Votes without Leverage*. Cambridge: Cambridge University Press.

Hatem, Mervat F. 1994. "The Paradoxes of State Feminism in Egypt" in Nelson, Barbara and Najma Chowdhury, (eds.). *Women and Politics Worldwide*. New Haven, CT: Yale University Press. Pp. 227–241.

Heinz, John, Edward Laumann, Robert Nelson, and Robert Salisbury. 1993. *The Hollow Core: Private Interests in National Policy Making*. Cambridge, MA: Harvard University Press.

Hernandez, Aileen. 1971. "Letter to Eve Norman dated April 29, 1971." Published by National Organization for Women. From a private archive.

———. 1975. "E.E.O.C. and the Women's Movement (1965–1975)." Paper presented at the Symposium on the Tenth Anniversary of the United States Equal Employment Commission, Rutgers University Law School, November 28–29, 1975.

Hilbink, Thomas. 2006. "The Profession, the Grassroots, and the Elite: Cause Lawyering for Civil Rights and Freedom in the Direct Action Era" In Sarat, Austin and Stuart Scheingold (eds.). *Cause Lawyers and Social Movements*. Stanford: Stanford University Press. Pp. 60–83.

Hilts, Philip J. 1993. "Inspector Ends a Hunger Strike Against Agency." *New York Times*. June 13, 1993 (late edition): A24.

Hine, Darlene Clark. 2003. "Black Professionals and Race Consciousness: Origins of the Civil Rights Movement 1890–1950." *Journal of American History* 89(4): 1279–1294.

Huddy, Leonie, Francis K. Neely, and Marilyn R. Lafay. 2000. "Trends: Support for the Women's Movement." *The Public Opinion Quarterly* 64(3): 309–350.

Human Rights for Women. n.d. "Human Rights for Women – Consent to Serve" in the papers of Human Rights for Women (83-M229), Box 1; Folder "HRW Directors." Schlesinger Library, Radcliffe Institute for Advanced Study, Harvard University.

Human Rights for Women. 1971. "Outline of HRW Projects as of August 1, 1971" in the papers of Human Rights for Women (83-M229), Box 1; Folder "HRW Fundraising." Schlesinger Library, Radcliffe Institute for Advanced Study, Harvard University.

Ingraham, Patricia Wallace. 1995. *The Foundation of Merit Public Service in American Democracy.* Baltimore, MD: John Hopkins University Press.

Jaquette, Jane. 2004. "Crossing the Line: From Academia to the WID Office at USAID." In Fraser, Arvonne and Irene Tinker (eds.). *Developing Power: How Women Transformed International Development.* Baltimore, MD. John Hopkins University Press. Pp. 189–199.

Jasper, James and Jeff Goodwin. 2003. *Rethinking Social Movements: Structure, Meaning and Emotion.* Landham: Rowman & Littlefield.

Jenkins, J. Craig and Bert Klandermans (eds.). 1995. "The Politics of Social Protest." In Jenkins, J. Craig and Bert Klandermans (eds.). *The Politics of Social Protest: Comparative Perspectives on States and Social Movements.* Minneapolis: University of Minnesota Press. Pp. 1–6.

Jones, Beverly W. 1982. "Before Montgomery and Greensboro: The Desegregation Movement in the District of Columbia, 1950–1953." *Phylon* 43(2): 144–154.

Jones, Lynn C. 1999. *Both Advocate and Activist: The Dual Careers of Cause Lawyers.* PhD. Dissertation. University of Arizona.

Kafer, Krista. 2001. "Wasting Education Dollars: The Women's Educational Equity Act." *Heritage Foundation Reports (Backgrounder) No.* 1490.

Kardam, Nüket. 1994. "Women and Development." In Beckman, Peter and Francine D'Amico (eds.). *Women, Gender, and World Politics: Perspectives, Policies, and Prospects.* Westport, CT: Bergin and Garvey. Pp. 141–153.

Kathlene, Lyn. 1994. "Power and Influence in State Legislative Policymaking: The Interaction of Gender and Position in Committee Hearing Debates." *American Political Science Review* 88(2): 560–576.

Katzenstein, Mary Fainsod. 1998. *Faithful and Fearless: Moving Feminist Protest Inside the Church and Military.* Princeton, NJ: Princeton University Press.

———. 1998a. "Stepsisters: Feminist Movement Activism in Different Institutional Spaces." In Meyer, David S. and Sidney Tarrow (eds.). *The Social Movement Society.* Boulder, CO: Rowman and Littlefield. Pp. 195–216.

Kenney, Sally. 1992. *For Whose Protection? Reproductive Hazards and Exclusionary Policies in the United States and Britain*. Ann Arbor: University of Michigan Press.

———. 2004. "Equal Employment Opportunity and Representation: Extending the Frame to Courts." *Social Politics* 11(1): 86–116.

Kerber, Linda. 1999. *No Constitutional Right to be Ladies: Women and the Obligations of Citizenship*. New York: Hill and Wang.

King, Desmond. 1995. *Separate and Unequal: Black Americans and the US Federal Government*. Oxford: Oxford University Press.

———. 1999. "The Racial Bureaucracy: African Americans and the Federal Government in the Era of Segregated Race Relations." *Governance* 12(4): 345–377.

King, Desmond and Rogers Smith. 2005. "Racial Orders in American Political Development." *American Political Science Review* 99(1): 75–92.

Kiplinger, W.M. 1942. *Washington is Like That*. New York: Harper and Brothers.

Kitschelt, Herbert. 1986. "Political Opportunity Structures and Political Protest: Anti-Nuclear Movements in Four Democracies." *British Journal of Political Science* 16 (1): 57–85.

Klein, Susan S., Carol Anne Dwyer, Lynn Fox, Dolores Grayson, Cheris Kramarae, Diane Pollard, and Barbara Richardson (eds.). 2007. *Handbook for Achieving Gender Equity through Education*, Second edition. Philadelphia: Lawrence Erlbaum Associates, Inc.

Kranz, Harry. 1976. *The Participatory Bureaucracy*. Lexington, MA: Lexington Books (D.C. Heath and Co.).

Kriesi, Hanspeter, Ruud Koopmans, Jan Willem Duyvendak, and Marco G. Guini. 1995. *The Politics of New Social Movements in Western Europe: A Comparative Analysis*. Minneapolis: University of Minnesota Press.

Kvistad, Gregg. 1988. "Radicals and the State: The Political Demands on West German Civil Servants." *Comparative Political Studies* 21(1): 95–125.

Laughlin, Kathleen A. 2000. *Women's Work and Public Policy: A History of the Women's Bureau, U.S. Department of Labor, 1945–1970*. Boston: Northeastern University Press.

Laurence, Leslie. 1994. "Bias in Medicine Hurts All Women" *The Orlando Sentinel*. April 12, 1994: E-3.

Leader, Ambassador Joyce E. 2001. "Women in the International Affairs Professions: A Speech Delivered at Penn State University, Harrisburg, PA, April 5, 2001. http://www.fundforpeace.org/media/speeches/leader02.php. Accessed July 16, 2004.

Levine, Susan. 1995. *Degrees of Equality: The American Association of University Women and the Challenge of Twentieth-Century Feminism*. Philadelphia, PA: Temple University Press.

Lieberman, Robert. 2006. "Private Power and American Bureaucracy: The EEOC, Civil Rights Enforcement, and the Rise of Affirmative Action" Paper presented at the annual meeting of the American Political Science Association, Philadelphia, PA, August 31, 2006.

Lorde, Audre. 1984. *Sister Outsider: Essays and Speeches*. Trumansburg, NY: The Crossing Press.

Luker, Kristen. 1984. *Abortion and the Politics of Motherhood*. Berkeley: University of California Press.

Lukes, Steven. 1974. *Power: A Radical View*. London: MacMillan.

Marshall, Anna Maria. 2006. "Social Movement Strategies and the Participatory Potential of Litigation" In Sarat, Austin and Stuart Scheingold (eds.). *Cause Lawyers and Social Movements*. Stanford: Stanford University Press. Pp. 164–181.

Matthews-Gardner, A. Lanathea. 2003. *From Woman's Club to NGO: The Changing Terrain of Women's Civil Engagement in the Mid-Twentieth Century United States*. PhD Thesis: Syracuse University.

──────. 2005. "The Political Development of Female Civic Engagement in Postwar America." *Politics & Gender* 1(4): 547–575.

Marcy, Mildred. 1974. Oral History for the Women in the Federal Government Oral History project. Schlesinger Library, Radcliffe Institute for Advanced Study, Harvard University.

──────. 1991. Oral History Interview, Foreign Affairs Oral History Collection. Georgetown University Library. February 15, 1991.

Martin, Janet. 1989. "The Recruitment of Women to Cabinet and Subcabinet Posts." *Western Political Quarterly* 42(1): 161–172.

──────. 2003. *The Presidency and Women: Promise, Performance and Illusion*. College Station: Texas A & M University Press.

Mayer, Margit. 1978. "The German October of 1977." *New German Critique* 13 (Winter) Special Feminist Issue: 155–163.

Mazur, Amy. 1995. *Gender Bias and the State: Symbolic Reform at Work in Fifth Republic France*. Pittsburgh, PA: University of Pittsburgh.

──────. 1995a. "Strong State and Symbolic Reform" in McBride Stetson, Dorothy and Amy Mazur (eds.). *Comparative State Feminism*. Thousand Oaks, CA: Sage Publications. Pp. 76–94.

──────. (ed.). 2001. *State Feminism, Women's Movements, and Job Training*. New York: Routledge.

──────. 2002. *Theorizing Feminist Policy*. Oxford: Oxford University Press.

McAdam, Doug. 1996. "Conceptual Origins, Current Problems, Future Directions." In McAdam, Doug, John D. McCarthy and Mayer N. Zald (eds.). *Comparative Perspectives on Social Movements*. Cambridge: Cambridge University Press. Pp. 23–40.

──────. 1996a. "The Framing Function of Movement Tactics: Strategic Dramaturgy in the American Civil Rights Movement." In McAdam, Doug, John D. McCarthy, and Mayer N. Zald (eds.). *Comparative Perspectives on Social Movements*. Cambridge: Cambridge University Press. Pp. 338–355.

──────. 1982. *Political Process and the Development of Black Insurgency, 1930–1970*. Chicago: University of Chicago Press.

McAdam, Doug, Sidney Tarrow, and Charles Tilly. 2001. *Dynamics of Contention*. Cambridge: Cambridge University Press.

McBride, Dorothy and Amy Mazur. 2004. "Conceptual Framework for the Comparative Analysis of Women's Movements: RNGS: Comparative Study of Women's Policy Offices 1970–2000." Unpublished Paper.

McCammon, Holly J., Karen E. Campbell, Ellen M. Granberg, and Christine Mowery. 2001. "How Movements Win: Gendered Opportunity Structures and the State Women's Suffrage Movements, 1866–1919." *American Sociological Review* 66: 49–70.

McCann, Michael. 1994. *Rights at Work: Pay Equity Reform and the Politics of Legal Mobilization*. Chicago: University of Chicago Press.

McConnell, Grant. 1970. *Private Power and American Democracy*. New York: Vintage.

McDonagh, Eileen and Laura Pappano. 2007. *Playing with the Boys: Why Separate is Not Equal in Sports*. New York: Oxford University Press.

McGlen, Nancy E. and Meredith Reid Sarkees. 1995. "The Status of Women in Foreign Policy." *Headline Series* No. 307 (Summer). Ithaca, NY: Foreign Policy Association.

McMillin, Lucille Foster. 1941. *Women in the Federal Service*. Third edition. Washington, DC: U.S. Civil Service Commission.

———. 1943. *The Second Year: A Study of Women's Participation in War Activities of the Federal Government*. Washington, DC: U.S. Government Printing Office.

McNemar, Quinn. 1969. *Psychological Statistics*, Fourth edition. New York: John Wiley and Sons.

Meyer, David S. 2004. "Protest and Political Opportunity." *Annual Review of Sociology* 30(2004): 125–145.

Meyer, David and Steven Bouchert. 2007. "Signals and Spillover: Brown v. Board of Education and Other Social Movements." *Perspectives on Politics* 5(1): 81–93.

Meyer, David and Sidney Tarrow (eds.). 1998. *The Social Movement Society*. Boulder, CO: Rowman and Littlefield.

Meyerson, Debra. 2003. *Tempered Radicals: How Everyday Leaders Inspire Change at Work*. Cambridge, MA: Harvard Business School Press.

Millsap, Mary Ann. 1988. *Advocates for Sex Equity in Federal Education Law: The National Coalition for Women and Girls in Education*. PhD. Thesis: Harvard University Graduate School of Education.

Moore, Kelly. 1999. "Political Protest and Institutional Change: The Anti-Vietnam War Movement and American Science" In Guigni, Marco, Doug McAdam, and Charles Tilly (eds.). *How Social Movements Matter*. Minneapolis: University of Minnesota Press. Pp. 97–115.

Morgan, Laura Dana. 1913. "A Report on the Status of Women in the Classified Civil Service of the United States Government in the District of Columbia." *The Journal of the Association of Collegiate Alumnae* 6(3, April): 88–94.

Morin Richard and Claudia Deane. 2001. "Women's Forum Challenges Feminists, Gains Influence. *The Washington Post* (Final Edition). May 1, 2001, A06.

Naff, Katherine. 2001. *To Look Like America: Dismantling Barriers for Women and Minorities in Government.* Boulder, CO: Westview Press.

Nash, Margaret, Susan S. Klein, Barbara Bitters, and William Howe, Sharon Hobbs, Linda Shevitz, Linda Wharton with Eleanor Smeal. 2007. "The Role of Government in Advancing Gender Equity in Education." In Klein, Susan S., Carol Anne Dwyer, Lynn Fox, Dolores Grayson, Cheris Kramarae, Diane Pollard, and Barbara Richardson (eds.) *Handbook for Achieving Gender Equity through Education,* Second edition. Philadelphia: Lawrence Erlbaum Associates, Inc. Pp. 63–101.

National Committee on Pay Equity. 2001. "The Wage Gap Over Time: In Real Dollars, Women See a Continuing Gap." *National Committee on Pay Equity Fact Sheet.* http://www.feminist.com/fairpay/f_change.htm. Accessed March 31, 2003.

———. 2002. "The Wage Gap By Education: 2001." *National Committee on Pay Equity Fact Sheet.* http://www.feminist.com/fairpay/f_education.htm. Accessed March 31, 2003.

National Organization for Women. 2002. "Facts about Pay Equity." http://www.now.org/issues/economic/factsheet.html. Accessed March 31, 2003.

Nienburg, Bertha. 1920. *Women in the Government Service, Bulletin of the Women's Bureau, No. 8.* Washington, DC: Government Printing Office.

NOW Legal Defense Fund. 1968. "Minutes of Meeting" of November 2, 1968. From the papers of Marguerite Rawalt (MC 478), Box 27, Folder 4. Schlesinger Library; Radcliffe Institute for Advanced Study, Harvard University.

Nyswander, Rachel Fesler and Janet M. Hooks. 1941. *Employment of Women in the Federal Government, 1923 to 1939. Bulletin of the Women's Bureau, No. 182.* Washington, DC: Government Printing Office.

October 17th Movement. n.d. "October 17 Movement" [flyer advertising meeting]. From the papers of Mary Eastwood (M-187) Box 6: Folder 55. Schlesinger Library: Radcliffe Institute for Advanced Study, Harvard University.

Office of Educational Research and Improvement. 2001. *Digest of Education Statistics, 2000.* Washington, DC: U.S. Department of Education, Office of Educational Research and Improvement, Center for Education Statistics.

Olmstead, Ambassador Mary Seymour. 1985. Oral History Interview, Foreign Affairs Oral History Project. *Women Ambassadors Series.* Washington, DC: Georgetown University Library.

Outshoorn, Joyce. 1994. "Between Movement and Government: 'Femocrats in the Netherlands.'" *Schweizerisches Jahrbuch für Politische Wissenschaft* 34: 141–163.

_____. 1997. "Incorporating Feminism: the Women's Policy Network in the Netherlands." In Gardiner, Frances (ed.). *Sex Equality in Western Europe*. New York: Routledge. Pp. 109–126.

Paterson, Judith. 1986. *Be Somebody: A Biography of Marguerite Rawalt*. Austin, TX: Eakin Press.

Patterson, James T. 2001. *Brown v. Board of Education: A Civil Rights Milestone and Its Troubled Legacy*. Oxford: Oxford University Press.

Pedriana, Nicholas. 2004. "Help Wanted NOW: Legal Resources, the Women's Movement, and the Battle over Sex-Segregated Job Advertisements." *Social Problems* 51(2): 182–201.

_____. 2006. "From Protective to Equal Treatment: Legal Framing Processes and Transformation of the Women's Movement in the 1960s." *American Journal of Sociology* 111(6): 1718–1761.

Pierson, Paul. 1993. "When Effect Becomes Cause: Policy Feedback and Political Change." *World Politics* 45: 595–628.

Pitkin, Hanna. 1969. *Representation*. New York: Atherton Press.

Piven, Francis and Cloward, Richard. 1978. *Poor People's Movements: Why They Succeed, How They Fail*. New York: Random House.

Poggi, Gianfranco. 1990. *The State: Its Nature, Developments, and Perspectives*. Stanford, CA: Stanford University Press.

Pringle, Rosemary and Sophie Watson. 1992. "'Women's Interests' and the Post-Structuralist State." In Barrett, Michèle and Anne Phillips (eds.). *Destabilizing Theory: Contemporary Feminist Debates*. Stanford, CA: Stanford University Press. Pp. 53–73.

Raeburn, Nicole C. 2004. *Changing Corporate America from Inside Out: Lesbian and Gay Workplace Rights*. Minneapolis: University of Minnesota Press.

Randall, Vicki. 1987. *Women and Politics: An International Perspective*. Chicago: University of Chicago Press.

Rawalt, Marguerite. 1969. *A History of the National Federation of Business and Professional Women's Clubs, Inc. Volume II: 1944–1960*. Washington, DC: National Federation of Business and Professional Women's Clubs, Inc.

Reinelt, Claire. 1995. "Moving onto the Terrain of the State: The Battered Women's Movement and the Politics of Engagement." In Ferree, Myra Marx and Patricia Yancey Martin (eds.). *Feminist Organizations: Harvest of the New Women's Movement*. Philadelphia: Temple University Press. Pp.84–104.

Ries, Paula and Anne J. Stone (eds.). *The American Woman 1992–93: A Status Report*. New York: W.W. Norton.

Ritter, Gretchen. 2006. *The Constitution as Social Design: Gender And Civic Membership in the American Constitutional Order*. Stanford, CA: Stanford University Press.

Rochon, Thomas. 1998. *Culture Moves: Ideas, Activism and Changing Values*. Princeton, NJ: Princeton University Press.

Rochon, Thomas and Daniel Mazmanian. 1993. "Social Movements and the Policy Process." *Annals of the American Academy of Political and Social Science* 528: 75–87.

Rockman, Bert. 1990. "Minding the State – Or a State of Mind? Issues in the Comparative Conceptualization of the State." *Comparative Political Studies* 23(1): 25–55.

Rohrschneider, Robert. 1993. "New Party versus Old Left Realignments: Environmental Attitudes, Party Policies, and Partisan Affiliations in Four West European Countries." *Journal of Politics* 55(3): 682–701.

Rosenberg, Gerald. 1993. *The Hollow Hope: Can Courts Bring About Social Change?* Chicago: University of Chicago.

Rosenfeld, Rachel and Kathryn Ward. 1996. "Evolution of the Contemporary U.S. Women's Movement." *Research in Social Movements, Conflict and Change* 19: 51–73.

Rossi, Alice S. 1982. *Feminists in Politics: A Panel Analysis of the First National Women's Conference.* New York: Academic Press.

Rucht, Dieter. 2003. "Interactions between Social Movements and States in a Comparative Perspective." In Banaszak, Lee Ann, Karen Beckwith, and Dieter Rucht (eds.) *Women's Movements Facing a Reconfigured State.* Cambridge: Cambridge University Press. Pp. 242–274.

Rung, Margaret. 2002. *Servants of the State: Managing Diversity and Democracy in the Federal Workforce, 1933–1953.* Athens: University of Georgia Press.

Rupp, Leila J. 1985. "The Women's Community of the National Woman's Party, 1945 to the 1960s." *Signs* 10(4):715–740.

Rupp, Leila J. and Verta Taylor. 1987. *Survival in the Doldrums: The American Women's Rights Movement, 1945 to the 1960s.* New York: Oxford University Press.

Ryan, Barbara. 1992. *Feminism and the Women's Movement.* New York: Routledge.

Salisbury, Robert and Paul E. Johnson. 1989. "Who You Know Versus What You Know: The Uses of Government Experience for Washington Lobbyists." *American Journal of Political Science* 33 (February):175–195.

Sandler, Bernice R. 1997. "'Too Strong for a Woman': The Five Words that Created Title IX." *About Women on Campus* (Newsletter of NAWE: Advancing Women in Higher Education) 6(2):1–4.

Santoro, Wayne A. 1999. "Conventional Politics Takes Center Stage: The Latino Struggle against English-Only Laws." *Social Forces* 77(3): 887–909.

Santoro, Wayne A. and McGuire, Gail M. 1997. "Social Movement Insiders: The Impact of Institutional Activists on Affirmative Action and Comparable Worth Policies." *Social Problems* 44(4): 503–520.

Sapiro, Virginia. 1994. *Women in American Society: An Introduction to Women's Studies.* Third edition. Mountain View, CA: Mayfield Publishing Co.

Sarat, Austin and Stuart Scheingold (eds.). 1998. *Cause Lawyering: Political Commitments and Professional Responsibilities*. New York: Oxford University Press.

———. 2005. *The Worlds Cause Lawyers Make: Structure and Agency in Legal Practice*. Palo Alto, CA: Stanford University Press.

Sartorius, Rolf H. and Vernon Ruttan. 1989. "The Sources of the Basic Needs Mandate." *The Journal of Developing Areas*. 23(April): 331–362.

Savage, Mike and Anne Witz. 1992. *Gender and Bureaucracy*. Oxford: Blackwell Publishers/The Sociological Review.

Sawer, Marian. 1990. *Sisters in Suits: Women and Public Policy in Australia*. Sydney: Allen & Unwin.

———. 1995. "'Femocrats in Glass Towers?' The Office of the Status of Women in Australia." In Stetson, Dorothy McBride and Amy Mazur (eds.). *Comparative State Feminism*. Thousand Oaks, CA: Sage Publications. Pp. 22–39.

Sawyers, Traci M. and David S. Meyer. 1999. "Missed Opportunities: Social Movement Abeyance and Public Policy." *Social Problems* 46 (2): 187–206.

Schattschneider, E.E. 1960. *The Semi-Sovereign People: A Realist's View of Democracy in America*. New York: Holt, Rinehart and Winston.

Schumaker, Paul. 1975. "Policy Responsiveness to Protest-Group Demands." *Journal of Politics* 37(May): 488–521.

Sedmak, Nancy and Chrissie Vidas. 1994. *Primer on Equal Employment Opportunity*. Sixth edition. Washington, DC: Bureau of National Affairs.

Shanahan, Eileen. 1973. "A.T.&T. to Grant 15,000 Back Pay in Job Inequities." *The New York Times*, January 19, 1973: A1.

Sharma, Ritu R. 2001. "Women and Development Aid." *Foreign Policy in Focus* 6(33): 1–3.

Shapiro, Harvey D. 1973. "Women on the Line, Men at the Switchboard." *The New York Times Magazine*, May 20. Pp. 26ff.

Shelton, Elizabeth. 1965. "Title VII Will Referee Sex by Common Sense." *The Washington Post*, November 23, B1.

Shuman, Jerome. 1971. "A Black Lawyers Study." *Howard Law Journal* 16(2, Spring): 225–313.

Skrentny, John D. 2006. "Policy-Elite Perceptions and Social Movement Success: Understanding Variations in Group Inclusion in Affirmative Action." *American Journal of Sociology* 111(6): 1762–1815.

———. 2002. *The Minority Rights Revolution*. Cambridge, MA: Belknap Press.

Skocpol, Theda. 1992. *Protecting Soldiers and Mothers: The Political Origins of Social Policy in the United States*. Cambridge, MA: Belknap Press.

Skowronek, Stephen. 1982. *Building a New American State: The Expansion of National Administrative Capacities, 1877–1920*. Cambridge: Cambridge University Press.

Smith, J. Clay. 1993. *Emancipation: The Making of the Black Lawyer, 1844–1944*. Philadelphia: University of Pennsylvania Press.

Smith, Selma Moidel. 1999. "A Century of Achievment: The Centennial of the National Association of Women Lawyers. *The Women Lawyers Journal* www.abanet.org/nawl/about/history.html. Accessed December 22, 2005.

Smith, Steven Rathgeb and Michael Lipsky. 1993. *Nonprofits for Hire: The Welfare State in the Age of Contracting*. Cambridge, MA: Harvard University Press.

Snow, David and Robert Benford. 1992. "Master Frames and Cycles of Protest," in Morris, Aldon and Carol McClurg Mueller (eds.). *Frontiers of Social Movement Theory*. New Haven, CT: Yale University Press. Pp.133–155.

Staggenborg, Suzanne. 1991. *The Pro-Choice Movement: Organization and Activism in the Abortion Conflict*. New York: Oxford University Press.

Stetson, Dorothy McBride and Amy Mazur. 1995. *Comparative State Feminism*. Thousand Oaks, CA: Sage Publications.

Stetson, Dorothy McBride. 1995. "The Oldest Women's Policy Agency: The Women's Bureau in the United States." In Stetson, Dorothy McBride and Amy Mazur (eds.). *Comparative State Feminism*. Thousand Oaks, CA: Sage Publications. Pp. 254–271.

Stigler, George J. 1975. *The Citizen and the State: Essays on Regulation*. Chicago: University of Chicago Press.

Stockford, Marjorie. 2004. *The Bellwomen: The Story of the Landmark AT&T Sex Discrimination Case*. New Brunswick, NJ: Rutgers University Press.

Strolovitch, Dara. 2007. *Affirmative Advocacy: Race, Class and Gender in Interest Group Politics*. Chicago: University of Chicago Press.

Swers, Michelle. 2002. *The Difference Women Make: The Policy Impact of Women in Congress*. Chicago: University of Chicago Press.

Talbot, Marion and Lois Kimball Rosenberry. 1931. *The History of the American Association of University Women, 1881–1931*. Boston: Houghton Mifflin Co.

Tarrow, Sidney. 1994. *Power in Movement: Social Movements, Collective Action and Politics*. Cambridge: Cambridge University Press.

———. 1998. *Power in Movement: Social Movements and Contentious Politics*. Second edition. Cambridge: Cambridge University Press.

Taylor, Verta. 1989. "Social Movement Continuity: The Women's Movement in Abeyance." *American Sociological Review* 54(5): 761–775.

The Washington Post. December 15, 1967. Photo and caption on p. B3.

Tilly, Charles. 1978. *From Mobilization to Revolution*. Reading, MA: Addison-Wesley.

Tinker, Irene. 1983. "Women in Development." In Tinker, Irene (ed.). *Women in Washington*. Beverly Hills, CA: Sage Publications. Pp. 227–237.

Tobias, Sheila. 1997. *Faces of Feminism: An Activist's Reflections on the Women's Movement*. Boulder, CO: Westview Press.

Towns, Ann S. 2003. "Women Governing for Modernity: International Hier-
archy and Legislative Sex Quotas." Paper presented at the Annual American
Political Science Association Meeting, August 28–30, 2003, Philadelphia,
PA.

Tully, Mary Jean. 1973. "Letter to the Editor." *New York Times Magazine*,
June 10, 1973, 78–79.

United Methodist Women. n.d. "Living the Legacy: The Continuing Journey
of Women in Mission, 1869–2002" http://gbgm-umc.org/umw/history/
legacy.cfm. Accessed July 5, 2006.

U.S. Bureau of the Census. 1957. "Educational Attainment: March 1957."
Current Population Reports: Population Characteristics. Series P-20, Nr. 77
(December 27, 1957). Washington, DC: U.S. Government Printing Office.
http://www.census.gov/population/socdemo/education/p20–077/p20–77.
pdf Accessed November 9, 2008.

———. 1972. *1970 Census of Population, Volume 1 Characteristics of the
Population. Part A Number of Inhabitants. Section 1*. Washington, DC:
U.S. Government Printing Office.

———. 1975. *Historical Statistics of the United States, Colonial Times to
1970, Bicentennial Edition, Part 2*. Washington, DC: U.S. Bureau of the
Census.

———. 2000. *Statistical Abstract of the United States*. Washington, DC: U.S.
Bureau of the Census.

———. 2002. *Statistical Abstract of the United States*. Washington, DC: U.S.
Bureau of the Census.

United States Civil Service Commission. 1949. *Hatch Act Decisions (Political
Activity Cases) of the United States Civil Service Commission*. Washington,
DC: United States Government Printing Office.

———. 1968. *Study of Employment of Women in the Federal Government
1967*. Washington, DC: Bureau of Management Services, United States
Government Printing Office.

———. 1969. *Study of Minority Group Employment in the Federal Government November 30, 1969*. Washington, DC: Government Printing
Office.

Van Dyke, Nella, Sarah A. Soule and Verta A. Taylor. 2004. "The Targets
of Social Movements: Beyond a Focus on the State" *Research in Social
Movements, Conflict and Change* 25:27–51.

Vargas, Virginia and Saskia Wieringa. 1998. "The Triangle of Empower-
ment: Processes and Actors in the Making of Public Policy for Women." In
Lycklama à Nijeholt, Geertje, Virginia Vargas, and Saskia Wieringa (eds.).
*Women's Movements and Public Policy in Europe, Latin America, and the
Caribbean*. New York: Garland Publishing. Pp. 3–23.

Verba, Sidney, Kay Lehman Schlozman, Henry E. Brady, and Norman Nie.
1990. American Citizen Participation Study, [Computer file]. ICPSR version. Chicago, IL: University of Chicago, National Opinion Research Center

(NORC) [producer], 1995. Ann Arbor, MI: Inter-university Consortium for Political and Social Research [distributor], 1995.

von Wahl, Angelika. 1999. *Gleichstellungsregime: Berufliche Gleichstellung von Frauen in der Bundesrepublik und den USA* (Translated: Equal Employment Regimes: Equal Employment Opportunities for Women in Germany and the USA). Leverkusen: Leske+Budrich.

Wald, Kenneth and Jeffrey Corey. 2002. "The Christian Right and Public Policy: Social Movement Elites as Institutional Activists." *State Politics and Policy Quarterly* 2(2): 99–125.

Walker, Edward. n.d. "Polity Membership, Movement Cultures, and Iron Laws: Three Types of Institutionalization in Social Movement Theory." Unpublished paper.

Walsh, John. 1972. "NIH: Protestors Try Going Through Channels." *Science* 177(4055): 1176–1179.

Ware, Susan. 1981. *Beyond Suffrage: Women in the New Deal*. Cambridge, MA: Harvard University Press.

The Washington Post. 1967. Photo and caption with no title. December 15, 1967, B3.

Watson, Sophie. 1990. "The State of Play: An Introduction." In Watson, Sophie (ed). *Playing the State: Australian Feminist Interventions*. Boston: Allen and Unwin. Pp.3–20.

Weldon, S. Laurel. 2002. "Beyond Bodies: Institutional Sources of Representation for Women in Democratic Policymaking." *Journal of Politics* 64(4):1153–1174.

Wellesley College Center for Research on Women. 1995. *The AAUW Report: How Schools Shortchange Girls: A Study of Major Findings on Girls and Education*. New York: Marlowe and Co.

Wells, Mildred White. 1953. *Unity in Diversity: The History of the General Federation of Women's Clubs*. Washington, DC: General Federation of Women's Clubs.

Werum, Regina and Bill Winders. 2001. "Who's 'In' and Who's 'Out': State Fragmentation and the Struggle Over Gay Rights, 1974–1999." *Social Problems* 48(3): 386–410.

White, Deborah Gray. 1999. *Too Heavy a Load: Black Women in Defense of Themselves, 1894–1994*. New York: W.W. Norton and Co.

Whittier, Nancy. 1995. *Feminist Generations: The Persistence of the Radical Women's Movement*. Philadelphia, PA: Temple University Press.

Wilson, James Q. 1989. *Bureaucracy: What Government Agencies Do and Why They Do It*. New York: Basic Books.

Wolbrecht, Christina. 2000. *The Politics of Women's Rights*. Princeton, NJ: Princeton University Press.

Wolfson, Mark. 2001. *The Fight Against Big Tobacco: The Movement, the State and the Public's Health*. New York: Aldine de Gruyter.

Women's Equity Action League Educational and Legal Defense Fund. 1980. "WEAL Fund Board of Directors." From the papers of Marguerite Rawalt (MC 478), Box 29, Folder 4. Schlesinger Library; Radcliffe Institute for Advanced Study, Harvard University.

Woods, Patricia. 2005. "Cause Lawyers and Judicial Community in Israel: Legal Change in a Diffuse, Normative Community." In Sarat, Austin and Stuart Scheingold (eds.). *The Worlds Cause Lawyers Make: Structure and Agency in Legal Practice*. Palo Alto, CA: Stanford University Press. Pp. 307–348.

Woods, Patricia and Scott Barclay. 2008. "Cause Lawyers as Legal Innovators with and Against the State: Symbiosis or Opposition?" *Studies in Law, Politics, and Society* 45:203–231.

Woodward, Alison. 2003. "Building Velvet Triangles: Gender and Informal Governance." In Christiansen, Thomas and Simona Piattoni (eds.). *Informal Governance in the European Union*. Northhampton, MA: Edmond Elgar. Pp. 76–93.

Yin, Robert. 2009. *Case Study Research: Design and Methods*. Fourth edition. Thousand Oaks, CA: Sage Publications.

Young, Iris Marion. 2000. *Inclusion and Democracy*. Oxford: Oxford University Press.

Young, Louise M. 1989. *In the Public Interest: The League of Women Voters, 1920–1970*. New York: Greenwood Press.

Zald, Mayer. 2000. "Ideologically Structured Action: An Enlarged Agenda for Social Movement Research." *Mobilization: An International Journal* 5(1):1–16.

Zald, Mayer and Roberta Ash. 1966. "Social Movement Organizations: Growth, Decay and Change," *Social Forces* 44(March): 327–340.

Zald, Mayer and Michael Berger. 1987 [originally published in 1978]. "Social Movements in Organizations: Coup d'Etat, Bureaucratic Insurgency, and Mass Movement." In Zald, Mayer and John McCarthy (eds.). *Social Movements in an Organizational Society*. New Brunswick, NJ: Transaction Books. Pp. 185–222.

Zelman, Patricia G. 1982. *Women, Work, and National Policy: The Kennedy-Johnson Years. Studies in American History and Culture: No. 33*. Ann Arbor, MI: UMI Research Press.

Index

United States
  movement–state intersections,
    effects of, 201–202
  policy agencies vs. other countries,
    191–192
  political appointees in, vs. other
    countries, 204
  understanding the American state,
    implications for future
    research, 201–202

velvet triangles, 5
Veterans' Preference Act, 42
Vietnam War, 81–82
Violence against Women Act, 143,
  168
Violence against Women Office, 143
Vocational Education Act, 154

Washington College of Law, 35–36
Weeks, Lorena, 144–145
*Weeks v. Southern Bell Telephone
  and Telegraph*, 144–145
Wirtz, Willard, 146
Wolfe, Leslie, 154, 175–176
Women in Development (WID),
  Office of, 157–159, 196, 201
women in government. *See also*
  feminist activists inside the
  state; government workers
  1848–1919, 39–42
  sex discrimination in hiring
    prohibited, 40, 57–58, 106,
    167
women in government (1920–1959)
  African Americans compared,
    44–46
  networking of, 57
  New Deal policies, influence on,
    17–18, 159
  opportunities for, 40–44
  women's organizations focus on
    increasing, 51–52
women of color
  dual activism inside the
    bureaucracy, 71–72

  in women's organizations, 48,
    54–56, 64–65, 70–71, 72
Women's Action Committees,
  109
Women's Action Organization
  (WAO), 110–112
Women's Bureau
  employee orientation, career vs.
    activism, 87–88
  information dissemination tactic,
    178
  limitations on influence of, 22,
    191–192
  location and influence of, 17
  networking through, 58
  protective legislation position, 99,
    100
Women's Christian Temperance
  Union, 47–48, 52
Women Scientist Advisors, 109
Women's Educational Equity Act,
  148, 153–155, 169,
  175–176
Women's Educational Equity Act
  Program, 201
Women's Equity Action League
  (WEAL), 67–68, 77–79
Women's Health, Office of,
  203
Women's Health Equity Act,
  131–132
women's movement. *See also*
  feminism, defined; feminist
  activists inside the state;
  feminists outside the state;
  movement–state intersections;
  women's organizations
  (1960–present)
  civil rights movement compared,
    8, 61–62
  femocrats vs. the, 6
  government workers in, 67
  mobilization factors, 30–31,
    92–93, 105, 113–114
  participants social status/
    education, 64